DOCTOR
TO THE
RESISTANCE

THE HEROIC TRUE STORY OF AN
AMERICAN SURGEON AND HIS FAMILY
IN OCCUPIED PARIS

HAL VAUGHAN

Potomac Books, Inc.
Washington, D.C.

Library of Congress Cataloging-in-Publication Data

Vaughan, Hal, 1928–
   Doctor to the Resistance : the heroic true story of an American surgeon and his family in occupied Paris / Hal Vaughan.— 1st ed.
      p.   cm.
   Includes bibliographical references.
   ISBN 1-57488-773-4 (alk. paper)
      1. Jackson, Sumner Waldron.   2. Jackson, Charlotte Sylvie, d. 1968.
   3. Jackson, Phillip.   4. World War, 1939–1945—Underground movements—France.
   5. World War, 1939–1945—France.   6. France—History—German occupation, 1940–1945.   7. Surgeons—United States—Biography.
   8. Americans—France—Biography.   I. Title.

D802.F8V345   2004
940.53'44361'092273—dc22   2004000052
ISBN 1-57488-774-2 (paperback)

Printed in Canada on acid-free paper that meets the American National Standards Institute Z39-48 Standard.

Potomac Books, Inc.
22841 Quicksilver Drive
Dulles, Virginia 20166

First Edition

10 9 8 7 6 5 4 3 2 1

DOCTOR
TO THE
RESISTANCE

For Phuong Gia

CONTENTS

PREFACE AND ACKNOWLEDGMENTS

IF YOU WALK into the Memorial Building of the American Hospital of Paris at Neuilly, you will see an immense plaque in heavy bronze, erected in May 1929 and dedicated to the memory of American men and women who served in France during the Great War: 1914–1918. Among those who served were Sumner Waldron Jackson and his wife, Toquette. Should you then turn right toward the doctors' offices that line the elegant corridors of the main building, you might see a more modest tribute, in bronze too, and covering events that took place some twenty years later. It is engraved:

IN GRATEFUL MEMORY
OF
DOCTOR S. W. JACKSON
EUROLOGUE OF
THE AMERICAN HOSPITAL OF PARIS
1925–1943[1]
FOR HIS UNTIRING ACTIVITY BEFORE
AND DURING THE WAR
DIED WHILE A PRISONER IN GERMANY

The plaque commemorates the end of an adventure in which an American family—the Jacksons—took great risks with the possibility in mind, always, that the reward would be death, or worse than death.

I have pieced together what follows from talking with Dr. Jackson's son, Phillip, who was called "Pete," and from family documents and eyewitness accounts. I drew on a memorial to Dr. Jackson left by Clemence Bock, a trusted family friend, and the papers of Dr. Morris

Sanders, a friend and colleague. I have also undertaken extensive research at government and university archives in the United States and Europe.

———————◆———————

I don't know where to begin to thank the many who helped me put together the historical pieces that are the core of this work. Many of you were generous with your time, and if I have failed to acknowledge someone's help, let me now say, "Thanks again."

I owe much to Phillip Jackson and I hope he knows of my gratitude and admiration for his bravery in the face of extraordinary adversity. Phillip helped me to understand the Jackson family and I caught in Phillip the spirit that made the Jackson family heroes. Loraine Riemer, his daughter, helped me with documents and photos.

Thanks to my agent, Edward W. Knappman, New England Publishing Associates, for believing in this work, and to his charming and astute wife and partner, Elisabeth.

A word of thanks must go to Don McKeon, publisher and vice president at Brassey's, Inc., who found this "a hell of a story," and thanks to Christina Davidson, associate editor, for a fine blue pencil. Her suggestions have made this a better book. The whole Brassey's team, from cover design to production, gets a "hats off."

A special thanks goes to Pamela Zimmerman Cohen for her detective work in finding sources and photographs, and for her keen eye and kind hand. Pam has been a mainstay.

Professor Charles L. Robertson spent many hours reading the manuscript and making valuable suggestions. His company and conversation have always been stimulating. I am also grateful to Lawrence Bond, an independent TV producer and consultant to the History Channel. He shared with me his work on the documentary, *The Typhoons' Last Storm*. Jack Eckert of the Francis A. Countway Library of Medicine and Michelle Marcella of Massachusetts General Hospital did a stellar job of tracking down key documents. The National Archives has many treasures, among them Herbert Rawlings-Milton, John Taylor, and James Kelling. Many thanks.

I owe a special debt of thanks to "Joe," Andre Migdal, Jean Langlet, and Maisie Renault. The members of this heroic group of "survivors" gave invaluable insights, particularly Maisie Renault, who shared her memories of Toquette with me. I am especially grateful to Serge Klarsfeld, who gave his time generously to assist with this project and let me use the only known photograph of Henrich Illers.

Much appreciation must be given to Lieutenant LeRoy at the Château de Vincennes and Mr. Atkins at Perpignan, both of whom put me on to Joe and to Phyllis Michaux for her early help. Mme. Noel of the Grande Chancellerie de la Légion d'Honneur sent me a file on Toquette. Mr. Rouby at the Ministère des Ancien Combattants et Victimes de Guerre was generous in allowing me to consult the Jackson file at the Ministry of Defense. M. F. Malassis at the Fondation de la Résistance was ever available to answer questions.

Thanks, too, to Larry Collins and Dominique Lapierre for introducing me to the elusive Erich Posch-Pastor von Camperfeld. If you haven't read their work, *Is Paris Burning?*, about the last days of the German Occupation of Paris, you've missed a treat. I'm grateful to have had the permission to quote from *La Traversée de la nuit* by Geneviève de Gaulle Anthonioz; *La grand misère* by Maisie Renault; and *l'Amérique déportée, Virginia d'Albert-Lake de la Résistance a Ravensbrück*, by Catherine Rothman-Le Dret.

At the American Hospital of Paris, Drs. Robert Steinmetzer and Yann Le Cocguic, both great "docs," kept me alive and encouraged me in dark moments; and Claude Boisseu des Chouartes has as always been wonderful and quick to help.

Finally, thanks to Roger Kaplan for his initial assistance and to his father, "Kappy," my *maître*, for his support way back when.

Thanks to you all. I am solely responsible for any errors of fact.

Hal W. Vaughan
Paris, October 2003

PROLOGUE

DR. JACKSON came to me by way of a few words on a document found in the dusty cellars of the American Hospital of Paris: "[T]he American Jackson, Medical Director of the hospital, was deported with his wife and son." That meant, in the parlance of World War II, interrogations by the Gestapo, often accompanied by torture, and then transport to an SS prison camp—where slow death by overwork and starvation awaited. Dr. Jackson and his wife had most certainly died long ago, but thoughts about the fate of their son began to haunt me.

It took weeks of research to unearth Dr. Jackson's "dossier" in the Paris archives. The thin file, which carried the tribute *"Mort Pour La France,"* confirmed that Dr. Sumner Waldron Jackson, medical director of the American Hospital of Paris, had been arrested and deported in 1944 for "Resistance." I also found files for his wife, Charlotte ("Toquette"), and son, Phillip, who was 16 when arrested. The family's last known address was given as Enghien-les-Bains, Seine et Oise. A search in the telephone directory turned up the name "Jackson" in that town—an outlying suburb of Paris.

I admit that my heart beat a bit faster when a female voice answered the telephone and became irritated when I made it clear that I was searching for the Jackson family.

"You're not one of those TV people, are you?" she demanded.

I explained that I was connected with the American Hospital and sought to contact Phillip Jackson. This seemed to appease her, and she asked me to write stating my business. Despite her hesitancy, the brief conversation at least confirmed one fact: Phillip Jackson was indeed alive.

Weeks later I visited Phillip in his room at l'Institution Nationale des Invalides. Founded by Louis XIV, the venerable complex houses a hospital for war wounded, various museums, and the tomb of Napoleon Bonaparte. Phillip had earned the right to have a room there as one of Gen. Charles de Gaulle's French Resistance fighters, deported by the Nazis. He had had an accident months earlier and was confined to a wheelchair, undergoing daily intensive physical therapy to regain the use of his legs. Despite his infirmity, Phillip could stand up by grabbing a leather-bound bar that hung above his bed. He did this often to relieve the cramps in his back and legs. And when he stood he was an impressive man, even at seventy-four years of age.

Later, when I saw the prewar photos of his father, I was struck by the father-son resemblance: both over six-feet tall, 180 pounds, mostly muscle with massive shoulders and arms. The father had the hands of a man from Maine who had cut wood and dug in limestone marble quarries. I noted that Phillip's features were softer than his father's, the cheekbones less prominent—but nevertheless he had a strong face, a firm handshake, and a real look-me-in-the-eye way about him.

I explained to Phillip that I was a writer interested in the story of his family and the American Hospital, with the idea of telling about the Americans who remained in Paris during those terrible days of German Occupation. I already knew a great deal about the complex story of the French Resistance to the Nazi Occupation of their country, and of the French men and women of every political shade who fought underground: the heroes, antiheroes, and traitors. And I had talked at length with men and women who had survived Nazi concentration camps.

He was reluctant and clearly uncomfortable that a total stranger wanted to pry into his past. I left his room feeling that aside from the immediate trauma of his recent accident, there resided deep inside Phillip Jackson a well of sorrow. The tone of his voice rose a pitch when he spoke about his mother and father and often, later, tears would cloud his eyes; after more than fifty years, the memory of their shared suffering as prisoners of the Nazis still cut deep. Phillip slowly came to trust me and invited me to visit with him on a regular basis.

One afternoon in late December 1999, we sat talking in Phillip's room at Les Invalides. The light was failing. Phillip was hunched over, his big hands clasped on his knees. He had something on his mind. I could barely read the expression on his face. Then his lips began to tremble, his voice cracked.

"I found these at the Enghien house this weekend," he said, referring to his family's lakeside home. And he handed me a folder and a handful of small leather-bound books. "You can read these . . . you'll be able to decipher the writing. The manuscript is from Miss Bock, who tutored my father when he returned here from America with my mother after the First World War. My father was the only man Miss Bock ever loved . . . you'll see that. There are some photographs, too."

We sat silently for a few moments. The lights went on in the courtyard. I could see his face was composed now. We shook hands and I wished him a happy Christmas.

During the holidays I went over the photos and read the Bock manuscript. One photograph struck me: it was a picture of Dr. Jackson grinning from ear to ear and holding Phillip—a boy of four—upright in his arms. The boy had the same happy look as his father and both wore radiant smiles—Phillip already looked like his dad even down to a pair of prominent ears. Then, a photograph of Phillip's mother, Toquette, came to hand: she had become an old woman, a skeleton, her face scarred by vermin, her head wrapped in a wool scarf. The photo had been taken in Sweden in 1945 immediately after Toquette's release from Ravensbrück concentration camp. The ironic disparity of those two moments depicted in the photos and separated by fourteen years clashed: a happy, normal family had been caught up in the Nazi Occupation of France, had volunteered to be part of the underground war and had passed through hell.

Almost fifty years later on a sunny day in July 2003, I was present at a photo session in the garden of the Institution National des Invalides. Phillip was in a wheelchair; his wartime decorations pinned to his coat jacket. Later, the photographer took me aside and asked gently, "What did he do?" I replied simply, "He was a hero in World War II," and left it at that.

There was so much more to tell about the boy who had been held by the Gestapo and deported to an SS concentration camp, and who had barely escaped from a frightful disaster at sea. He had returned home in 1945 a young man barely 18 who had missed out on most of his adolescence and a college degree, and yet still managed to look after his mother and to prosper. And I thought of all the others like Phillip who returned home from German captivity that summer of 1945—survivors, people who had been caught up in extraordinary, often heroic circumstances and who had returned to lead mostly mundane lives.

Toquettte was, of course, a survivor. Energetic, stubborn, and courageous Toquette, fifty-six years old when repatriated home in June 1945 and awarded a one-hundred-plus dollar disability pension for the infirmities she suffered at the hands of the Nazi SS. Her diaries after World War II begin in 1948. They're banal—speak of the weather, the cellar filled with water when the lake overflowed, a film shared with Phillip. Toquette had a haunting need to note every detail: "rain all day, T&H caught cold, stayed at hotel; cleaned a bit of my garden; wrote to Freda Jackson, got tax forms; Pete [Phillip] can't skate, ice too thin; and the ever-present ghostly inscriptions of her loneliness: *"personne venu,*—no one came-by."

Her diaries are snapshots of a courageous lady, the youngest child of a Protestant Swiss family of six children, a Red Cross nurse at 25 with the guts to work in the crude wartime surgeries where broken and maimed men were cut and sewn up and sometimes healed. One admires her self-assurance and faith to marry a foreigner at age 30 and to follow Sumner to a strange and exotic land, and when that didn't work out to construct a new life from scratch. Through it all Toquette manages to be ever-strong, frugal, and gentle, taking immense joy in her pet animals, never without a dog, a cat, a tamed fox, a rabbit, a goat.

After the New Year 2000, Phillip and I continued to meet routinely. I was now actively researching the Jackson family story at archives in Paris, London, and the United States. Phillip and his daughter Loraine helped with pieces of the story—but much was hidden. Such is the nature of clandestine work.

One winter's day we were going over the portfolio of photographs that Phillip had given me. He was sitting on the edge of his bed when it occurred to me that there was a question I had long wanted to ask.

"Phillip," I said, "How could your mother and father allow their 15-year-old only son to get involved with the underground Resistance? If you had been caught, you would have been shot!"

He looked at me and cocked his head. Then he stretched out his hands, palms up. Tears filled his eyes as he shook his head as in disbelief. "We thought it was all a game."

Months later as I dug deeper, I realized that for a short period when Phillip was 15, he did indeed think that dodging about Paris, delivering clandestine mail was a game. But his father and mother knew otherwise. By May 1943, German security services were everywhere in Paris: on the street, in the subways, at train stations; checking identities, arresting anyone suspicious—searching for downed Allied flyers. The SS had already captured and tortured General de Gaulle's chief agent in France—Jean Moulin, alias "Max," who spent the last few days of his life shackled to a wall at SS headquarters, a few blocks from the Jackson apartment on the Avenue Foch. The German Occupation engulfed Paris in a climate of fear, and though Phillip may have undertaken his Resistance work with a boyish sense of adventure, Sumner and Toquette were wise enough to realize that exposure of their illicit activities could lead to arrest, deportation, or worse.

I once asked Phillip how he felt about those people who had imprisoned and enslaved him and his parents, beat him, tried to kill him. He answered that as a guide and translator with the British Army immediately after his escape from the Nazis, shortly after the war was over, he had carried a gun.

"Could you have used it?" I asked.

"I thought about it," he said. "But I couldn't do it . . . ."

"Was it worth it?" I asked.

He shook his head and was silent for what seemed like many minutes. I feared instantly that my question was inconsiderate.

"I don't know," he replied. "They would have been defeated anyway . . . but then we could not have held our heads up high."

I remembered how Phillip had told me something his father had said back in 1941, how the family *had* to be part of the Resistance so they could hold their heads high when the Nazis were defeated as Sumner knew they would be. He had borrowed his father's words of almost sixty years earlier.

What was Sumner like, this man from Maine who managed a good life in Paris during the heady days of the Jazz Age, and who loved medicine and being a physician as much as he loved anything—maybe even more? We know he was large and imposing, and he gave the impression that his heart was as big as his body. He was a man who gave of himself: full of energy, as quick to anger as to smile, who needed to sweat, to cut wood, to box, to play tennis, to canoe, hunt, and fish, but who could work all hours with hardly a wink of sleep. He gave his blood to his wounded patients in World War II, and was tender as a lamb. The men and women under his care said so in documents I uncovered. Sumner's comrade and fellow prisoner, Michael Hollard, already a Resistance leader and hero when arrested by the Gestapo—thought that 60-year-old Sumner was "a remarkable American: upright, a stern man of great energy and forcible character who never talked about why he and his son had been arrested by the Gestapo." That was Dr. Jack: the physician, the father who refused to escape, when he could have followed Hollard to freedom, because he couldn't leave his prostrate dying prisoner patients. The man who chose for his 1914 medical college yearbook the motto: "He doeth well who doeth his best. Anon"[1]

We shall never know what impulse led Sumner and Toquette to remain in Paris as the German Army moved in. Where did Sumner find the courage to play tricks on his own pro-Vichy chief at the American Hospital, and on the Gestapo, hiding men in hospital beds that were wanted by the German police and SS and at the Jackson apartment on the Avenue Foch?

And Toquette? How had she managed to play the role of a mother, a wartime nurse, and a Resistance agent working under the nose of the Gestapo? How did she delicately balance all of these activities . . . arranging to use the Foch apartment as a mail drop, a bank, and a courier center for the Resistance while endangering her life and those of her husband and son? Was it all a game? Did the Jackson family believe they were playing some desperate *jeu interdit*, as Phillip suggests? Or was this American family in Paris made of the stuff of heroes?

Walter Lippmann wrote that "what each man does is based not on direct and certain knowledge, but on pictures made by himself or given to him. . . . The way in which the world is imagined determines at any particular moment what men will do."[2]

1

AT THE WESTERN FRONT ON THE SOMME

June 1916

Sumner Waldron Jackson got his first taste of war at the Somme. Like Verdun, the name "Somme" evokes disaster. For there in the summer and fall of 1916, not far from where English archers defeated French knights five hundred years earlier, the English, French, and German high commands wasted over three-quarters of a million men—the best of their citizen soldiers. Lt. Sumner Waldron Jackson, late of Boston's Massachusetts General Hospital (MGH), a volunteer for Britain's Royal Medical Corps, survived the battle. He had sailed to France in June 1916 with a number of Americans who had joined the "Harvard Group." Many volunteers were physicians and surgeons like Sumner, but there were also artists like Walt Disney and writers like e.e. cummings, Louis Bromfield, Ernest Hemingway, and John Dos Passos. Men and women of all types—bankers, cooks, drivers, and nurses—wanted to be part of the war to end all wars. This was clearly defying President Woodrow Wilson's 1914 edict that U.S. citizens should not "enter into the service of either of the belligerents."[1]

Shipping out to France was dangerous. German U-boats prowled the Atlantic, indiscriminately sinking Allied and American shipping. Indeed, the steamer Sumner sailed on, the Cunard's 13,405-ton *Andania*, was later sunk by a torpedo from the German submarine, *U-46*.

Upon his arrival in France, Sumner was assigned as a surgeon and medical officer (M.O.) to the British General Hospital No. 22 located at Dannes-Camiers, in the Pas de Calais, just north of the Somme on the English Channel.[2] Before 1914 the surrounding countryside had been pastoral: great moors and grazing fields along the coast cut by watercourses; and on the Plateau de Picard to the east, ominously hard, dry, chalky soil where the Germans had dug in since 1914. By Sumner's arrival in 1916, however, the bucolic landscape appeared torn and crowned with barbed wire, its verdant fields turned to a pitted wasteland where men drowned in mud.

The second Battle of the Somme began on the first day of July—a clear, sunny, and pleasant morning of the third year of the Great War. The planners forecast a great offensive, the leaders assuring all that everything was planned and assembled. Two million English and French infantry and cavalry were stretched along a thirty-mile front from Amiens to Perrone, facing the German Kaiser's elite troops dug into fortified trenchworks protected by barbed wire. The British thought they could destroy these works and overcome the Boches with massive artillery barrages before and while the "Tommies" attacked. The "boys" would then meet the enemy with the bayonet, the cavalry with the naked sabers.

Sumner must have watched the battalions forming up. The English, Irish, Scottish, and Welsh boys were eager and young and came in all sizes, except the Welshmen, who were stunted from poor diet and work underground—but nonetheless, brave and strong. Pink-cheeked boy-officers just out of school led the men. The Scottish regiments wore kilts, and pipers accompanied them. One boy said the skirl of the pipes made him piss in his pants.[3] French infantry called *poilus* (literally, "hairy"), who had already been in the lines for many weeks, would join in the attack.

Torrential rain had already saturated the countryside that June 1916, and the roads leading to the frontline trenches were deep in mud. Camions, horses, and mules loaded with wood boxes—some of them coffins—were everywhere as the materials of war clogged the roads going up the line. At the communication trenches the men disembarked and stumbled single file into the front lines. The Tommies carried 60-pound packs, hard rations, water, clean socks, and a sweater. They toted entrenching tools, gas masks, rifles, and grenades, and bandoliers of ammo around their waists and over their shoulders.

The great man Sir Douglas Haig, booted and spurred, shiny, neat, shaved, and keen of eye, was there. He told newsmen that his "Lancers" would be in Bapaume, ten miles behind the Boche lines, on the second day of the offensive. However, almost everything that Haig expected of the enormous artillery barrage failed. And despite advance information that the German wire defenses and dugouts remained intact, he ordered the troops to attack.[4] So when the whistles blew and the rockets burst, the units to attack went up and over, advancing straight into a barrage of German fire. Many immediately got caught on the barbed wire and floundered in the mud, pinned down by enemy fire. Soon Tommies and *poilus* lay bleeding, dying, and dead only a few yards from where they had scrambled over the top of the trenches.

Still Haig ordered wave after wave of men forward, long lines of young men lugging sixty pounds of equipment. They clawed their way up and out of the protection of their trenches, plodding forward shoulder to shoulder only to discover the uncut wire and the German troops firing frantically at them. The men were being massacred in the wire entanglements: brave men, straddling the wire, while the German "Maxim" machine guns swept their ranks firing six-hundred rounds a minute.

A German survivor describes how, at "the shout of a sentry, 'They are coming,' we sprang up the stairs . . . and there they come, the khaki clad boys not twenty meters in front of our trench. . . . They advance slowly, fully equipped . . . our machine guns tear holes in their ranks."[5] In some places the machine guns penetrated the British front line to strike down troops who had not even reached no-man's-land. An Irish sergeant recalled seeing "long lines of men to my right and left; I hear the machine guns; and when I advanced another ten yards there were only a few men left around me; by the time I had gone twenty yards, I seemed to be on my own. Then I was hit myself."[6] The advance was checked, halted, and finally stopped dead.

When the men retreated to their trenches, German artillery lobbed 750-pound shells into their dugouts. Jagged bits of hot metal from grenades and cannon burst randomly among the men, ripping their flesh. Chlorine, phosgene, and mustard gases blistered exposed skin, scored the men's eyes, and often suffocated them. Ninety-one percent of the men who went over the top that day were either killed or wounded. There was work aplenty for the litter bearers, the surgeons. The ambulances were busy around the clock.

And still it went on.

Sumner was often assigned to medical teams that went up to the lines to work with the volunteer ambulance corps and in the dressing stations near the trenches.[7] The volunteer ambulances went everywhere. Most rigs had four places in the back for the badly wounded, called *couches,* and four places for those who could sit up, called *assis.* Many of the *couches* were blind from poison gas—some were without limbs, some had broken faces. The *assis* were lightly wounded and would go back into the lines in a few days.

The medical teams traveled the tortuous roads to reach the dressing stations where M.O.s like Sumner treated the men as best they could, often under artillery fire. Then the terrible cargo—men gassed and ripped apart by grenades and bombs and maimed by machine guns—were loaded into the Packards, Renaults, and later, Fords that lumbered back along the muddy shell-torn roads. The gruesome work continued night and day. The ambulances bore paths deep into the earth; their drivers changed tires in a foot of mud surrounded by land littered with debris and the fetid carcasses of animals.[8] The drivers hated jarring the wounded. Still, they drove at full speed, often at night with no lights, over the rough roads and around the shell holes lest their cargo expire before reaching medical aid. In the mass confusion and the shelling, the drivers sometimes got lost. But the transport system marked a great improvement over the previous year, when the "Frenchies" hauled the wounded out on horses and mules. Now they parked the ambulances on the front—at the mouth of the trenches.

Being a medical officer in the Royal Army Medical Corps at the Battle of the Somme was a deadly business. Capt. Noel Chavasse, VC (Victoria Cross) and Bar, was at the Somme at the same time as Sumner. Chavasse's citation for the Victoria Cross reads:

> During an attack he tended the wounded in the open all day, under heavy fire, frequently in view of the enemy. During the ensuing

night he searched for wounded on the ground in front of the enemy's lines for four hours. Next day he took one stretcher-bearer to
the advanced trenches, and, under heavy fire, carried an urgent case
for 500 yards into safety, being wounded in the side by a shell splin-
ter during the journey. The same night he took up a party of trusty
volunteers, rescued three wounded men from a shell hole twenty-
five yards from the enemy's trench, buried the bodies of two officers
and collected many identity discs, although fired on by bombs and
machine guns. Altogether he saved the lives of some twenty badly
wounded men, besides the ordinary cases which passed through his
hands. His courage and self-sacrifice were beyond praise.[9]

Clarence Mitchell, an ambulance driver on the Western Front,
wrote: "The English Red Cross men are nervy beyond belief, the casualties among them are very high, even among the ambulance drivers
who run up in daylight to the second line of trenches."[10]

At Dannes where Sumner was posted, Dr. Hugh Cabot, a renowned urologist and accomplished surgeon, headed the Harvard
Surgical Unit and commanded the 22nd General Hospital. (He had
been one of Sumner's earlier chiefs at MGH before coming to France,
and would later promote Sumner to specialize in genito-urinary surgery.) In 1916 Sumner's unit served thirteen hundred beds, laid out
in rows and rows of huts. During the Somme offensive five hundred
beds were added. In 1916 there were more than sixty MGH volunteer
physicians and surgeons and as many as two hundred nurses serving
in the unit.

Dr. David Cheever of Harvard led a contingent of the Harvard
Surgical Unit to Dannes. He describes his team of thirty volunteers as
"specialists in surgery, medicine, and X-ray work, and dentists, an
ophthalmologist, an aurist [hearing], an orthopedist and a bacteriolo-
gist." The men landed first in England and went to London to "pro-
cure appropriate uniforms as commissioned officers. Their dress
corresponded to the British regular officer's uniform except in the absence of certain insignia indicating a commission under the crown,
which would have required the men to give up American citizenship."[11]

The unit treated the *couches*: "gassed" soldiers, men with terrible burns from "liquid fire" (today's napalm), and shell and machine-gun wounds with severe infections, extensive bone damage, and "dreadful" facial wounds involving the mouth and jaw. The physicians and surgeons were inventing avant-garde techniques and, for the first time, systematically using antitetanus serum to prevent acute infection.[12]

> Dr. Harvey Cushing describes one case of trauma he treated on Good Friday, 1916:
> The man suffered facial paralysis from a bullet wound in the mastoid. He got his during an engagement at a place called Croult, and, with a field full of other wounded, was left for dead. The enemy came over [him] a day or so later, a soldier poked at him and, finding him alive, swung at his head with the butt end of his musket, breaking his jaw. He was finally picked up during a counter-attack. . . .
> [It was] amazing the patience of the seriously wounded, some of them hanging on for months; their dreadful deformities, not so much the amputations but broken jaws and twisted, scarred faces; and the tedious healing of the infected wounds, with discharging sinuses, tubes, irrigations, and repeated dressings.[13]

The gravely wounded were sent back to hospitals in Paris or London. The American Hospital of Paris at Neuilly was so renowned that it was reported—perhaps a kindly exaggeration—that some British soldiers going into battle put a note inside their pockets asking to be sent there if they were hit.[14] At Neuilly fine bits of shrapnel were removed by a giant magnet, a broken face repaired, a wooden leg fitted, a glass eye installed. There were cases of a newly diagnosed condition named "shell shock." When not a variety of "malingering," the severe cases involved men deaf and dumb, some suffering "shakes and tremors" and various grades of paralysis of the arms and legs.

Shell shock? Indeed, thousands of these men were diagnosed and treated for hysterical psychoneurotic conditions. Daily they witnessed the dead put to use as stepping stones, only to slip out of sight. Edward Campion Vaughan, a distant cousin of the author, described no-man's-land in 1916:

> From the darkness on all sides came the groans and wails of wounded men: faint, long, sobbing moans of agony and despairing

shrieks. It was too horribly obvious that dozens of men with serious wounds must have crawled for safety into new shell-holes, and now the water was rising about them and, powerless to move, they were slowly drowning. Horrible visions came to me with those cries—of Woods and Kent, Edge and Taylor, lying maimed out there trusting that their pals would find them, and now dying terribly, alone amongst the dead in the inky darkness. And we could do nothing to help them; Dunham was crying quietly beside me, and all the men were affected by the piteous cries.

Later that day Vaughan wrote, "The cries of the wounded had much diminished now, and as we staggered down the road; the reason was only too apparent, for the water was right over the tops of the shell holes."[15]

The Battle of the Somme ended in November 1916. Tragically the Tommies and *poilus* had advanced a mere six miles. The Lancers never reached Bapaume; the battle was a catastrophe. It was recorded as the greatest loss of life in British military history.[16]

But the fighting had not abated. Through the dreary autumn and winter of 1916–1917, the men in the lines suffered abominably. Dannes was repeatedly bombed; there was no British breakthrough, and the fighting consumed itself and died down. The whole campaign of 1916 ended in a bitter deadlock.[17]

Helen Jordan Lamb, a nurse from Cape Cod, Massachusetts, worked with Sumner that winter. In her memoir, she tells of Christmas 1916:

We went into the country woods, taking two of our Tommies, and brought back a wee Christmas tree and many greens. We all helped to decorate the ward—it looks very gay and quite like Christmas. About 20 of us, NCO's, Officers and Sisters went from tent to tent singing Christmas songs. . . . Many M.G.H. people are here; Dr. Jackson is M.O. [Medical Officer] . . . having heavy surgical cases.

For Christmas dinner the boys had imitation chicken—a canned rabbit and vegetable and a steamed pudding. For tea, Grata (my chum) and I gave them the Canadian puddings. And all day they had been eating oranges, nuts, and candies from their Christmas bags.

We have a stove about the size of a bushel basket to keep the place a bit warm. Officers ever surround it. They sit facing it and freeze their backs, and back to it and freeze their faces. There really is no warm, homey place in the camp.[18]

By 1917 the character of the war had changed. At Dannes even the nursing "sisters" were now overcome by the wounded. Many patients were burn cases due to what the nurses described as "liquid fire." Miss Noyes, an operating sister, fell dangerously ill from plural pneumonia. "She raves," writes Nurse Lamb. "I told them to take these men a way [*sic*]! There is not a whole man here; they are all wounded and cut to pieces."[19]

A German described the war in 1917 from his side as "the turnip winter. . . . [At home] hunger demolished solidarity, children started to steal other people's rations. Soon, women in long queues outside shops spoke more of their children's hunger than of the deaths of their husbands."[20]

Then Tsar Nicholas abdicated, French units mutinied, and Wilson got America in the war.

————————————◆————————————

As the Germans bombed London, the "Teddies" (as the French called the Americans) crossed the Atlantic to France under constant threat of German U-boat attack. It was July 1917 and Gen. John J. Pershing had arrived in France only a few weeks earlier. He would command the A.E.F., the American Expeditionary Force, for the next three years.

Sumner was still at Dannes when Queen Mary came to visit the hospital on July 6, 1917. Nurse Lamb, his colleague, writes that Her Majesty

> looked very stunning in a light gray suit, a smart black hat encircled with pink feathers and a gay white parasol with pink roses. The Royal party arrived in a limousine with a white flag flying from the top, proceeded [*sic*] by several cars. Bugles sounded and everyone stood at attention—trim and polished and shining along the Queen's path from ward to ward. Tall, stately, of fair complexion and somewhat of a blonde with a quiet dignity, the Queen spoke to

the boys in the wards and asked the sisters how long they had been there. As she turned to go, three rousing cheers were given. The moving-picture man was busy and we expected someday to see it all in the "movies." A great day for No. 22![21]

That very evening the nurses organized a dance in Sumner's honor. A festive and sad time it was, for Sumner was leaving No. 22. He had been recruited into the American Army and ordered to serve at a military hospital in Paris. Things "up the line" were getting bloodier, and Sumner wanted to stay ahead of what was to be an innovation: a permanent up-front dressing station staffed by a team composed of a surgeon, his assistant, a sister, and her orderly. The U.S. Army was desperate for physicians and surgeons with battlefield experience, and Sumner was one of the few military surgeons who knew what trench warfare did to the human body and mind.

One minute Sumner was a British Army officer and surgeon and the next minute, Sumner Waldron Jackson, M.D., was a first lieutenant (and later a captain)[22] in the U.S. Army Medical Corps. And his luck held. A few days after Sumner left Dannes, an American officer, Lt. Louis J. Genella of the British Medical Corps, suffered a shell wound on the front lines. He was the first American casualty. Dannes was still a dangerous place; a few weeks later four American medical personnel serving at the hospital were killed when the Germans bombed the building again.[23]

As America entered the fight, the former European War became the Great War. The Teddies brought hope and a cocksureness that the English couldn't stomach. But the French adored the Teddies—except maybe some Frenchmen who went crazy when those skinny, long-legged, pink-cheeked boys from Iowa and Nebraska started eyeing their wives and girlfriends and got a wink back.

With almost two years of war behind him, Sumner must have bristled at the attitude of those brash and bright boys from across the ocean, who looked down on the French and English troops. Sumner had seen the worth of the French *poilus* and Tommies. He knew firsthand how they'd fought—and he let it be known that his fellow Yanks had yet to be bloodied. He wasn't shy in telling his friends and colleagues what a battlefield was like when the guns went off.

Sumner left Dannes to work as an Army surgeon under Dr. Joseph A. Blake at Red Cross Hospital No. 2 on Rue Piccini in Paris' chic 16eme *arrondissement*. Dr. Blake, a renowned New York City surgeon, had established the hospital at the outbreak of the European War with private donations from America and France.

When Sumner arrived, the hospital had three hundred beds, of which a third were reserved for French wounded and the rest for American soldiers and personnel of the American Red Cross. Sumner made his hand as a surgeon here dealing with severe wounds and fractures that the troops had suffered up front. After being treated at dressing stations, they were transferred to hospitals by ambulances or hospital-trains to Red Cross and state hospitals located behind the battle lines. Paris was at times only a few miles away and the sound of cannon could be heard at the Place de la Concorde.

The Piccini hospital also housed the Red Cross central research laboratory, where a corps of bacteriologists studied patient records to advance the treatment of trench fever—a disease transmitted by body lice in filthy quarters and in the trenches. By today's modern standards the hospital would hardly pass muster by the American Hospital Commission. But for Sumner working at Blake's side in 1917, it was a boon and an honor.

Sumner met his future wife at the Piccini hospital. To twenty-nine-year-old nurse Charlotte "Toquette" Sylvie Barrelet de Ricou, the six-foot-one, handsome thirty-one-year-old surgeon from the Somme battlefield must have seemed exotic and heroic.

Phillip would say years later: "I guess that by the time Dad showed up, Mom had sown her wild oats."[24] Sumner himself had been engaged six years earlier to Mary Louise Darariscotta in Philadelphia, when he was an assistant professor of pathology at Jefferson University; but he never let slip a word about his amorous life before Toquette. Phillip can remember his father saying, perhaps in jest and to tease Toquette, something like, "The first time I kissed your mother was in a linen closet at the Rue Piccini."

Phillip exclaimed, "Dad! A closet?"

And Sumner replied, "A big room where they stored linens . . . a very long kiss. I was in love with your mother."[25] Then he winked at Toquette and she blushed.

Toquette, who had been a nurse since 1914, was a good catch for Sumner. In her memorial, Clemence Bock, Sumner's tutor and a close friend of the family, writes: "Toquette not only spoke English, which made for an easy and at first flirtatious relation; but she shared a passion for tennis, swimming, and boating. Sumner was a regular visitor to [their] house . . . and Toquette's mother and sisters and brothers took him in, indeed would help him realize his future dreams."[26]

They were married at her family home at the lake of Enghien, just outside of Paris, on November 29, 1917.[27] The one-time Maine backwoodsman, somewhat polished in the salons of Philadelphia and Boston, made quite a match for the attractive, lithe, petite, *a la Française* woman who was awarded the Red Cross Gold Medal 1914–18.[28] The youngest of six children born in the French-speaking Swiss canton of Neuchâtel, Toquette was from a decidedly well-off Protestant family. Her father was a lawyer and *notaire* specializing in the acquisition and transfer of property under a complicated and obscure Franco-Swiss legal system involving rights, taxes, and ancient laws of inheritance. *Notaires* were prosperous, and Toquette's father had moved the family to France to deal with the affairs of a number of rich Swiss families. He was himself a man of property, not the least the house at the lake of Enghien. (He died there in 1907.)[29]

Toquette's mother, Anna-Julia de Ricou, and Toquette's siblings warmed to Sumner. He may have been a Teddy from across the ocean but he clearly shared their values: respect for learning, for good manners, and for money. Toquette's brother, Paul-Eugene, was a lieutenant in the French Army decorated with the Croix de Guerre and Légion d'Honneur.

Courting Toquette in Paris must have been something special for Sumner even as he was busy working under Dr. Blake. The team was on the cutting edge of medicine, during a war when there were no sulfur or antibiotic drugs. Sumner and his colleagues experimented and developed techniques to treat the terrible wounds caused by the flying shrapnel and explosives of modern warfare. And they made good headway, successfully treating trench fever.[30]

Gangrene, a major scourge of earlier wars, killed soft tissue, particularly in wounded extremities. A friend of Sumner's, Dr. Kenneth Taylor of the University of Minnesota and a volunteer at the American Hospital of Paris, had successfully treated laboratory animals against this evil by injecting a preparation of chloral hydrate and quinine. However, the remedy had not been tested on humans. Mary Davis, a British nurse and Taylor's assistant at the hospital, saw what the gangrene did to her "boys." She decided to secretly contaminate herself with gangrene, and when she fell ill had Dr. Taylor use his remedy. Mary Davis, the human guinea pig, was cured in 48 hours.[31]

In Paris, Sumner discovered a singular symbol of how the war was changing attitudes. It arrived in the form of a man from New York, Washington, D.C., and Alabama, the son of a slave and a freeborn woman: the inventor of ragtime. His name was Lt. Jim Reese Europe, and he brought jazz to the continent. Jim Reese Europe and William Handy had written the music for the fox-trot, and with William Tyres, Jim wrote the first tango for the famous dancing couple Vernon and Irene Castle. The U.S. Army was so taken with his music that upon his arrival in Europe, they sent Jim's all-black "Hellfighters" band on a tour of France.

The music was an immediate success. The Hellfighters even put on a performance for Sumner's Hospital No. 9. A photograph of the event shows the band playing in the courtyard. Jim Reese Europe is directing, baton in hand and eyeglasses perched on his nose. He's dressed in full uniform, sporting an officer's Sam Brown belt, peaked service cap, and leather puttees.[32]

Jim Reese Europe became a raging success. His African-American band with some one hundred fifty instruments had played all over Paris, and indeed all over France by 1918. Their premiere concert at the Théâtre des Champs Elysées drew the likes of French president Poincaire and generals Pétain and Pershing, who relished the popular syncopated music.

Thus "jazz," as Jim explained it, "[l]iquefied harmony—half moan and half hallelujah,"[33] was introduced to Europe. But Jim's real forte was getting people to dance. He had couples dancing in the streets of Paris and across a dozen towns and cities in France.

Later, when Jim was gassed in action in the Champagne region, General Pershing's staff ordered Jim and the band out of the trenches.

No one in the U.S. high command wanted anything to happen to Lieutenant Europe. Unfortunately, no one in the U.S. high command could protect Lt. Jim Reese Europe when he was murdered by his drummer at a concert in Boston a few months after the end of the war.

Between July 1917 and August 1919, Sumner was a staff member at four hospitals in Paris and a mobile hospital unit. The war was grinding out American casualties on the battlefields of the Aisne-Marne, St. Mihiel, Meuse-Argonne, Champagne, Somme, and Vosges regions. About a million American combat troops were deployed in these engagements, 191,000 troops in hospitals at any one time. American battlefield casualties totaled fifty-two thousand, and many more would die in the influenza-pneumonia epidemics that swept U.S. military camps in France in 1919.

At the eleventh hour of the eleventh day of the eleventh month of 1918, the Great War ended. A generation of young men had been lost, including almost one-and-three-quarter million Germans, one-and-a-half million French, and three-quarters of a million British.[34] The Great War killed ten million and wounded twenty million.

Sumner's actions at the Somme and during three years of war, and Toquette's deeds as a wartime nurse for almost five years, forever marked the Jackson family. Eric Leed notes in his book *No Man's Land: Combat and Identity in World War I,* that what men (and women, too) learned in the Great War set them irrevocably apart from others who stood outside it. The Jacksons evolved a view of the Red Cross, Wilsonian neutrality, the nature of war, and the character of the French people and French values that sharply contrasted with public sentiment in America. In a way, the Jacksons had chosen their destiny.[35]

2

COMING HOME—GOING HOME

There is a special thrill about coming home to America via New York—and by steamer: the briny gives way to the land, to the perfumes of the earth. The view of the mouth of the Hudson River and the Statue of Liberty strikes something in all of us. As the steam whistles blast out a chorus and Manhattan comes into view, one can almost feel the beat of the city—and New York was certainly beating in August 1919.

When Sumner with Toquette on his arm arrived at the piers of Hoboken, New Jersey, in the last days of August 1919, the country he had left three years earlier had since matured and prospered. Americans believed they had won "over there." Industry had created enormous wealth by arming and supplying the more than two million men sent to Europe; and President Wilson, Nobel Peace Prize winner that year, was now working to realize his vision of a peaceful postwar world through a nascent League of Nations. Sumner and Toquette, who throughout their lives took an active interest in world politics and current affairs, had to notice that despite President Wilson's quest for peace, the world was—in 1919—as it had always been: a very dangerous place. The Red Army was abroad in Finland and in the Crimea. Benito Mussolini launched his Fascist party that would rule Italy two years later, and despite Germany signing the peace treaty in Versailles, that country was in political turmoil.

Sumner returned to a culture, certainly in rural America and in Washington, of "America first, America the best," growing isolationism, and suspicion of things foreign. Toquette must have been struck by the vastness of America and the dynamic of it all. One can only guess at her expectations.

Sumner was processed out of the Army at Camp [*sic*] Dix along with thousands of other officers and enlisted men.[1] On September 12, 1919, Dr. Sumner Waldron Jackson was a civilian again. He had served his country well, gained light-years of experience as a surgeon—especially the year before, when he practiced at a mobile hospital during the great push by the Teddies along the Meuse-Argonne that ended World War I.[2] Now he was free to take Toquette home to Maine to meet his family. Sumner had rarely visited Maine after his graduation from Bowdoin College in 1909. He had worked as a companion in Philadelphia to pay his way through medical school and then held an internship at Mass. General in Boston.

He had been away for ten years. His parents were now elderly; his brother and sister were grown up. And here he was, returning home as an American doctor, British officer, and Paris surgeon. He was bringing along his pretty French wife to the family farm at Spruce Head, a village in southeast Maine on the edge of the sea and what is now Camden Hills State Park, close by the Canadian border. Of course, Sumner was considered a hero; he had financed his siblings' schooling and served his country as Maine men traditionally had. But a lot of soldiers had come and gone by 1919. Paris was an alien and suspicious place, and the folks in Spruce Head were more interested in how the buttermilk had turned out that autumn. They were busying themselves with smoked hams and bottling fruits and vegetables in earthen cellars—provisions for the rigors of the coming winter when Spruce Head would be snowed in for weeks.[3]

We can only imagine what Toquette was thinking while she traveled from New York, the most cosmopolitan city in America, to rural Maine. Quaint? Probably not, for she was neither a snob nor a cynic. She must have loved the countryside, the lake and nearby ocean, the changing colors of the maple leaves, and above all, the domestic and wild animal life of Maine. (In Paris, she kept several dogs and cats at the apartment in the chic 16th arrondissement of Paris, and some pet goats and foxes at the lake house at Enghien.)

Sumner had made connections in Philadelphia while at Jefferson Medical School, and he had no trouble obtaining a post with an established urologist there. The couple moved to Philadelphia sometime in late 1919, and he began to prosper and build a reputation as a serious clinician. But Toquette never took to American ways, and Sumner's experiences had set him forever apart from the America he'd left. By 1920 the economy was booming, and colleagues and "company" wanted to talk about their new Fords, Packards, and Pierce-Arrows. They chatted about tennis and golf and the peccadilloes of their neighbors, and the market: shares and stocks, bonds and oil and railways. It all bored Sumner to death. He preferred telling war stories, rarely to the delight of the male company and always to the utter boredom of the women. He'd sit back, light a cigar, sip from a glass of whisky, and in plain "Maine-speak" tell about life on the Western Front during the Great War. His favorite story, certainly apocryphal, was about a man who drove a Ford ambulance:

> Unbeknown to the driver, the wounded *poilu* in the back awoke and drank from a canteen full of red wine. When the driver got to the hospital up front, the soldier was drunk, sitting upright and singing. Albeit badly wounded, the man greeted the hospital orderlies with a smile, offered a swig of red and a drag on his cigarette. Furious, the hospital orderlies dropped the cover on the Ford and told the driver he had no business bringing the soldier to a hospital reserved for *couches*—the seriously wounded.
>
> "Get to the damn dressing station for *assis*—the lightly wounded," they barked.
>
> It was some twenty miles away. Off the driver went, while the man in the rear fell into a deep boozy sleep.
>
> At the dressing station the orderlies found a comatose hulk of a man on the stretcher. They sternly admonished the driver, "Get that man to the hospital for *couches.*"
>
> The driver was furious; but he took off at top speed, indifferent to the jarring bumps in the road. The bouncing eventually woke the *poilu*. The wounded man began shouting and pounding on the walls of the cab, cursing the driver. When they arrived again at the entrance to the hospital for *couches,* the driver bopped the man over the head with a tire iron, putting the cursing *poilu* to sleep. The orderlies complimented the driver: "Glad to see you got it right this time."[4]

Sumner would invariably end with, "Did you folks know that at Chemins des Dames, a hundred men fell every minute? Did you know it took 448 shells to kill one man up there?"[5]

His dinner companions didn't give a damn about the Great War. They wanted to talk about profits, penny stocks, real estate, and golf. Yet nothing could stop Sumner. He wanted to speak of the brave men—brave Frenchmen, brave Englishmen, brave Germans and Yanks—all mixed up in the muck. And he would say something like: "Let me tell you folks, I know the Hun, they'll never forget that defeat." Toquette would plead with "Jack" (as she called him) to change the subject and talk about Maine and what she had heard from Sumner's sister: that Sumner and his brother once chased a bear out of Spruce Head.

Toquette's French ways did not endear her to the women in the City of Brotherly Love. The gentlemen in Ben Franklin's town must have been bowled over by her flippant attitude but certainly the ladies were less than impressed. And to tell the truth, Toquette was similarly disenchanted with her new life in America.

It was obvious, very soon, that Philadelphia was not going to work out. Toquette missed her mother, the family house on the lake at Enghien with its long weekends and conviviality, good food, and good company. She missed swimming in the cold lake, the sailing and canoeing, tennis, and her animals. And she fell ill; there is a hint that she might have had a miscarriage, but she recovered. Sumner finally realized that Toquette felt like an exiled and displaced bride—as did so many other French wives brought to America by returning servicemen in 1919.

Toquette was thirty-two and Sumner thirty-six years old when she convinced her husband to leave Philadelphia and return to Paris. Given the new developments at the American Hospital of Paris, it may have seemed like a promising time to make the move back across the ocean. The American Hospital, no longer in the hands of the American military, was newly dedicated to its mission as a private establishment to bring American medicine, surgical techniques, and care to Americans living in or visiting Paris. Privately financed since 1909, in 1921 the board of governors launched a drive to raise money for the construction of a building to replace the hospital built at the turn of the century. The new U.S. president, Warren G. Harding, called on citizens to give their support.

Tat, Toquette's sister, wrote to the couple that everyone was talking about the new building: 120 beds for medical, surgical, and maternity cases, three operating rooms—and the governors had bought the land next to the old hospital.

Sumner wrote to Dr. Edmond Gros,[6] whom he had known as the hospital's director during the war. Gros confirmed that they were indeed looking for American physicians and surgeons and that there would be a continued need for them if the hospital's mission to care for Americans were to be realized. He told Sumner as he told everyone, "The hospital is a bit of the United States right here in Paris. We never lose the feeling that we are thoroughly American."[7] Gros told about how Dr. Charles Bove—an American surgeon who had come to France when America entered the war—had just passed the French baccalaureate and was going on to do medicine at the faculty of Paris. Sumner would have to enter the practice of medicine in France by the same route—which meant going back to school and learning medicine all over again. If he could accomplish this tedious undertaking— and Bove later told Sumner that the "whole business was a nightmare"—the hospital would certainly hire him.[8]

Toquette's family offered to help them financially until Sumner could qualify to practice in France. Toquette arranged the storage of their few things and their steamship tickets on the *Aquitania* to sail from New York to Le Havre. She also, in advance, located a tutor in France for Sumner: Miss Clemence Bock, a "plain spinster" and teacher of Latin and French.

They sailed for Paris in September 1921; Toquette was going home with great expectations, Sumner was leaving home with grave doubts.

Awaiting their arrival in Paris was thirty-year-old Clemence Bock. Toquette and her sister, Tat, had chosen Miss Bock to help Sumner pass the French baccalaureate examinations: either Sciences-Languages or Languages-Philosophy. Clemence was to develop a great love for Sumner and wrote a seventeen-page memorial to him sometime after 1945, titled *Souvenirs sur le Docteur Jackson*. It is a pretty and strikingly old-fashioned piece, this tribute to Sumner and to the family that befriended her.

Over the years, as Clemence and Toquette became friends, it seems that Clemence became Toquette's scribe. (Clemence, however, certainly had her own ideas about Sumner.) If Clemence's idyllic, pastoral, and Homeric record of Sumner's adolescence is to be believed, Sumner's arrival at her place on the Boulevard Haussmann in the fall of 1921 was anything but heroic. He was a six-foot-one, 185-pound lamb—a docile hulk of a man willing to submit to the tortures of tutorship, first in the sciences, and later, having failed to master "obscure" French sciences, English, Latin, and French. These were secondary-school exams for the French baccalaureate (*Bachot*), which the French government insisted he pass before redoing his medical studies at the University of Paris.[9]

Sumner, Clemence reports, would sit "sad and forlorn, very correct in a gray business suit; and so tall I had to raise my eyes to look at him." She noted he had "American features and bushy eyebrows joined above blue eyes that seemed small and deep. However, he did appeal to Clemence's eye.

Later, at the lake house at Enghien, she watched Sumner getting out of a dinghy. "He wore only a brief bathing slip and at a distance he looked like one of the heroes of a Fenimore Cooper novel. I wondered if there wasn't 'red-skin' blood in the Jackson family, despite their Scotch origins." Clemence admired his robust physique: "Physical exercise was a must for the Doctor's muscular body, and he played tennis, sailed, or worked the garden; cutting and sawing wood was his hobby. He loved animals and played with a wild fox Toquette had tamed."

Regarding his studies, Clemence wrote, "The Doctor had difficulty expressing himself in French, and I realized his mouth actually ravaged and harmed the pronunciation of French words." Nevertheless, she managed to get over her allergy to Sumner's French (which was adequate if not quite poetic) and found Sumner "conscientious," memorizing his lessons verbatim.

Still, after studying for a year under her tutelage, Sumner failed the crucial *Bachot* examination: Philosophy. It must have been a bitter moment for the decorated front-line surgeon from the Great War. But

Clemence and another professor counseled the Jacksons to abandon Paris and try to do the *Bachot* at Algiers, where the examining professors were "less strict."

It is almost impossible to imagine what indignities this non-French, mature physician had to endure to be licensed to practice medicine in France at a time when there were no reciprocal agreements. Still, the Paris Medical Society objected strenuously to foreign physicians being licensed in France, as did the Minister of Education and the French bureaucracy. Sumner's friend and colleague at the American Hospital of Paris, Dr. Charles Bove, relates his own experience:

> If I had realized exactly what my decision to practice medicine in France would involve in terms of personal heartache and a variety of professional obstacles, I would not have entered into my commitment so lightheartedly. I recall an elderly professor who, during the oral test, got me in so tight a fix I thought for certain I would be flunked. He hadn't a tooth in his head, but he managed somehow to chew tobacco. The yellow juice ran out of the corners of his flaccid lips and down his chin.
>
> Suddenly he shot at me a problem in geometry. At this time I was still groping with the French language and I did not understand his meaning. There was a silence during which I watched with fascination the tobacco juice drip from his chin. Then he screwed his loose, wrinkled face into a tight knot and ordered me to sit down. I did not move.
>
> "Sit down! Enough!"
>
> I continued to stand where I was and he seemed about to have a fit. "Sir, if you will enunciate clearly enough for me to understand what you are saying I shall try to work out the problem."
>
> He glared at me and grunted. Then he went to the blackboard and furiously jotted down some problem in algebra.
>
> "Work that!"
>
> I did so and luckily quite rapidly. Had I sat down as any young student would have done, it would have cost me an additional year's study.[10]

Sumner must have been very determined, and Toquette must have been very stubborn, about their goals. In any event they took Clemence's advice, packed their dog and pet fox in a small 5cv Citroën car, and sailed from Marseilles to Algiers and an exotic life of studying "philo" in the Casbah.

After achieving success with the *Bachot* during their nine-month stay in Algiers, Sumner and Toquette returned to Paris early in 1923. He studied at the Ecole du Médecine in Paris, defended his thesis in 1925, and was admitted to practice at the American Hospital as a surgeon and urologist that same year. They took an apartment on Avenue Foch, which in 1925 was as chic as it is today. The apartment had two entrances: one through a garden giving onto the avenue, and one on the side street, the Rue Traktir. Patients coming to Sumner's Paris office would enter through the garden.

Up until then, and despite help from Toquette's family, they had been living an almost bohemian existence while Sumner finished medical school. The move to Avenue Foch, however, was an extravagant new beginning. To celebrate, Toquette organized an elegant surprise housewarming party. But when Sumner walked into the parlor and found it lit with candles and hung with crepe streamers, he looked around and yelled, "But where is Mademoiselle Bock? Someone fetch Bock!"

Clemence was introduced at the party as the artisan of Sumner's victory over French "bullshit bureaucracy." The guests—mostly physicians—sang a bawdy tribute to the doctor's thesis on anorectal fistulas while a big dog Toquette had just brought home howled. The song went something like:

Jack can you find an anal fistula? . . . It's south of the sigmoid . . . and north of the anus . . . and it's hell when a patient sits down, sits down. It's hell when a patient sits down. . . .

Bock remembers the evening as "memorable . . . and I wasn't shocked because I know doctors are different from lay people. They don't see people the way we do, it's a kind of deformation in their character; and they love a good time." Clemence never forgot that evening; she writes, though "Toquette may have had a bit too much champagne because as she said good-bye, she stepped outside in the small garden on the Avenue Foch and took my arm in hers.

"'Clemence,'" she whispered, "'I hope you're not in love with my Jack.'"

But she was, of course.

Clemence thought that Dr. Jackson

> towered over most men. I can see him now at the American Hospital in a long surgical coat that reached his ankles. He invariably wore a white shirt with a tiepin joining an oxford collar—always Mr. Correct. But with a terrible temper. His patients feared and loved him. He was often intimidating, but he was mostly gentle, well read and forever telling interesting stories about America and the Great War. [His] patients were wealthy Americans and the wives of rich Parisian businessmen. Some of the most beautiful women in Paris came to his office at avenue Foch or to the hospital. . . .
>
> Mademoiselle Diplarakos, the beauty queen of Greece, was in love with him, and while he never talked about his patients' ailments or personal lives, I do know that he treated Ernest Hemingway and his wife, all the bankers at Morgan, and Scott and Zelda Fitzgerald. . . . When he was elected to the hospital medical board, one of his fellow physicians, a sculptor, had him pose for a bust of Hypocrites. The bronze statue is still at the house on the lake.[11]

According to Clemence, the first years of Dr. Jackson's practice were "brilliant." The Jacksons bought an Amilcar and took vacations on the Côte d'Azur. Sumner and Toquette were present on May 12, 1926, when the new Memorial Building at the American Hospital was inaugurated by French president Gaston Doumergue, Marshal Foch, and U.S. ambassador Myron T. Herrick. U.S. president Calvin Coolidge sent a message about the heroic work of the hospital in the Great War.[12] The ceremony marked the hospital's foray into a New World.

From its opening in 1909–1910, the founders dedicated the hospital to the service of the American community in Paris. In the early years, needy Americans were treated in wards, free of charge; the more fortunate, wealthy patients had private rooms and paid handsomely for their care and services.

From 1914 to 1917, during World War I, when the hospital was converted for military use, the French government and American charitable contributions financed care for the sick and wounded. When America entered the war in 1917, the hospital became a U.S. military institution managed by the American Army. (The same held true during World War II.)

As time passed and the hospital expanded, the need for sophisticated treatment and modern high-tech diagnostic equipment put an additional burden on the organization's finances. All patients were eventually asked to pay something, but no one was turned away. It was understood that admitting physicians, like Sumner, would do their share of pro bono work. By 1925 the hospital had already been awarded approval by the American College of Surgeons, and was deemed "comparable" to American medical institutions. The demand for a "bed" by then was considerable.

Throughout the 1920s when Sumner was chief of urology (known as a genito-urinary specialist in 1925), and during the Great Depression, the American Hospital's stated mission was: care for Americans in Paris.[13] But as the Depression bit into the expatriate community, the hospital and attending physicians such as Sumner suffered from the loss of income from a once-wealthy clientele, and were taxed with donating more and more of their time to pro bono medical work. Many wealthy patients were literally "wiped out" by the stock market crash of 1929. Families sank into destitution—one patient even left her fur coat to the hospital as payment for services. There were hundreds of such stories, some no doubt anecdotal, but many were true.

The hospital launched a campaign in the big American cities of Boston and New York, and in Paris, asking the public to help their expatriate fellow Americans and to give, "each according to their means." The hospital's governors declared that "this institution recognizes neither race, religion, social class. . . . We remain a symbol of charity for all in this age of materialism." The Morgan Bank in Paris responded by giving the hospital a "considerable" overdraft facility at a preferential rate of 5 percent per annum, unheard of at the time.[14]

Regardless of the egalitarian nature of the hospital, Sumner was "a key player in the hospital's team composed of Drs. Edmond Gross [*sic*], de Martel, and Jackson providing general and internal medicine and surgery that was envied at the time for bringing American advanced procedures to France."[15]

And Sumner did indeed treat the "elite" of Paris and some members of the so-called Lost Generation—expatriate writers and artists and their families. Sumner, according to Clemence, knew Gertrude Stein and Zelda and F. Scott Fitzgerald, and as we shall see treated Ernest Hemingway—with whom Sumner shared a love of boxing. Fitzgerald and Hemingway were the nucleus of the group that had abandoned America for Paris. Clemence says, "Sumner was well known in Paris and sought after by the American community, and I marveled at how he always managed to be a gentleman." His patient roster also included folks like Edward E. ("e.e.") Cummings, who drove an ambulance for the Norton unit in France in 1917,[16] and Michael Arlin. The Astor, Vanderbilt, Harriman, and Morgan families also sought medical consultations with Sumner.[17]

The American Hospital played host to a variety of ex-pat writers and journalists: Harold Stearnes, Henry Miller, and James Thurber, for example. This "lost" pack hung out on the Left Bank, seeking the company of other "artists" and drinking at the Dome, the Select, or the Rotonde cafés and sometimes doing "a deck of snow," as cocaine was called in Paris at the time.

As the genito-urinary specialist, Sumner very likely assisted Dr. de Martel when Zelda Fitzgerald underwent an exploratory operation for chronic gynecological problems in June 1925. The "right ovary was inflamed . . . the appendix removed, in very bad shape . . . near peritonitis"—not a benign matter, given the state of Zelda's health and chronic alcoholism. But any question that Gros, de Martel, or Sumner was involved in an abortion or curettage must be ruled out. The hospital's medical board forbade abortions unless the pregnancy was life-threatening. And there were clinics in Paris that "specialized" in such procedures. It would have been too risky to perform an abortion at the "American" on such a "notorious" person as Zelda, with staff and nurses assisting.[18]

Drunkenness and stomach disorders were common among the American expatriates and accounted for many of the ailments seen by Sumner in his private practice and at the hospital. It should be remembered how "broke" most of them were in 1925–1929; few of the "Lost Generation" in Paris had money. Most were living from hand to mouth and, like the Fitzgeralds, on overdrawn advances from Maxwell Perkins, Scott's publisher at Scribner's. Hemingway enjoyed playing the "starving artist," getting Fitzgerald and the publishers who hung around the Dome café to pick up his tab. He cried out once at the Dome, "Some of you rich guys ought to buy the old man a pair of pants so he wouldn't freeze his ass off in the winter." It worked. Harold Loeb, who published avant-garde magazines, ran home and fetched a pair of pants for Hemingway.[19]

On one occasion, Ernest Hemingway was brought to the emergency room of the hospital with his head swathed in thirty layers of toilet paper.[20] He had gone into the bathroom of his apartment at night, and in the dark pulled the wrong cord. A skylight came crashing down on his head. The toilet paper was used to stop the blood flow until Sumner, who was on call, could sew him up.[21] The writer was left with a permanent scar.[22] In *Michael Palin's Hemingway Adventure*, the author speculates that the accident brought back memories of the battle wounds Hemingway suffered in 1918, when he ran a frontline canteen for the Red Cross on the Piave River near Fossalta in Italy. Out of those memories was born *A Farewell to Arms*.[23]

After the stock market crashed, the "Lost" group moved away. Zelda, tragically, went in search of medical care for what eventually would be diagnosed as *"une folie a deux"* and schizophrenia.[24] The members of the "Lost Generation" enjoyed a brief but glamorous hold on the city of Paris—a flash in the pan, but a brilliant flash at times.

Hemingway wrote to Maxwell Perkins from Paris on October 31, 1929: "Hope to Christ you weren't caught in the market. They're liquidating now." The writer left Paris the following year, not to return until World War II.

————————

Meanwhile at the hospital on January 10, 1928, a great event occurred. Sumner was forty-three and Toquette thirty-nine when she gave birth to their first and only child, Phillip, nicknamed "Pete." Someone showed up at the hospital with a number of bottles of Bollinger 1921, and Phillip was toasted until the nurses shut the party down.

The years after Phillip's birth became a strange interlude in world history. By 1933 there were almost fourteen million unemployed in the United States, three million in Britain and as many in France; worldwide, thirty million people were unemployed, according to the statistics of the time.[25] Neither Paris nor the Jackson family escaped the ravages of the Great Depression: labor unrest, devaluation of the French franc, street riots, erratic public transport sometimes set aflame, news *kiosques* burned, and bloodshed on the streets as Communists fought Fascists.

Clemence reports that it was about this time that Dr. Jackson treated a patient who was the victim of what would become an infamous public scandal.[26] The event was a crime of passion, or so the newspapers alleged. It began on a night in 1933, the year Hitler was appointed German chancellor. The hospital telephoned Sumner because an American lady was being brought to the emergency room with a bullet wound. Sumner was one of the few surgeons experienced in gunshot trauma.

It turned out that the "American lady," twenty-four-year-old Dorothy Wright, was not American but the English mistress of Roland Coty, the son of the millionaire publisher and manufacturer of Coty cosmetics and perfumes. Coty was labeled "bizarre" by Parisian newspapers; married with two children, he and his wife apparently shared the favors of Miss Wright.

Upon examination, Sumner declared Miss Wright dead on arrival, three hours after a bullet—shot at close range from Coty's revolver—struck the girl behind her right ear. The newspapers claimed that Miss Wright's murder and liaison with a married man were being hushed up and that millions of francs had been passed around. (Sumner's name was never mentioned in the files—and the hospital refused to even confirm that Miss Wright was admitted.) Maurice-Ivan Sicard, a journalist, wrote under the headline, "Why hasn't Roland Coty been arrested?" that the girl had had a terrible argument with Coty and his wife. He reported that Coty was an "alcoholic and drug user, a degenerate," and that he and his wife engaged in what Sicard called, "inversion parties." Sicard explained that on the night of Miss

Wright's death, Coty had been out drinking and grew angry because the Wright girl had refused to keep him company. Coty then returned to the Hôtel George V and went to the suite he had rented for Miss Wright. The floor maid heard three distinct voices in the apartment. There was shouting. Then, at about 5 A.M., the maid heard a shot.

Coty told the maid that Miss Wright had killed herself. He called the Coty family physician, Dr. Iselin, who called the American Hospital—presumably because Iselin believed the Wright girl was an American. The hospital woke Sumner, who arrived in the emergency room to find the girl brain-dead.[27]

Sumner was frequently called into the hospital to treat strange cases. As time went on and the older surgeons retired, he and Dr. Bove were the only surgeons experienced with trauma—mainly gunshot wounds. One winter's evening, Sumner removed a bullet from an American's tongue. The poor man had gotten mixed up in a right-wing political riot at the National Assembly. A stray bullet, fired either from the police or one of the rioters, had entered through his neck. Somehow the wounded man had managed to request transport to the American Hospital. The patient, whose name has been lost with time, was comatose when he arrived. Dr. Jackson was the duty surgeon that week, but one of the nurses called in Dr. Bove, too. It's a tribute to the medicine of the time that they located the bullet through an X-ray. The little .25-caliber slug was extracted in the base of the tongue and the man walked out of the hospital a few days later, none the worse. Dr. Bove insisted that Dr. Jackson keep the forensic evidence. Sumner walked around with the bullet in his vest pocket for months. According to Clemence, Sumner would say, "Bove and I took it out of a tongue," and then he'd roar with laughter.[28]

These were the years when the American Hospital became a center for Franco-American scientific and medical exchanges. Men like Charles Mayo, renowned American surgeon and founder of clinics that bear his name; Albert Calmette, inventor with Guerin of a tuberculosis vaccine; and Emile Roux, Institute Pasteur, a renowned toxicologist who discovered antidiphtheria serum, all visited the hospital and gave lectures at the Memorial Building. Physicians and scientists from American medical colleges and associations, Japanese, British, Australian, and Chinese shared their discoveries and techniques with the elite of European medical circles. The hospital at Neuilly became a hub for international medical and scientific exchange.[29]

All this was snuffed out after the Anschluss of March 11, 1938. War with Germany seemed inevitable. Still, many Parisians clung to the hope of "an arrangement with Mr. Hitler."

Indeed, by 1938, Hitler shocked the majority of the French people as they watched newsreels of his entry into Vienna at the head of German troops. The Führer received a delirious welcome from the Austrian people as he proclaimed Austrians members of the "master race." And Pierre Flandin, a former prime minister of France (who later would figure in Vichy governments) wrote in *Le Figaro*: "Germany has to find in the world an outlet for its over-industrialization and its overpopulation. The question is whether you allow [Germany] to find this or, wherever it goes, it finds France in opposition. I do not agree that France can play policeman in Central Europe or in any other country."[30]

Abwehr and Gestapo services were active in establishing agent networks in France in 1938 and 1939, often recruiting among Red Cross officials, Poles, and Latin Americans.[31] A story circulated in 1938 about a visit to the American Hospital by Carl Oberg, a German SS colonel posing as a diplomat. Oberg is believed to have toured the hospital to scout its future use by the SS in wartime. As head of all German security forces in France during the Occupation, Oberg would ultimately play a fateful role in the lives of the Jackson family.

Throughout 1938, the hospital's medical board, of which Sumner was a member, prepared for catastrophe. The Fitzgeralds, Ernest Hemingway, the Vanderbilts, and the many lesser society lights, businesspeople, and tourists, had long since gone home. The board set out to remake the image of the hospital, which had unfairly been characterized as a watering hole for rich American and French society "dames," and revamp it into a premier military hospital.[32] With the help of U.S. ambassador William C. Bullitt, Edward B. Close, an American World War I hero and managing governor of the hospital, prepared to transform the beds at Neuilly into a French military facility as in 1914.[33]

Sumner was burdened with meetings, conferences, and new responsibilities as the hospital prepared for a war. Many of the governors, staff, and physicians had been through it all before. Certainly Sumner's knowledge was indispensable. The board provided for the worst cases: shrapnel wounds, gas attacks, aerial bombardment, blackouts, and electrical outages. Sumner agreed to do standby anesthesia during surgery when he wasn't operating. A special unit for blood donations was set up. And the board planned to close the maternity ward and transfer mental cases. The American Red Cross was called on for support. When French staff were mobilized, Americans and volunteers picked up their work.

Unlike many Europeans and Englishmen who believed that Herr Hitler could be accommodated, the Jackson family spoke of nothing but war after the Anschluss. Tat writes in her diary at this time: "Situation grave; Hitler bears down on Rumania . . ." and later, "We arranged for our passports to be updated." Tat visited England that summer, where she had "tea with Miss Grey and her niece . . . here they say Hitler will invade Czechoslovakia."

On September 12, back at the lake house, Tat reports in her diary that the Jacksons gathered to hear Hitler's live radio broadcast that evening. The next day at lunch with Clemence Bock, the family pondered Hitler's next move. They didn't need to wait long for an answer. On September 30, the Reichsführer forced Czechoslovakia to concede the Sudetenland to Germany.

It snowed at Enghien on Christmas Eve 1938: "Snow on the roofs," writes Tat, who tells of a Christmas feast with the Jackson and Barrelet de Ricou families: a lunch of crayfish, jellied eggs, ham, fries, salad, *marrons glacés,* and Christmas pudding with hard sauce. It was to be their last Christmas feast together.[34]

The year 1939 opened with Western Europeans in a panic. Hitler swallowed all of Czechoslovakia, rightly predicting to his worried generals that England and France would merely protest but not intervene.[35] Then Italy invaded Albania and signed a war pact with Germany, while Hitler agreed to carve up Poland with Stalin.

On September 3, 1939, as German Stukas bombed Warsaw, Great Britain declared war on Germany. A few hours later, France followed, as did Canada, Australia, and New Zealand.

At the lake house Sumner was certain that Roosevelt would join the Allies—America, too, would fight against the evils of Nazism and fascism. He was convinced that it was only a matter of weeks before America would declare war. So he kept busy cutting wood with Pete while Toquette went around the marketplaces with Tat, buying sugar, canned goods, and other essentials.

Tat notes that they were allowed one kilo of sugar (2.2 pounds) per person. Scrawled in a shaky hand in her red leather diary for September 3, she records: "Jack cut lots of wood . . . an alert that night; woke early, a few minutes after 5 A.M. Learned France under attack, listened to radio. It's war! War!"

The phony war that would last barely nine months had begun. Phillip was eleven years old. Like millions of other youths of his generation, his life would forever be marked by the events that would follow.

3

THE DEBACLE

Paris 1940

The cabarets and movie houses of Paris were full as the first winter of the war drew to a close. But despite the wine and chocolate, despite the cabaret life and Greta Garbo's *Ninotchka,* a grim, impending sense of doom hung over the city. A *Paris Herald Tribune* editorial, "The Promises of Spring," observed: "The tragedy of it all is that few minds will be without a gnawing consciousness that at the front and in many other areas of the world the season of promise has been blacked out."[1]

The days were full of fear and uncertainty and Sumner and Toquette argued over whether to return to America. Sumner suggested they send Phillip to live with Sumner's siblings in Waldoboro, Maine. Toquette refused. She tried to convince Sumner that the French Army could defeat the Germans. Sumner, who may have been better informed through his contacts at the American Hospital, knew the situation was critical. The pressures on the Jacksons were hardly bearable.[2]

Most French believed, as did Toquette, that the Germans would never penetrate their fortified Maginot Line. Even as late as 1939 French marshal Philippe Pétain—the victor of Verdun in 1916—claimed that the country's safety was best guaranteed by a continuous front buttressed with fortifications: *La Ligne Maginot.* Few imagined, aside from General de Gaulle, that the invading German armies, spearheaded by panzer tanks, would simply maneuver around the fortress line.[3]

On April 7, 1940, the *Herald Tribune* reported the full-scale German invasion of Norway and Denmark, two neutral countries that had managed to stay out of the Great War. Then a banner headline of May 10, 1940, announced what everyone in France was dreading: the invasion of Holland, Belgium, and Luxembourg.

Earlier Hitler had ordered his generals, "Do not wait for the enemy to come to us . . . but take the offensive immediately ourselves. . . . [Use] ruthless methods. Once time is lost it cannot be recovered." Hitler and his generals knew there wasn't sufficient fuel, spare parts, or armaments to risk a long war. Indeed as late as November 1939, Gen. Franz Halder had written in his diary, "None of the higher headquarters think that the offensive [in France] . . . has any prospect of success."[4]

Then Hitler struck! On May 13, German armies crossed the Meuse River and entered France. The Maginot Line built to protect France against a German invasion became a defensive millstone around the neck of the French Army. The Wehrmacht's panzer-led Blitzkrieg, supported by Luftwaffe dive-bombers, bypassed the fortifications or ran through them with lightning speed as their armies raced across France to the sea. In just one month Dutch, Belgian, and Norwegian forces surrendered. (Denmark capitulated on April 9th.) Italy declared war on France and Britain. The withdrawing British and French armies were trapped at Dunkirk. The French high command seemed helpless, traumatized by the dramatic use of German air power and the mechanized advance of the Wehrmacht armies. At strategic points, many command levels disintegrated because of inadequate and archaic communication systems between French Army units.

Prime Minister Paul Reynaud's government fled Paris. The mass exodus was wild beyond description. As the front collapsed and the capital was threatened, American diplomats were caught up in trying to follow Prime Minister Reynaud and his cabinet—first to Tours and then to Bordeaux (and eventually to Vichy, where Marshal Pétain would form a new government).

Cabinet ministers, bureaucrats, and soldiers mixed with hundreds of thousands of terrified refugees who jammed the highways. Reynaud was constantly harassed and often out of touch with military headquarters, and when he did hear from his generals it was to announce some new disaster as German armies advanced west and south toward the coast. On Reynaud's shoulders rested the fate of the country and its people in the final weeks before France capitulated.

But Reynaud had other troubles on his mind—including a boudoir scandal that held major political significance at the time.[5] It turns out that he had lived illicitly for years with a certain Mme. Helene des Portes, a former friend of his wife. He and Mme. des Portes would often cycle together in the Bois de Boulogne. Whenever the prime minister and Mme. Paul Reynaud, his legal wife, were invited to attend any of the various official events at foreign embassies, gossip had it that the host ambassador was never certain which lady would attend. At one dinner both his wife and mistress arrived, providing a troubling protocol problem.

Besides her good looks, Mme. des Portes was a determined lady and she had serious doubts about the outcome of the war. She persistently urged her lover and his ministers to negotiate peace with Hitler's Germany. According to the scuttlebutt, she was exceptionally persuasive in her boudoir. (It was a fact that the women who were intimate with members of the French government were ambitious to play political roles. The Nazi and Soviet espionage agents stationed in Paris found them a fascinating source of secret information.)

Rather than accept an armistice, Reynaud finally ceded power to his vice premier, Marshal Henri Philippe Pétain, a hero of World War I. As part of the handover of his government and right-wing cabinet to Petain, Reynaud arranged with the marshal to be appointed the new government's ambassador to Washington. This was said to be Mme. des Portes's wish, and she planned to accompany Reynaud to Washington.

But it was not to be. As Mme. des Portes drove Reynaud to the Spanish frontier in her automobile overloaded with baggage, she lost control of the car. The automobile hit a tree, killing her and injuring Reynaud so badly that he was unable to travel.

Reynaud, acknowledged as the most effective of the Third Republic's statesmen, was immobilized for months, and the Nazis imprisoned him and other prewar French premiers for the duration of the war. Georges Mandel, a left-wing Jewish minister in Reynaud's cabinet, was arrested at the same time and later murdered by the SS.[6]

For Sumner and his colleagues at the American Hospital, each day after the initial attack brought tragic and confusing news reports. The press and radio announced small French victories here and there on a shifting battlefield, but mostly the military situation was reported as grim, then hopeless, while an exodus of refugees continued to crowd the roads. Historians have estimated that six to ten million of France's forty million inhabitants left their homes fleeing the German advance.

By the first days of the German invasion, the American Hospital had been cleared of civilian patients to free up beds for wounded French and British military and refugee cases. The civilian patients were transported in ambulances and auto to a temporary hospital at Etretat on the English Channel. The Memorial Building and the hospital's annexes at Neuilly became a French auxiliary war hospital.

As the Germans advanced on Paris, Sumner and his colleagues, Drs. Edmond Gros and Morris Sanders, set up a temporary dressing station in the nearby town of Fontainbleau. Their ambulances took the wounded to the hospital at Neuilly—serious head and bone cases.[7]

Toquette put on her nursing whites and worked at the hospital. Sumner and other surgeons rotated between Paris and Fontainebleau, where the dressing station for French soldiers and wounded refugees was jammed with casualties. He set up an operating facility at a deserted gambling casino near Fontainebleau, where he operated side-by-side with Dr. Bove in a kind of makeshift field hospital. The wounded were placed atop the casino's baccarat, roulette, and craps tables. Bove took a woman's arm off while she lay on the baize-green table screaming, "My silver, my silver!" (All her silver tableware had been stolen as she tried to flee the oncoming German forces. It was all she had left in the world.)[8]

Outside the casino, a French "75"—friendly fire—went through one of the Ford ambulances, wounding a French *chasseur alpin*.[9] Sumner removed the boy's nearly severed leg. It was a neat piece of work done in bad light in a way that would allow the boy's stump to heal and be fitted for an artificial limb. The boy was very brave—most of them were.

———————————————

At the Memorial Building the wounded lay on stretchers in the corridors, waiting for someone to die to free up a bed. The staff worked the ambulances around the clock. The young women drivers—the cream of Paris society—followed in the wake of the French and British troops falling back on Paris. It was as in World War I— sickening chaos, the roads choked with fleeing civilians and frightened troops. Stuka dive-bombers would shriek out of a cobalt-blue sky—the weather was wonderful throughout June 1940—and women and children would wander aimlessly, dragging and pushing their meager belongings down endless tree-lined roads. They slept in ditches, begged for food and water, and pleaded with people in cars, "Take my son, save him."[10]

Later, in Bordeaux, Toulon, and Marseilles, newspapers ran notices like: "Mme. Filippi, Hotel de la Gare, seeks news of her daughter Chantal, abandoned at Chateauroux."

Despite French losses and defeatist leaders, individual French and British soldiers and airmen fought hard against the German machine. Squadron leader Paul Ritchey of the Royal Air Force was brought to the American Hospital at Neuilly in mid-May 1940 after his plane was shot down and crashed near Paris. An armor-piercing bullet had struck him on the side of the neck. He remembers:

> I heard a woman's voice speaking French with a slight American accent say, "*Ils ont le courage.*" I tried to get out of the stretcher and walk. I felt damn silly lying down, but I was pressed back gently. As I was carried through the door into the cool darkness inside, a pretty woman with blonde hair in the uniform of the American Ambulance Corps pressed my hand in which I was still clutching my bloodstained flying helmet and said, "It's going to be all right!" She spoke English with an American drawl, and I thought at the time she had the sweetest voice I had ever heard and looked more beautiful than anyone I had ever seen. I felt my eyes fill with sudden tears, and all I could do was to nod and smile my gratitude. The doctors worked over me. Dr. de Martel, the celebrated head specialist, took

the bullet out of me. Sally, a young American nurse, very kindly held my hand until I went under.

It came back to me the sight of French soldiers in panic throwing women and children out of air-raid shelters so they could get in themselves. . . . Then those same women and children were blown to bits, arms and legs and miscellaneous bits of flesh flying all over the place.

When I awoke I was lying there in quietness between cool white sheets, my once sweaty and verminous [*sic*] uniform again clean and draped on a chair; I had only a hole in my neck to remind me of what had happened. Then I remembered our squadron had destroyed 140 aircraft in nine days. It made me feel better as I shared a room with a captain who was blind.

A lot of French wounded were arriving now. . . . Dr. de Martel and others were busy all the time. When I got better I spent hours puttering about the garden and on the roof . . . a wonderful view of Paris. . . . I even watched de Martel operating on a man's head. A piece of skull about 4 inches by 4 had been removed, and as de Martel probed and delicately cut with his marvelously steady hands, at last producing a shell-splinter, I was surprised to feel suddenly sick and to have to get outside . . . out into that beautiful garden.

Now that the wounded were coming in, the American and French doctors worked day after day continuously from seven in the morning until four the following one. The hospital was full, the staff working to capacity. Several of the women ambulance drivers had disappeared without a trace and were presumed to be casualties. The Huns were deliberately strafing vehicles marked with the Red Cross, and the hospital authorities ordered all insignia removed. The doctors and the nurses never lacked in courage, energy, or cheerfulness. They were all magnificent and I shall never forget their kindness.[11]

A young Zouave[12] named Longuet, hardly twenty years old, had been a dispatch rider before German shell fragments took him down. An ambulance got him back to the Memorial Building, where he was patched up. He would live—but be crippled for life. General Lannois came to his room to pin both the Médaille Militaire (a decoration at the level of the U.S. Congressional Medal of Honor) and the Croix de Guerre on the boy's pajamas. A few staff members including Sumner and Toquette and Drs. Gros, de Martel, Bove, and Mr. Close gathered in the boy's room to honor him and his veteran father. The man sat at his son's bedside, wearing a black patch over the eye he had lost at Verdun in 1916.

"*Tel père, tel fils*," Sumner told Bove.

About this time Dr. Bove remembers Sumner and Toquette sitting together on the veranda of the Memorial Building overlooking the well-manicured hospital gardens. (The scene reminded Bove of how, only a few years earlier, he had posed for a group photograph there with the Jacksons, Dr. Thierry de Martel, and hospital nurses on the occasion of Toquette completing a course in advanced nursing.)[13]

On this day, just before German troops entered Paris, the weather was warm and balmy with a light breeze sweeping over the garden. The last British walking wounded had been evacuated. It was hard to believe that disaster was only a few hours away as General de Gaulle's tank division fought and stopped a German panzer advance at Moncourt. Nevertheless, it was here that Bove told Sumner and Toquette that he was leaving France. Toquette was shocked. Sumner was dismayed.[14] Bove insisted: "It's only a matter of a few weeks before Roosevelt brings America in and declares war on Germany. But this time the Boches will have Paris, and if we stay they'll lock us up." Bove left the hospital, never to return.[15] (His timing for America's entry into the war was, of course, off by almost two years.)

Sumner and Toquette remained on the veranda into the late afternoon as the light faded. Sumner told her that the advancing German troops could not be stopped. He knew through hospital sources that the Wehrmacht panzers were advancing and German units were headed for the west coast of France. Indeed, the British Army was evacuating France by ship at Dunkirk, taking French soldiers with them. And the young English pilot, Ritchey, the fighter pilot with a hole in his neck, flew out of Paris in a mail plane.

As the Germans advanced on Paris, there were ghastly stories in the Paris press of physicians abandoning their sick and putting elderly patients "to sleep."[16] Then Dr. Thierry de Martel, who was exhibiting signs of acute depression, disappeared.[17] Dr. de Martel was a decorated World War I veteran who had lost his only son in the same war. He told friends that he couldn't bear the thought of the Germans occupying his Paris. He wrote his friend, U.S. ambassador William Bullitt, saying, "I made you a promise that I wouldn't leave Paris. I didn't say whether I would stay in Paris alive or dead. Alive, I give the enemy a blank check; dead, an uncovered one." When he heard the sound of German tanks and troops marching down the Champs Elysées, Dr. de Martel injected strychnine in his arm as he lay on the divan in his study. His housekeeper found him a few hours later. A copy of Victor Hugo's play, *Hernani*, lay next to him, opened to the line, "Since one must be tall to die, I arise."[18]

Sumner was shattered by the death of his friend and colleague. Then Dr. Gros, his mentor at the hospital and the "godfather" of the Lafayette Flying Corps in France in 1914, had a stroke and was evacuated from Paris to return home. Sumner was exhausted and assumed that the worst was to come: the ambulance services would have to be shut down. The Germans would grab the Fords for their own troops when they occupied Paris. They'd use the beds at Neuilly as a military hospital for the Wehrmacht. He may have believed that Paris was going to be under siege as it had been in 1870—or worse—that German "shock troops" would parachute into Paris. One thing was certain: Sumner wanted Toquette and Phillip to leave the city.[19] He became convinced that it was time to go home if only for their son's sake. Phillip remembers how Toquette was adamant that they stay in France. She was sure that if her husband left the hospital for America, the French staff would also leave.[20] The fact that de Gaulle was taken into the Reynaud government as undersecretary for war gave her hope that the French and British would counterattack and hold the German armies.

The newspapers of the day told of a new government under Marshal Pétain, who would appeal to the Germans for surrender terms. Pétain was one of many patriotic Frenchmen who had come to believe that only an authoritarian regime could cleanse the corruption in French public and private life. His ideas fitted nicely into Hitler's plans and the Nazi design for a New Order in Europe. No sooner had German armies entered France when Marshal Pétain broadcast to the nation: "You, the French people, must follow me without reservation on the paths of honor and national interest."[21] (When he had his way, Pétain would dissolve the Republic and sign a permanent peace treaty with Nazi Germany.) At the same time, Admiral Darlan promised Winston Churchill he would move the fleet to Algeria—away from German control. News reports later claimed that Darlan left the fleet at Toulon when Pétain offered to make Darlan minister of the navy.[22]

On June 1, 1940, the hospital's managing governor, E. B. Close, called Sumner to his office and without ceremony appointed him "Resident Physician in Charge" of the hospital. As American staff and governors packed to leave, Gen. Aldebert de Chambrun was asked to serve as acting governor general in their absence. Thus began an American exodus from Paris. American governors, physicians, and French staff evacuated the city for the south of France or to return home to America. Only a few days later, the quiet, orderly departure from Paris turned into a chaotic flight. Anyone who could left the city.[23]

The dean of the American Pro-Cathedral of the Holy Trinity was nervous about leaving. His cathedral was a focal point for the Anglo-American Protestant community in Paris. Dean F. W. Beekman, a Harvard and Amherst man, was a patient of Sumner's and a friend to the Jackson family, though the Jacksons were agnostics. But despite his misgivings, he fled Paris on June 11, 1940, when he was informed by the American Embassy that the French government had left for Bordeaux in the south of France.[24]

On June 10, Paris was declared an open city. Then the *Herald Tribune* of June 12, 1940, failed to appear. Hachette, the delivery agent, had lost all its trucks. General de Gaulle bade farewell to his former mentor, Marshal Pétain, at Bordeaux. De Gaulle would tell his family later, in London, "The Marshal died in 1926. But he is the only one who doesn't know it."[25]

But most Frenchmen adored Pétain—certainly the French masses did. And apparently the Roman Catholic Church worshipped him, too, judging from a number of French primate declarations: *"La France c'est Pétain, et Pétain c'est La France,"* and "God is at work through you, M. le maréchal, to save France."[26]

De Gaulle ceased being an active soldier and flew from Bordeaux to London to join Winston Churchill. De Gaulle became a traitor in the eyes of Vichy and Marshal Pétain. He raised the standard of revolt against the legal government of France by broadcasting his famous

Appel du 18 Juin, imploring Frenchmen everywhere in the world to fight on with the British. The French Resistance was born on a BBC broadcast that day.[27]

Toquette, Phillip, Tat (Toquette's sister), and Rosalie the maid left Paris by automobile just in front of the advancing German armies. Sumner moved into a small apartment on the third floor of the hospital.

The fight for France ended in barely four weeks. The Nazi swastika was raised over the Arc de Triomphe and the Tour Eiffel on the morning of June 14. That day German troops in field-gray uniforms led by mounted saber-bearing officers marched down the Champs Elysées. The pictures of the day show Parisians in shock, watching the passing conquerors. Many of the men, women, and children in the crowds bowed their heads as tears ran down their cheeks in humiliation.

A month later, Bastille Day, July 14, 1940, Sumner awoke to a world turned upside down.

For Toquette and Phillip and Tat exiled in a hotel on the Allier River south of Clermont-Ferrand, it must have seemed no different. Tat wrote about how, on a beautiful summer's day, Toquette chased butterflies with a small boy, Phillip fished for salmon in the Allier, and Tat herself gazed into an azure sky as two men in fighter aircraft, an Englishman and a German, tried to kill each other.[28] War was still on between the British and the Germans.

For most Frenchmen, except perhaps those few who had joined Gen. Charles de Gaulle's newly formed Free French in London, it was a humiliating Bastille Day. France had been conquered—occupied by a people most of the French loathed and remembered as the Boches from the bloody battles of 1914–1918. France had been betrayed. Marshal Pétain had established his Vichy regime, appointing himself head of state after banishing the Third Republic, imposing stringent rationing, and arranging for de Gaulle to be condemned to death by a military tribunal. Later, in October, the old marshal would publicly shake hands with Adolf Hitler in a symbolic gesture for all of France to see that Germany was in and Britain was out. Pétain had committed France to the "path of collaboration" with the Third Reich.[29]

Sumner often went to the Memorial Building's roof for a moment away from hospital business, and to gaze at the former lands of the Duc d'Orléans, Louis Philippe, who became king of France. From his perch on the roof, Sumner would smoke a cigar and survey the expensive villas and gardens that dotted the orderly paths of the chic Paris suburb. But all that had changed. In under a month's time, most villas had been requisitioned by the Nazis, as Neuilly became the favored residence of the SS and the Gestapo. The minimal traffic was comprised of handsome Mercedes-Benz touring cars with miniature swastika flags on their fenders, Wehrmacht Army cars and lorries, some with SS pennants, and an occasional panzer tank painted in field gray and bearing the symbols of the German Reich.

Now Paris was part of an Occupied France that ran from the Atlantic to the Swiss border. In the north of France they created a forbidden zone where entry was strictly controlled by the Germans and other zones administered by Nazis. An Italian zone of occupation bordered the Italian frontier, while a so-called free zone was administered by Vichy and ruled by Pétain. Two zones bordering German territory were annexed or reserved for German colonization. And now, systematically, the Germans began transporting French soldiers to Germany where they would be held as hostages—two million men taken in just six weeks of battle. Their number was twice all the French captured in World War I.

Paris descended into what would become four years of a grim, terrifying, and ugly occupation. It was a time of cowardly collaboration, of every man for himself, of resistance, and near civil war.

In the early days of the Occupation, the Germans were under orders to be "correct" and behave.[30] They were loaded with deutschmarks and early Occupation currency: the conquerors had become tourists, hunting for souvenirs from the conquered. Paris became the playground of the Wehrmacht. The Germans were everywhere and into everything.

All the signage was in German. The Feldgendarmerie, or Bulldogs, patrolled the grand boulevards, and every day the army staged a display of power by marching down the Champs Elysées, a mounted officer astride a white stallion of French origin at the head of the troops. (The soldiers formed up just below Avenue Foch, a stone's throw from the Jackson apartment.)

They inflicted their law, their language when they could, and tried but failed to impose a kind of ersatz Nazi philosophy. What the Germans didn't or couldn't purchase, they took. As in the Great War—twenty-two years earlier—they had a mania for looting, for collecting and carting away French bed linen—real linen—along with machinery, tapestries, surgical instruments, milk, mutton, and sweet champagne. They systematically began to strip the country. The humiliation was powerful.

Sumner was sickened by the German Occupation and the gross, swaggering ways of the Germans. He was heartsick over the capitulation of France and the French—a country and people he and Toquette loved. His frustration and dismay were due in part to his absolute belief that his country—the United States of America—would not abandon France. He had a long time to wait. Alone now, he listened to London and de Gaulle's appeals on the BBC for resistance, while Toquette and Tat and Phillip listened religiously, too, in their hotel rooms on the Allier River.[31]

Still Sumner had a hospital to run and sick and wounded patients to care for. There were some two hundred fifty beds occupied with French soldiers, Allied prisoners, and refugees. He managed to keep the hospital full, and there were no German "guests." Counting staff, the number totaled five hundred mouths to feed, three times a day.

Meanwhile, the man the hospital's governors had appointed as governor general—their personal representative while they stayed at home to wait out the war—had moved into the hospital. Général, Le Comte, Aldebert de Chambrun was, according to his American wife, no easy man. "He seldom does things in halves,"[32] she pointed out. He was a soldier up from the ranks and knew nothing about running a hospital. But he was unquestionably Marshal Pétain's man and supported the Vichy regime. De Chambrun was a descendent of Général de Lafayette (and, as such, held U.S. citizenship). A Catholic, married to a wealthy Francophile from Cincinnati, Ohio, de Chambrun had been decorated by Pétain in World War I and by Marshal Lyautey during the pacification of the Barbary States: Algeria, Tunisia, and Morocco.

Toquette had met Countess de Chambrun ("a long-stemmed American beauty" born Clara Longworth)[33] and found her to be refined, haughty, and very determined to be taken seriously. The countess never hesitated to talk about her dissertation on Shakespeare's knowledge of Italian literature, which had earned her a doctorate at the University of Paris. She liked to refer to her days in North Africa as "living under the Crescent," remarking on the "cadaverous Jewish traders of the Fez souk" and the highlights of "dining in Mohammedan fashion." (To her credit, she devoted herself to protecting the American Library of Paris during the Occupation.)

Sumner and Toquette had lived over a year in Algeria and had no taste for French colonial rule. In fact, there could not have been two men more different than Sumner Waldron Jackson and Gen. Aldebert de Chambrun. Sumner simply didn't trust French aristocrats.[34] However, de Chambrun maintained good relations with the German Occupation authorities on a soldier-to-soldier basis. He was cordial with the new Vichy regime and with top French officials and businessmen in Paris. The general was also instrumental in helping Sumner to keep the hospital full. He even arranged with the French railroad bureaucracy to have their employees treated at the hospital.

After the armistice between France and Germany, it became clear that if the American Hospital were to stay independent of German control, something had to be done. General de Chambrun was able to use his considerable influence in Vichy to have the hospital put under the flag and the protection of the French Red Cross. (The General's son, René, was married to the daughter of Pétain's principal minister, Pierre Laval.)[35]

The Memorial Building—a bijou with its secure location, fine grounds, and modern facilities—became a working French Red Cross institution functioning under the name *Centre d'hospitalisation pour blesses de guerre libérés* (Center for the Hospitalization of War Wounded). Thus, the hospital was spared from falling into German hands and being appropriated by the SS.[36]

It is impossible to know when Sumner began hiding "patients" from the Germans. By 1941, he may have already been allied some-how to one of the early escape and evasion groups set up by de Gaulle or the British Special Operations Executive (SOE). We do know that right after the Occupation of Paris in June 1940, Sumner hid Donald Coster in the basement of the hospital until papers were arranged to smuggle him out to Lisbon. Coster, a member of the American Field Service in Brussels, had fled to Paris to escape the Gestapo. Sumner often hid escaped French and British soldiers—sick and wounded men who had no place to hide and who came to him because some fledging Resistance agent knew about the "big" American doctor at the American Hospital.[37] Sometimes, desperate men simply walked into the hospital, thinking they could find help. Sumner could not abandon them.[38]

General de Chambrun would never have approved of Sumner using the hospital to, as Otto Gresser put it, "hide airborne Ameri-cans who had been shot down—or British soldiers." Gresser, the hos-pital's administrator, described how Sumner would "hide and take care of them. Of course, it was very serious. This continued for a long time and I remember very well there were two British soldiers wan-dering the corridor of the hospital." Thus, Sumner became one of the early *résistants* as General de Gaulle and the British secret services in London began organizing intelligence networks in Occupied France.

In the early years of the Occupation, Sumner probably used the hospital exclusively to hide people from the Gestapo and German Se-curity Services. (How much General de Chambrun knew about Sum-ner's Resistance work at the hospital is unknown. What *is* known is that the general hated the English.)[39] It may not have been until early 1943 that the Jacksons began to use their apartment at Avenue Foch for secret underground work as members of the official French Resis-tance. What is certain is that their lake house at Enghien was never used for clandestine activity. The town was small, neighbors couldn't be trusted, and many German officials and military men were lodged there.

Sumner and his trusted team—Otto Gresser and Elisabeth Comte, his head nurse—had their hands full. Pharmaceuticals, bandages, sheets, crutches, and surgical instruments were in short supply. They had to beg, borrow, or steal everything needed to run a hospital.

Providing for patients and staff was a recurring nightmare. Meals were cooked on open wood fires in large cauldrons. The beautiful Memorial Building gardens were dug up and vegetables planted where once roses bloomed; water was found at 15 meters (45-plus feet) but was still scarce. Coal was rare, gas supplies diminished, and electricity frequently cut off—though they did buy fuel on the black market. Acids were used to sterilize the operating instruments and rooms. The ambulances at first ran on natural gas—two bottles on top of the cars. Then the hospital car engines were converted to burn charcoal.

Things got tighter and tighter. Within a few days after German troops arrived in Paris, everything was snatched from the marketplace to be resold later for two to three times its original price. The Germans imposed a regime of virtual starvation. Indeed, Field Marshal Hermann Goering decreed that the French people would have to subsist on 1,200 calories a day—half the number of calories the average human needs to survive. The elderly were rationed to 850 calories a day. The measures were staggering.

When de Chambrun arranged with his wealthy landowner friends to purchase potatoes, the produce was transported to the hospital by ambulance.[40] Otto Gresser tells about bartering wine for more potatoes:

> We had 250 patients. . . . The French authorities allowed each patient one-half a liter of wine [a pint] per day and soon we had more wine than the patients could drink. The farmers, however, couldn't get enough wine. We took 500 liters of wine [almost a hundred gallons] and bartered the wine for 5,000 kilos of fertilizer. One farmer gave us 10,000 kilos [about 22,000 pounds] of potatoes for the fertilizer. . . . We gave 50 kilos of potatoes to each staff member and it was very important for them to feed their families.[41]

Meat was almost impossible to come by and was desperately needed to stave off malnutrition. Sumner and Gresser arranged to obtain meat on the black market. When 300 kilos of beef were delivered to the hospital in a big "borrowed" German car, the suspicious German authorities asked to inspect the hospital kitchen. Gresser was able to hold them off long enough to have the meat hidden in the garden.

The effect of the penury of food on the French people was staggering. A number of French newspapers printed public notices warning: "Cat Eaters Beware." It called on the public to stop killing and eating cats: "In these days of terrible restrictions some famished people don't fear to capture cats to make a good stew. . . . They don't realize the danger. . . . Cats readily capture and eat rats, rats carry one of the most dangerous bacteria to human beings."[42]

As to wine, a more pleasant subject, the French needed it. In *Wine and War*, Don and Petie Kladstrup tell in a chapter entitled, "The Growling Stomach," how wine production halved between 1939 and 1942. The Germans loved and knew about wines—particularly French ones. Their *Weinführers* managed to take away not only the best of the annual French production but also massive amounts of ordinary table wine for their armed forces. The Germans shipped more than 320 million bottles of wine to Germany each year at fixed prices.[43]

Goering's *Weinführers* took from those who needed wine the most. "The old and the ill needed wine," French doctors advised German and French authorities. "It is an excellent food . . . it is easily digested . . . and a vital source of vitamins and minerals. The population needs the caloric value."[44]

Every commodity was rationed. In Paris old people, particularly, risked serious illness or death from hypothermia when they couldn't heat their apartments in the long cold and wet months of the war years.

When the Germans began systematically commandeering property in the Paris suburbs, Sumner asked Toquette to return to Paris in August 1940. He wanted her sister, Tat, to stay permanently at the house at Enghien out of fear that the Germans would requisition their property on the lake. From then on the family would use the house during the week and on weekends, bicycling back and forth between the apartment at Avenue Foch, the hospital, and the lake. Because of fuel rationing, there was little traffic, and the round trip between Paris and the lake was less that an hour by bicycle—or a half-hour when they could use their automobile. Sumner slept most weeknights at the hospital, but tried to join his family for breakfast early in the morning. When possible, he would spend weekends at the lake.

Sumner met Toquette, Phillip, Tat, and the maid at the Paris Austerlitz station on August 19, 1940. Tat thought he looked a "bit better." (She didn't know then that he was routinely donating blood at the hospital.) But they were shocked when they reached the lake house to find that their home had been looted and damaged by German troops.

Together, they listened regularly to "London" (as the BBC was called at that time in France, as its broadcasts began with, "This is London"). They followed the ups and downs of the war, not the least General de Gaulle's appeals on behalf of the Free French. But they were shocked when in September 1940 the Germans ordered a census of Jews in the Occupied Zone. While in Vichy the Communist Party was dissolved and the first laws defining Jewishness were issued. Jews were now banned from higher public service or "influencing public opinion."

The Jacksons were caught up in something monstrous and dreadful—and the family agreed that there was no turning back. There was an important job to do at the hospital. And Toquette, without knowing exactly how, wanted to be part of de Gaulle's Free French Resistance.

Indeed, resistance against the enemy would begin in small ways: refusing collaboration, shunning the occupiers, misdirecting a German soldier lost in Paris, passing on underground anti-Nazi literature, scrawling pro–de Gaulle slogans on a wall, and even blowing a bugle in a courtyard after an early curfew.[45] But in the days to come, selfishness, bigotry, and cowardice would play parts as great as courage and idealism. It wasn't until November 1940 that the first public demonstration against Germany erupted in Paris and later, that a German soldier was killed by a Resistance fighter. The public's view toward mass public resistance came only when the enemy's good behavior gave way to brutality and the Allies showed they could defeat the Reich.[46]

The year 1940 ended with sinister German notices on Paris signboards and walls announcing how Jacques Bonsergent, a French engineer, had been shot as punishment for "attacking" a German officer—the first Frenchman shot in Paris. A "papillon" stuck to the poster advised that destroying German billboards was considered an act of sabotage and anyone found doing so would be severely punished. This didn't prevent Parisians from tearing down the notices of Bonsergent's fate from the walls. The billboards were then guarded by French sentinels—who couldn't stop the Parisians from laying bouquets of flowers at the foot of the posters. The floral tributes often covered the sidewalk.[47]

Above all, Sumner worried about keeping German troops out of the American Hospital. He repeated ad infinitum that the building had to be kept at full capacity. "No empty beds!" he ordered. "Never a room for the Boches."[48]

Winter came and with the change of season, gray skies, wet roads, cold, hunger, and deprivation. Perhaps Jean Paul Sartre's essay, "Paris Under the Occupation," best captures the mood of the city:

"Paris would grow peaked and yawn with hunger under the empty sky. Cut off from the rest of the world, fed only through pity or for some ulterior motive, the town led a purely abstract and symbolic life. Dozens of times during those four years, on seeing bottles of Saint-Emilion or Mersault wine stacked in grocery-shop windows, Parisians would hurry up to find, below the display, a notice saying, 'All these bottles are dummies.' Paris too, was a dummy."[49]

When Toquette and Phillip returned to Paris, Sumner was still battling what he called the "bullshit bureaucracy of old men."[50] He was appalled by the French, the Germans, and even the Red Cross, who were falling down on distributing American and other aid packages to refugees in the camps.

At Neuilly, Sumner and Otto Gresser waged a daily battle to keep the hospital supplied with the barest necessities. Sugar was selling for the equivalent of three U.S. dollars per pound, a carton of cigarettes for thirty dollars, and onions (a critical source of vitamin C) were nowhere to be found. Vegetables had disappeared from the hospital garden. The wine cellar was nearly empty.

Fuel had run so scarce that French authorities curtailed cars; only public service vehicles were allowed on the roads. The French citizenry put their automobiles on bricks and took to their bicycles. By then most everyone except German collaborators got about on bicycles. Sumner had one made to order for his large frame, and he cut an unusual figure that winter sitting high upon the oversize two-wheeler, his head covered in an aviator's wool-lined helmet, his hands in fleece mittens.

At this time, the staff who had fled with the German Occupation returned to the American Hospital. Sumner had two eminent surgeons serving with him—Doctors Leriche and Carrel, Frenchmen he could count on and who worked prodigious miracles every day. Sumner's old friend, Dr. Maurice Sanders, helped with anesthesia, using the latest American techniques in oxygen therapy.

But he was still racked with doubt. Should the Jacksons stay in France? They might still be able to get to America via Spain. It didn't help his state of mind when the Gestapo and the Reich security police took over buildings only a few hundred meters from his apartment on Avenue Foch.

On one of the rare weekends that the Jacksons spent together at the lake house, Sumner took a letter from his pocket and handed it to his wife. As she scanned it, Toquette began to smile, and then called Phillip into the room. She read aloud:

Dear Dr. Jackson,

Please advise the medical staff that the Republic has awarded the Croix de Guerre with Palm to the hospital and named physicians and staff—I believe one of the last acts of General Huntziger before his untimely death.

I am pleased to advise you personally that you are among those decorated and cited for "A magnificent effort, voluntarily treating the wounded and aiding prisoners day and night in the face of the enemy . . . saving a great number of human lives."

Please accept my warmest thanks and appreciation for your exceptional devotion to duty in this trying period.[51]

Général Aldebert de Chambrun
Director General
October 10, 1940

Phillip says that his father never said a word as Toquette read the letter and its accompanying citation aloud. The documents were passed around for all to examine as Sumner stood with his back to the wall, an unusual taciturn expression on his face and his arms folded across his chest.[52]

To be decorated with the Croix de Guerre, created for the Great War of 1914–18, was not unusual during the 1939–1945 period. But the American Hospital's award is extraordinary for a number of reasons. (A copy of the citation is included in this book.)[53] First, it is dated after the armistice came into effect and therefore after the Republic was dissolved. Second, it is signed by General Huntziger, who at the time was a member of the Vichy government.[54] Third, the citation itself mentions the generous, charitable conduct of the hospital and physicians under enemy—and sometimes friendly—fire. It describes how these men and women cared for soldiers and civilians alike—day and night, nonstop. After the armistice, they turned to aiding thousands of refugees.

Those mentioned by name in the award tell a story, too: E. B. Close was the managing governor who appointed Sumner just before Close left for America. Close is the only nonmedical person named in the award. (Note that Général de Chambrun, with all his influence, was not named.) Also named are Mlle. Comte, who became Sumner's head nurse and confidante, and six physicians. (Dr. Jackson's name is spelled without the "c.")

The Jacksons were lucky to have the lake house. There were few German soldiers around—and even fewer German civilians. Toquette and Tat scoured the markets for vegetables brought in from the nearby farms. They sometimes found bread—good bread, not loaded with sawdust—though meat, vegetables, and eggs were rare; even rarer were duck eggs, butter, milk, and cream. The prices were outrageous. At Vichy, the capital of Pétain's new pro-Nazi government, Wednesdays, Thursdays, and Fridays were declared meatless days. In Paris, butcher shops closed for days on end. There was no meat, and a rabbit sold for a small fortune when one was to be found on the flourishing black market. The cost of chocolates and cigarettes was astronomical. Parisians were forced to reduce consumption of heating fuel by 30 percent.[55]

In the autumn and winter of 1940–1941, Tat's diary has almost daily entries about obtaining rationing cards for food. She mentions the long lines, growing longer and longer, to be endured in all weather; a line for bread, for milk, for meat, for vegetables; there always seemed to be one more line to wait in. Tat observes that in late winter she saw more and more German soldiers here and there, "hanging about" as the town loudspeaker announced that 125 grams of green coffee were available to families.

She tells how Sumner and Phillip went about gathering and cutting wood for the winter. A touching entry reveals how they "made a small fire, the wind has turned, out of the east getting cold." (Frenchmen would remember the winters of 1940–41 and 1941–42 as the coldest winters in ninety years.)

Throughout her diary entries for those years, Tat mentions the incessant difficulty of feeding the family. One entry is intriguing: she writes, "Toq. [Toquette], Jack [Sumner], Piet [Phillip] came by at 10:30." The last entry on the page reads: "*Courage et Vive de Gaule* [*sic*]." It seems that quiet, demure Tat, like the Jacksons, was already a *résistant* and cheering for the Free French leader in London.

Learning to survive, staving off malnutrition, keeping warm, biking to and from the hospital and to the lake house took all their energy. France entered into a period of hardship, discontent, and sacrifice.

4

INTERNMENT

Fleet Admiral William D. Leahy and his staff at the American Embassy at Vichy suffered terribly from the cold of the winter of 1941–42. The admiral tells of how he had to seal off the doors and windows of his rooms with cloth and paper strips and use coal-burning fireplaces (salamanders) to heat his quarters at his Avenue Thermal residence. It was there on Sunday evening, December 7, 1941, in a room adjoining his bedroom that President Roosevelt's ambassador plenipotentiary to Vichy listened on a U.S. Navy radio receiver and learned that the Japanese had "delivered their barbaric sneak attack" on the American naval base at Pearl Harbor.[1]

America, finally, was in the war.

There was now a grim and determined faith among the Jacksons that America would fight as it always had when provoked—and win. Hitler's armies were not invincible. Sumner believed in a final and decisive American victory against Nazi Germany and the Axis. But most French felt that the United States would be tied up in the Pacific. Certainly the average Frenchman did, as did the leaders at Vichy. They believed that Hitler's declaration of war on the United States showed how sure the Nazi leader was of his strength on the continent; the battle for Stalingrad was nine months away.[2]

By now the hospital had been cut off from all communication with New York, and General de Chambrun announced that expenses had to be further reduced because their funds in Switzerland were running low. It was a struggle to find medicine and food to care for the gravely ill prisoners, refugees, escapees, and demobilized soldiers who filled the beds and corridors of the Memorial Building. A few could pay; most could not. There were even "Brits" who regularly came to the hospital for care—a handful of old soldiers left from the Great War of 1914–18, whom the Germans semi-interned in a house at Neuilly. Sumner would turn no one away. But his orders still stood: no Germans in the hospital!

Under the stern management of Elisabeth Comte and Otto Gresser, no one asked any questions about who came and went or why they were there. Sumner was very proud of what he called "my organized confusion." And then he would add: "Don't let the bastards grind you down."[3] He told Otto Gresser that the Gestapo probably had informers in the hospital but in the end, "They'll never figure out this mad house."[4]

Despite the hardships the Jackson family was forced to endure, they did their best to maintain some semblance of normalcy in their lives. One Sunday in early September 1942, Toquette asked Clemence Bock and a few friends to come out to the lake for lunch. There was strict rationing and penury regarding basic foods, but Tat and Rosalie, the housekeeper, managed a decent lunch for their friends.

Around the table after lunch, the talk was mostly about the weather and ways to find fuel to heat the house that winter. Tat reported that there was nothing but turnips and a few potatoes at the market, and observed that before steaming potatoes—when you could find them—one should dip them in boiling water with a bit of salt. Rosalie countered that there was almost no salt available. Then she emerged with an immense *tarte aux pommes* and a bottle of Eau de Vie.[5]

Phillip remembers how he pored over a world atlas that day. When he asked his father about the location of Pearl Harbor, Sumner explained that it was on the Hawaiian island of Oahu.[6] Dr. Jackson then hooked his thumbs in his vest, cocked a cigar between his teeth, and announced something to the effect that "the Boches will surely put me away. They'll try to barter Americans for Germans in the States." And with a sly smile, he added something like, "Of course, we could pack up and get out of here. People are making it to Spain." This was guaranteed to make Toquette furious.

Sumner was, according to Clemence Bock, "*Tres prudent*"—very wary of the German physicians and officials with whom he conducted hospital business. He had at that time considerable influence with French and German authorities. Nevertheless he was to be interned by the Germans at Compiègne for almost a month in September 1942.[7] He treated it like a joke, telling Clemence:

> You want to know how I spent my paid vacation? Thursday morning they came to arrest me. My bags were packed. I called Toquette. They had interrupted me while I was examining a patient.
>
> Before leaving I was given food packages, a few good bottles, and I stuffed it all in my pockets. I really didn't know what to do with it all. And then at the police station I ran into friends. We all had tags hung around our necks. They made me sign my name, and then we were shipped to the Gare du Nord, where I had the good fortune to come across a worker who had been one of my patients. He was good enough to tell Toquette where I was.
>
> Then at Saint Denis, I got there at lunchtime, and the English were getting aid packages from the King and Queen. So we had an hour and a half lunch that was better than we had at the hospital and at home. I also bought a pair of suspenders, the kind I never found in the Paris shops. And a reamer to clean out my pipe.
>
> They made me write my name and my date of birth to prove I was indeed Doctor Jackson.
>
> That evening we were at Compiègne, the food was far inferior to the Saint Denis camp, but friends surrounded me and they gave me a small room with a small rug. Nearby was a camp where Jews were held. And the majority of my fellow prisoners were veterans of World War I, some prisoners were American veterans of the Great War but many were the sons of Teddies, abandoned in France after their fathers had gone home.[8]
>
> The Boches continued to annoy me with their paperwork. I had to sign and re-sign their papers. I've never written my name so often.[9] But I got out thanks to the General. . . . [de Chambrun] came to get me in a Red Cross car with a chauffeur. He handed me copies of press clippings. We were famous!
>
> Vichy, Jan. 25 (UP)—Two hundred of the most prominent expatriates in Paris have been seized by the Germans and taken to the crude wooden barracks in Besancon[10] to be held as hostages for the good treatment of German nationals in the United States, it was learned today.

The hostages were apparently hand-picked, because they included most of the best-known expatriates such as Lawrence Whipp, organist of the American Church of Paris, who took charge of the church after its pastor, the Rev. Frederick W. Beckman [*sic*], had left.

Others included prominent doctors and dentists, many of them from the American Hospital at Neuilly, which continues to function as an American institution.

The prisoners were taken to a Besancon camp and interned in wooden barracks occupied by Senegalese prisoners of war. The barracks provide almost no comforts.

When other Americans in Paris and sympathizers, including many American women who married into French nobility, learned of the arrests, they organized an emergency committee to aid the hostages, and have provided them with toilet articles, cigarettes, and other comforts.

Countess Adelbert [*sic*] de Chambrun, the former Clara Longworth, sister of the late Nicholas Longworth, who has been director of the American Library since the Occupation, opened a branch at the camp. Meanwhile, negotiations are underway to obtain the release of certain of the hostages whose professional services are needed at hospitals and other institutions.

An attempt has also been made to obtain Mr. Whipp's release so he can conduct church services. Through friendship and close association with a son of Madame Benoit, patroness of the arts, Mr. Whipp has made his home in the Benoit apartment for a number of years.

The General wanted to know what I thought about the news clipping. All I could say was, "It's free publicity. Good for the hospital. Show 'em we're still in business. We need the money." Then de Chambrun complained because his wife's name had been spelled incorrectly.[11]

Sumner was released long before the other American captives probably from the influence of General de Chambrun's connections either at Vichy or within the German high command.[12]

Despite his making light of his internment, Sumner told Toquette that all the same, it galled him to be a prisoner of the Germans, the very "Boches" he had fought in 1916. He was given a firsthand look at how the Germans treated their "guests." Jews were held in a camp next to the American compound at Compiègne. African troops were imprisoned in ramshackle wooden hutches with primitive sanitary facilities in the same compound. The soldiers would beg for water and a handout from behind their barbed-wire enclosures. Sumner was allowed to treat the black prisoners when he complained bitterly to the camp commander about their abominable living conditions.

He told Toquette later how the guards found a hundred ways to abuse and humiliate the Americans. But the black soldiers, mostly from Senegal—then a French colony—were treated like cattle. In one incident, Sumner watched a black soldier being disciplined by a guard. The German guards beat the man and forced him to drink from a communal piss pot. But as angry as he was, Sumner wasn't going to give in to the "Boches."

While "in the hole," as he called it, Sumner befriended Lawrence (Larry) Kilbourne Whipp, one of some fourteen hundred Americans interned by the Germans. (Charles Knight, the architect of the American Hospital Memorial Building, was also a prisoner.) The tall, gangly Whipp was the organist and choirmaster at the Holy Trinity Episcopal Church in Paris—also known as the American Cathedral.

Whipp had arrived in the camp well before Sumner. He carried a pianist's silent keyboard to keep up his finger practice. But he was singularly unpopular with the other prisoners. Whipp complained to Sumner that he was being treated better by the German guards than by his compatriots, who were mostly the sons of American soldiers and Frenchwomen sired in World War I. These orphans of Teddies, many who did not speak a word of English, had exercised their right to be Americans at twenty-one to avoid French military service. The German guards claimed they were a lazy, slovenly, insubordinate lot. They caused so much trouble that Whipp and two others were appointed by the Germans as judges to try offenders and fix sentences. The German guards would then administer the punishments. This did not add to the organist's popularity, and Sumner warned him to be careful.[13]

One of Whipp's fellow prisoners became a bitter enemy. The man was a French-American chauffeur—no doubt the son of a Teddy whose mother remained in France. Whipp managed to get permission from the stalag commandant (whose unlikely name was Nachtigall) to give a concert for the German guards and their American prisoners. Whipp's fellow prisoner had kept a meticulously written record of the concert. He truly despised Whipp, whom he called a "giraffe" (presumably because he had a long, graceful neck) and a "lunatic," because he practiced his fingering on an empty wooden box. The man's diary entry goes on:

> Commandant Nachtigall and aide Kuntz make entrance and sit at table of honor. . . . Tall devil comes in; goes with long strides to the stage. His eyes are turned up so he does not see that there are five steps. He stumbles and falls forward. His legs begin to falter. He rubs his knees, straightens, and looks at ceiling with eyes rolling like marbles. His left cheek swells under pressure of his tongue. . . . He's thinking in English and mumbling in German, then he speaks in a French worthy of a Spanish cow. In a trembling voice he says, "I'm going to play some old pieces for you, first the choral prelude 'I beseech Thee, Lord,' by J.S. Bach."
>
> The more he strikes the keys the more he appears 100 times taller than he is. The guy next to me says, "Oh! Oh! This guy knows how to tickle the ivories; this tall guy is an ace."
>
> . . . Then he announces "Sicilienne" by Mozart. Like demons on the loose his long fingers move over the harmless old piano. The enthusiasm is delirious, cries of bravo and encore. . . .
>
> At intermission, tea and delicacies from Red Cross packages, including chocolate and cakes, were served to the German officers—the prisoners never got a smell of packages and our mouths watered. . . .
>
> (Personally I detest Whipp and gnash my teeth seeing him; but as he plays number after number there is frantic applause. . . . I am carried away too by the atmosphere of feverish joy.) Then he plays Kreisler's masterpiece, "Alt Wien." Nachtigall leaned over to Kuntz. "Jew music." He didn't even bother to whisper. We all heard him.
>
> The applause is unbelievable. . . . It lasts for five minutes. . . . Whipp stands up and shakes his head like a giraffe. . . . Nachtigall grasps his hand and congratulates him so respectfully that I ask myself, which one of the two is the prisoner?[14]

Later, Sumner learned that Commandant Nachtigall was de-
nounced by the Gestapo on a charge of "spoiling the Americans,"
and was transferred out of the camp to the front.

The story of Lawrence Whipp is extraordinary. In an article
about him in *Time* magazine from March 12, 1945, he is described as
"an impeccable ornament of Paris' pre-war community, a man aloof
yet religious and deeply committed to his vocation." *Time* goes on to
explain how Whipp, "served in the cathedral for twenty years—even
under the Wehrmacht during the German occupation—as the organist
and choirmaster." When most Americans fled Paris—including the
cathedral's dean, the Reverend Beekman—Whipp stayed at his post
as lay reader. He is said to have been caught listening to the BBC by
the Gestapo, arrested, and imprisoned. But there was still rumor, at
least at the American Cathedral in 1999 that Whipp, a homosexual,
had been imprisoned to make him cooperate with the Gestapo.[15] Apparently the Gestapo was still trying to recruit Whipp in 1944. A letter addressed to him from the Swiss Consulate (the Swiss represented
the United States during the Occupation of France) telling him to appear before a certain *Obersturmführer* Hoferichter (an SS rank) to
discuss a possible repatriation to the United States bears the notation
in Whipp's handwriting, "Gestapo—I refused!"[16] Whatever the case,
after the liberation of Paris in August 1944, Whipp mysteriously disappeared.

In the words of the Rev. Benjamin Shambaugh, canon, the American Cathedral of Paris, the story continues:

> Some say Whipp was killed by zealots of the Resistance who ac-
> cused him of siding with the Nazis. After the Liberation he had
> given sanctuary to a French Wagnerian opera singer named Mme.
> Lubin, who had sung for the Nazis and was thus considered a trai-
> tor. Having found out Whipp's "compassion" for the woman, the
> Resistance killed him in her place.

But other theories abound. One has it that the penniless Whipp
was about to be fired from his only job at the cathedral by Dean
Beekman (who had returned to Paris after the liberation) because he
had hidden Mme. Lubin in the dean's bedroom—and in desperation

Whipp committed suicide. Another theory has it that Whipp broke when interned and agreed to work for the Gestapo. His *Ausweis*, a German pass issued to him in October 1942 that allowed him to live and travel freely in Occupied France, was approved by the SD, the security service of the SS, Befehlshaber der Sicheerheitspolizai. In any case his body was found floating in the Seine in late April 1945.[17]

If Lawrence Whipp's life during the Occupation and his death after the liberation of Paris remain shrouded in mystery, the life of Dr. Morris B. Sanders seems to be an open book until one begins to search a bit deeper.

Dr. Sanders was a colleague and close friend of Sumner at the American Hospital of Paris dating back to 1929. He was a fellow alumnus of Massachusetts General Hospital (MGH) and a member of its urology service. Before that he had been a surgical resident in China at the Yale-in-China Medical School and Hospital.

In 1942 Dr. Sanders, who occasionally was called in to assist Sumner at the hospital, was interned at Compiègne but released through the efforts of Dr. Alexis Carrel,[18] a Nobel Prize winner and eminent French biologist and surgeon who was pro-Vichy and espoused some Nazi theories.[19] Upon release from internment, Dr. Sanders became a consultant to Carrel's foundation.[20]

But nagging questions remain: Why did he and Sumner have no visible relationship after 1942 following Sumner's release from internment? After America went to war with Germany, how could Sanders, an American, justify his liberty in front of an ever-hostile Nazi bureaucracy and security services? Nowhere in his papers does he explain how and why he was able to live and work in Occupied France under a Nazi régime. Then, after the war Sanders was appointed an attaché at the U.S. Embassy in Paris. It must be stressed that such an appointment requires—as for all Foreign Service employees—a thorough background investigation. It would be exceptional for him to have received the requisite security clearances had he collaborated with the Germans.

Thus, the puzzle remains unsolved. It is possible that Sanders cooperated with American intelligence services in China and France; and after 1941, with the OCI—Office of Coordinator of Information (later the OSS). This would have been possible through the U.S. Embassy in Paris up to Pearl Harbor, and after 1942 through clandestine means and via Alan Dulles's OSS office in Bern, Switzerland. (The same Alan Dulles would later head the CIA.)

Dr. Sanders obviously loved Sumner and was close to him. He spent the last years of his life trying to write a book about the Jackson family. In May 1961, he succeeded in publishing an 800-word article in a hospital publication, *The News of MGH*. Dr. Sanders wrote:

> I don't know how a . . . college publication . . . could impart the importance and influence, which was Jackson's, to the American community in France, especially Paris, and to the traveling American public from 1920. . . . Later he used his home on avenue Foch (about three blocks from Gestapo headquarters) [and the American Hospital] as a shelter and stepping-stone for fallen Allied aviators en route back to England.
>
> Two or three days after the beginning of the German Occupation of Northern France . . . Sumner Jackson and I drove an ambulance to Fontainebleau to set up a first-aid station for French wounded with the permission of the Nazi medical authorities. This allowed us to bring back to the American Hospital seriously wounded patients. . . .
>
> But before that Jackson (he was known as Dr. Jack) helped make the American Hospital of Paris a veritable American medical home where Americans living in Paris and American visitors found a place in sickness . . . like at home. And he made the hospital a "showcase" of American medicine, a demonstration hospital not only for the French but for other European physicians as well, and an exhibition center of American medical paraphernalia and instruments.
>
> With the Occupation of Paris Dr. Jack worked long hours, gave his blood numerous times and slept in the building, and visited his family only on weekends. His patients numbered the few Americans remaining in France, repatriated French prisoners of war and American and British women sent to the hospital from German concentration camps. By declaring that they should not be returned to enemy camps because of ill health, Jackson was able to help political prisoners.

During the long cold winter of 1941 and 1942, Sumner and Toquette watched as their neighbors, some French Jewish families, fled to the Unoccupied Zone—to Vichy, southern France, and Lyon. There were mass arrests now of Communists and Jews with a rumor that Jews were being transported on eastbound trains to "nowhere." The clean-cut German "boys" were no longer buying souvenirs. The "correct," stiffly polite "visitors" were acting like masters. While French families went without food, a German officer wrote: "In times like these, to eat well and eat a lot gives a feeling of power."[21] Germany attacked Romania, Bulgaria, Yugoslavia, and Greece, and the Wehrmacht was close to taking Moscow. All of Europe bowed to Hitler's rule.

By 1941 there was a burgeoning resistance. In Paris, Frenchmen were killing German officers in train stations out of a sense of humiliation, hate, and envy. German officers, corrupt French bureaucrats, black market operators, and some perfectly decent, so-called patriotic Frenchmen were buying swanky foreign cars. Needless to say, money for such luxuries was earned through collaboration with the occupying powers or through illegal activities—and they went hand-in-hand.

French police took part in the first mass arrests in the Occupied Zone in May 1941, when thirty-six hundred Polish Jews were picked up around Paris; that August, another group of foreign Jews was arrested. Then a wave of assassinations by Resistance fighters at the end of the year was followed by the arrest of a thousand Jewish notables. The Germans levied a fine of a billion francs on the Jewish population of the Occupied Zone. The first systematic deportation of Jews from the Occupied Zone would begin a year later, when Jews were required to wear a yellow star on their clothes. In June 1942 Himmler would set massive quotas for the deportation of Jews to extermination camps at Auschwitz.

But it was the atrocious events of the spring of 1942 that "shocked and shook the French."[22] Even anti-Semitic and extremely right-wing citizens were disturbed by the roundups and deportation of Jews— more than 42,000 were sent to "nowhere" that summer. French police, named *agents capteurs,* arrested 12,884 non-French or stateless Jewish families between July 16 and 17.[23] Forcing Jews to wear yellow Stars of David in German-occupied France was one thing (although

Pétain refused to force Jews in the Vichy-run part of France to wear them). Sending men, women, and children to holding camps pending deportation was too much for the average Frenchman. Many suspected, if they didn't know, that there was a Nazi extermination drive in progress and that Vichy had put the apparatus of the state, above all its police, at the service of the Nazis.[24]

The Jacksons were all too aware of what was going on. Sumner arranged for the American Hospital's ambulances to go to the holding camps and bring the sick back to the hospital for treatment. The French police carefully monitored this activity, and German authorities forced patients back into camps when they were well enough to leave their hospital beds. It broke the hearts of the American Hospital staff. They knew these men, women, and children would be deported.[25]

After being freed from internment, Sumner embarked with Toquette upon their own intrigue: setting up a Paris center for de Gaulle's Resistance group, Goélette. Their apartment on Avenue Foch was to become a key locale for Goélette's underground work against the German Occupation. It would also be a target of the German and Vichy French police apparatus, which sought to bring down all resistance by what the Nazis and Pétain's Vichy agents called "terrorists."

SS Maj. Gen. Carl-Albrecht Oberg, the Gestapo officer who may have scouted out the American Hospital on one of his prewar visits to France, arrived in Paris in the spring of 1942. The tall, stocky, bespectacled Nazi from North Germany was stationed as Reichsführer-SS Heinrich Himmler's personal representative and commander of all the security police and Gestapo apparatus in France. Oberg had been a member of the SS Schutzstaffel (Protection Squad) since 1932. He had served as the right-hand man of Reinhard Heydrich, known as the "Blond Beast" and infamous for his devious methods of blackmail, terror, and persecution. Together, they worked to carry out Heydrich's "Total solution of the Jewish question in those territories of Europe under German influence."[26]

Carl Oberg stood no nonsense from anyone—even Wehrmacht generals, as we shall see. He didn't really want to be in Paris. He thought Paris immoral. And he had a particular hatred for the intellectual French Jew. Oberg had lobbied to stay in Berlin near the real power. Paris was beautiful and exciting, but overcrowded with French and German bureaucrats vying for control. He despised the petty office seekers who schemed and exchanged pseudo-secrets. He felt there were enough politicians and their wives and mistresses around to govern Europe. Oberg saw France as only a remnant of a country. He saw the French only capable of talking about doing things, while only the Germans were allowed to rule.

His first order of business from Himmler was both to organize German security forces and French-Nazi police agents in France to crush General de Gaulle's nascent Resistance force, and to manage the deportation of Jews in France to slave labor death camps. One of Oberg's key operatives was Dr. Heinrich Illers, chief of Gestapo in Paris. Dr. Illers helped Oberg prepare the Kaltenbrunner Report dated May 27, 1943—a treatise on General de Gaulle's secret French underground army and Resistance organizations.[27] Using the report, German and French security forces "rolled up" Resistance cells. The men, women, and adolescents arrested were tortured without mercy to reveal their plans and name their fellow agents—and then murdered or deported to Nazi slave-labor death camps.[28] Many of the atrocities committed against de Gaulle's underground agents took place at Gestapo and SS headquarters near the Jackson apartment.

Oberg knew he could count on an important number of French police. There were also French military and naval officers, rigid bureaucrats, and hard-core Fascists all too eager to work with the Gestapo. They wanted a new order in France to sweep out the Communists. Oberg and his Nazi SS colleagues in France believed that God-fearing men and women would rally to Germany. The Catholic Church would become an ally. France and the Christian world would become Germany's partners. Together, they would crush the Marxist Jews and Soviet Russia. Britain would sue for peace.[29]

The forty-five-year-old Oberg, a veteran of World War I and the son of a German professor of medicine and physician, would earn the title "Butcher of Paris" because of his activities against Jews and de Gaulle's Resistance agents.[30] As the Nazi police leader in France, he was to play a sinister role in the life of the Jacksons.

5

RESISTANCE

"Goélette" means schooner, a fore-and-aft rigged ship having two masts. As part of de Gaulle's Force Françaises Combattantes de l'Interieur (FFCI), Goélette's principal mission was to collect intelligence. Agents also worked to sabotage the German war effort while helping Allied servicemen and Resistance fighters escape capture. The group's operations, including radio transmissions, air and sea pickups and deliveries of agents and materials by plane and parachute, were managed from France in coordination with London.[1]

In the beginning, the Goélette agents concentrated on collecting intelligence about Vichy and German relations with Pétain. Their work was centered in the city of Vichy, the capital of unoccupied France where Marshal Philippe Pétain resided. Goélette had agents among the marshal's staff; in the early years of the German Occupation, Vichy intelligence officers (Deuxième Bureau et Cinquième Bureau de L'armée) played an important role in organizing de Gaulle's Resistance groups and teaching the ABCs of underground work to neophyte agents.[2] It was in Vichy that Goélette had planted a secret radio transmitter and agents to code and decode messages to London.[3]

By 1942 it became necessary for Goélette to have an "office" in Paris. Paul Robert Ostoya Kinderfreund, a thirty-eight-year-old former gendarme and journalist, was picked to run the Paris operations.[4] He took the alias Renaudot, known here as "R," because there were twenty in the Paris telephone directory. The Jackson family was ideal for recruitment as Resistance agents. Their Avenue Foch apartment and doctor's office with two entrances was a perfect place for covert comings and goings. They carried German passes, *Ausweis*. Phillip had a student identification card.

It is not known whether Toquette first approached Renaudot— *R*—at the suggestion of her neighbor, the Goélette agent Francis Delouche de Noyelle, or if *R* just came to the door one afternoon. We do know, however, that Renaudot set up several independent networks around Paris, with the Jacksons' apartment on Avenue Foch as the hub. Each group was isolated (no matter how small), and there was no contact among the groups except via courier. By 1943 *R* had already lost five agents to the Gestapo—and this was just the beginning.[5]

Phillip, who knew almost nothing about his father's Resistance work at the American Hospital, says that his parents decided to join Goélette in 1943 when they arranged to use their apartment on Avenue Foch as a mail drop, bank, and meeting place in Paris for agents.[6] It was a big step for the Jacksons. Phillip says that his parents felt obligated to be part of the Resistance and were outraged by the Nazi régime, the German Occupation of France, and the Vichy government. "We had no idea of the danger we were running. It was all a game," he explains today. But naïveté probably applied only to Phillip as a teenager. Certainly Sumner and Toquette knew the risks, and they kept Phillip mostly out of their work until sometime in early 1944.[7]

What motivated Sumner and Toquette? Why were they different? How did they justify risking the life of their fourteen-year-old son? The family certainly stood apart from many of their friends. Indeed, half the wealthy and upper-class Parisians kept portraits of Marshal Pétain on their walls. The other half may have been listening to the BBC and de Gaulle broadcasting from London, but many still approved to some extent of Vichy's collaboration with the Nazi régime as a way to get on. For the Jackson family, this was unthinkable. Any collaboration with Vichy—not to mention the enemy that occupied France—was abhorrent.

Sumner was, of course, already involved in his secret work at the hospital. And Toquette, with her pent-up nervous energy, couldn't sit idly by. If she wasn't digging up the garden or bailing out the cellar at the lake house, she was planning to carry secret messages, hide someone at Avenue Foch, or arrange false papers and escape routes for downed Allied aviators.

With the help of his network of Resistance spies such as Sumner and Toquette, the tall, gangly *R*, ever in need of a good shave, supplied London with valuable intelligence. Messages went by courier to Vichy for transmission by wireless to B.C.R.A., London. (*R* sometimes used an air courier service, but the schedule of aircraft landings and take-offs depended on the moon.)

When *R* had decoded his messages he would go to the street opposite the Madeleine Cathedral and mingle with the ladies of the night who frequented that quarter of the city. When he felt comfortable, he would telephone his courier and say something like: "I have some cheese for you. Drop by the concierge's lodge at ———." *R* painstakingly, literally sewed messages inside cheeses bound by sheer, coarse cotton. By the time the courier got to Vichy by train, the cheeses would be so pungent that even the Germans wouldn't go near them.

Renaudot's reports by radio and courier covered the enemy's order of battle and airports, the results of Allied bombings, advice on targets and about German secret weapons and the transport of munitions, and movements of German troops and materials including senior staff and headquarters' units.[8]

One secret Allied document released after the war gives a list of reports transmitted to London by Goélette agents working for the railroad in Chalon-sur-Saone and from an agent spying at Le Bourget airport. These messages went out under a radio "VVV" code taken from a dictionary supplied by London. The message opened with a set word or phrase—"La Cygne," for example—which certified to London that the message originated from *R* and not from the Germans.

Another agent's report on German airfields reads: "st. omer: ju-88s painted all black land/take-off day/night; one me210 parked/repairing. bethune: Six h129s, various marks, land/take-off day/night. arras: 12 ju88 wings w/cannon holes at railhead." And so on. There were nine locations and their map coordinates.

Other agents gave the results of an Allied bombing: "New information: tunnel near Saumur untouched. Torpedoes in tunnel make it unusable for moment. . . . Passage between Paris and Le Havre for motorized barges re-established. Must lower water level by bombing points indicated by following map coordinates."[9]

——————

Sometime after the Allied invasion of North Africa, Phillip remembers being caught "with my pants down." Louise Heile, the family maid, had taken his trousers to be washed. When she reversed one of the pockets, bits of white chalk fell on the rug. Her suspicions were confirmed. She ran to Toquette and informed her that her "adorable Pete" was marking the walls of the neighborhood with 'V' for victory signs. What's more, Louise suspected he was scrawling obscenities about the German occupier that she had seen on neighborhood walls. (Other boys in Phillip's class were doing the same thing.)

Toquette was appalled: this was the very thing that could attract the French police or, worse, the Gestapo.

Later, in the woodshed at the lake, as father and son set about cutting wood, Phillip caught hell from Sumner for doing "stupid tricks" that could jeopardize the family. Sumner told his son that he could be shot if the French police turned him over to the Germans. Phillip said something like, "The Boches don't shoot people for chalking V's, Dad." Sumner then replied that if he got caught, he "might endanger the family. Mom and I are . . . doing some other things."

The BBC announced a singular event on the morning of November 8, 1942: American and British forces had landed in North Africa. Two weeks later, Eisenhower arrived in Algiers. The German armed forces occupied all of France on November 11, 1942 (the anniversary of the end of World War I on that day in 1918). The French fleet was scuttled in the Bay of Toulon, and Admiral Darlan was assassinated in Algiers on Christmas Eve by a group of so-called Free French fighters.

By the new year, 1943, the war had changed: the sieges of Leningrad and Stalingrad were lifted, and Field Marshal von Paulus's Sixth Army surrendered. With the invasion of North Africa, Vichy ended all pretense of independence, bowed to the Nazis, and disbanded the French military.

Now General Oberg controlled the French and German security and police apparatus throughout France. His blueprint of French Resistance organizations allowed the SS and Gestapo to carry out a sustained and systematic program of reprisals against, and the extermination of, Resistance groups and members of the Free French secret army. French police rounded up some four hundred leading "terrorists," arrested 5,460 so-called Communists, and seized 40 tons of illegal arms. A joint French-German radio detection team equipped with fake French ID cards uncovered nine radio transmitters. Security became ferocious during 1943—arrests occurred for "Gaullism, Marxism or hostility to the regime." The French arrested nine thousand people while the Germans arrested thirty-five thousand, causing the German security service to complain to Vichy about their poor record compared with that of the German police.[10]

As the year 1943 opened, Sumner was all the more confident[11] that the Americans would liberate France. He took his staff onto the roof of the hospital to watch Allied bombers plaster the Renault factory a few miles down the Seine. It was a great show. But the pressure on Sumner at the hospital grew as the number of Allied airmen downed in air raids over northern France multiplied. More and more soldiers quietly trickled in to Neuilly on their way to Spain and to freedom in England. Getting them to England was acknowledged as enormously valuable. Aside from the humanitarian aspect of keeping the airmen out of prison camps, putting airmen "back to work" benefited the U.S. Air Force and their British allies. The men had valuable knowledge about French Resistance networks and their escape routes. In the early days of the war, a British fighter pilot was a priceless human resource.

As the war dragged on, Resistance activities expanded in various forms in addition to chalking "Vs" and obscene epithets on buildings: distributing underground newsletters and papers (featuring some fine prose and poetry), tearing down official German propaganda posters, even shooting or otherwise killing German soldiers on the Paris metro. The Resistance had clever ways of trapping Germans involved in forbidden activities, and they turned them and used them when they could. Germans were subject to blackmail—and if caught, it meant assignment on the Russian front.

Some citizens joined formal underground Resistance groups. Sumner, Toquette, and Phillip joined Goélette. Other individuals who weren't connected to an official Resistance network did what they could in their everyday lives to hurt the occupier.

One example of individual sacrifice and heroism is the Migdal family with its eleven members. André, the sixth of the Migdal children, started work at fourteen at the German-controlled Villacoublay airport near Paris.[12] (Although Jewish, he and his siblings refused to wear the yellow stars on their clothing.) His brothers, Robert and Henri, who were Resistance "delinquents" and already carrying guns, showed him how to pry open the fuel caps of German trucks and pour sugar mixed with sand into the Wehrmacht fuel tanks. André managed to sabotage German transport before he and his brothers were arrested. "Mickey," as family and friends called André, spent the night of his first arrest in a dark, wet cell. In the morning, a French cop took pity on him: "If we catch you again, you little 'Yid' bastard . . ." Those were the last words he remembered hearing from a representative of French law and order before being tossed into the street. Robert, age twenty, and Henri, twenty-six years old, were deported to Auschwitz, where they died in gas chambers in 1942.

André was arrested again by the French police for having anti-Nazi propaganda in his school case. He spent a year in various French prisons and finally reached Compiègne, from where he was deported to Hamburg-Neuengamme via Büchenwald. At the Neuengamme camp, he eventually met up with Sumner and Phillip Jackson and a man named Jean Langlet.

The Migdal family's fate was typical: André's mother and father, Joseph and Sophie Migdal, were arrested by the French police in December 1942 and deported to Auschwitz in convoy no. 42. They were exterminated with the other members of the convoy.

Fanny, André's oldest sister, pregnant with her first child, was arrested in the Paris metro by French police in 1943 and imprisoned at Drancy, where her baby, Annie, was born. By a miracle, she and her baby escaped with the help of her husband, and survived the Occupation. Charles, Odette, Huguette, Roger, Micheline, and Arlette Migdal—André's remaining brothers and sisters—survived in various hideouts in the French countryside thanks to their sister, Marcelle, who systematically placed them in safe French homes far from Paris.

In the Pantin cemetery in a section called Carré des fusillés ("The Circle of the Assassinated"), there are two crosses bearing the names Edouard and Jean Rodde—the grandfather and father of Jeannine (Mrs. André) Migdal. Both men were members of the French Resistance (FTPF). They were taken by the French police and murdered along with ninety-three other hostages by German firing squads on the heights above Paris at Mont-Valerien.

Yet another example of resistance is the case of Jean Langlet, who was the commercial manager of his father-in-law's Bronzavia aero-engine works at Lyon. He and members of his family helped sabotage the factory in January 1944. With the help of British agents, they blew up machinery, spare parts, and Gnome and Rhone engines, and set fire to the workshops to prevent the German Luftwaffe from using the machinery and plant against the Allies. The family was arrested and turned over to SS Lieutenant Klaus Barbie at the infamous l'Ecole de Santé militaire on Avenue Berthelot.[13] They were tortured in the *baignoire*: their heads thrust under icy water and held there.

Langlet recalls, "One's lungs felt they would burst; and then one passed out. After a while you got smart and played dead. Then the thugs would take a drink of schnapps and start all over again."[14] Langlet, his brother, and his father-in-law were deported to Neuengamme.

There were, of course, thousands of acts of defiance and bravery all over France in those years of resistance, and the price paid if arrested was death or deportation to "nowhere." De Gaulle's agents had some notable successes: an engineer stole the plans for the German submarine base at Lorient and delivered them to London. Another engineer named Keller managed to tap the telephone lines linking Berlin to the Paris headquarters of the Wehrmacht. He fed valuable tactical information to de Gaulle's headquarters, which allowed agents in Normandy to give the Allies detailed plans of the German fortifications along the "Atlantic Wall"—a fortress area to repel the Allied invasion of France.

As the Occupation reached its climax, the price in savage brutality against civilians grew. One of the least known and more terrifying attacks of retribution for French Resistance took place in the village of Tulle, southwest of Clermont-Ferrand. There, in the last days of the war, German troops forced the townspeople to watch as they hanged ninety-nine of Tulle's menfolk from trees, telephone poles, and from apartment balconies in the center of the town.[15]

German atrocities lit a fire under the Resistance and made unlikely bedfellows and unpredictable alliances. The French poet Charles Peguy, killed at the battle of the Marne in 1914, wrote, "In wartime he who refuses to surrender is my friend, whoever he may be, wherever he may come from and whatever party he may belong to."[16] In the cities and towns of France, there was a newfound spirit—a belief that the end of the struggle against the barbarian was within reach. Listening to the BBC, Sumner and Toquette were linked somehow to America, England, and the *résistant* French nation in a great crusade to defeat the Nazis. Despite the deprivations and grim and somber moments, Sumner, Toquette, and Phillip knew victory was near. Their optimism spread to others and was shared by their companions in the Resistance and colleagues at the hospital.[17]

At Saint-Nazaire, where the river Loire empties into the Atlantic, Allied air raids had destroyed 85 percent of the town's houses and reduced its public buildings to piles of bricks and mortar. Most Nazairiens had fled, but every day thousands of workers were transported to and from the town to service the shipbuilding yards and German submarine pens where U-boats were fueled and repaired before returning to sea to attack Allied shipping.

But just how badly had the Flying Fortresses damaged the German submarine works? General de Gaulle's intelligence services in London needed to know—for apparently, Allied reconnaissance photography wasn't detailed enough.

In June 1943, de Gaulle's group asked "Pigeon Bleu" (as *R*, head of Goélette in Paris, was known in radio traffic and BBC broadcasts) to put a man on the ground to take photographs.[18]

This assignment was particularly challenging. *R* knew about the destruction of Saint-Nazaire and about the men and women who were transported daily in special trains from the neighboring towns of

Trignac, Montoire de Bretagne, Pontchateau to the north, and La Baule. The rail station at Saint-Nazaire overlooked the town and was less than a mile from the basin where the submarines entered from the Atlantic. How could he get someone with a camera to slip in and out of one of the most heavily guarded German installations in France?

Somehow, *R* reached the conclusion that a boy might be the ideal candidate. He thought that Toquette Jackson's son, then fifteen years old and speaking passable German, might be able to get in and around to take photos of the town's destruction, undetected by German eyes. With luck Phillip might even be able to take pictures at a safe distance of the submarine pens and the 88mm antiaircraft batteries that were supposed to surround them. *R* knew that the British had ways of enlarging photos that allowed specially trained technicians to observe amazing details. But how to get Phillip in and out of Saint-Nazaire on the trains patrolled by the German military police—*les boule-dogues,* as the French called the German Feldgendarmerie? His plan required some research.

R went to meet "Dorsal," his agent in the city of Nantes, a town located on the Loire River, inland from Saint-Nazaire. Dorsal ran a bicycle repair shop there off the Rue Doumergue. Dorsal told *R* that Allied bombers and their crews of ten men did a round-trip from airfields north of London, then down the English coast crossing the Atlantic east of Plymouth, making landfall near Brest. From there the Fortresses flew over Nantes and the Saint-Nazaire targets. German fighter planes and antiaircraft batteries protected the whole area. It was a deadly business, and the Americans had lost fifty Flying Fortress planes and more than three hundred aircrew since they began their raids in September 1942.

Agent *R* learned, too, that security in La Baule and Saint-Nazaire was tight—for it was here that the Germans were building a part of the Atlantic Wall. But the northern towns were outside the German "forbidden zone." Dorsal apparently confirmed to *R* that a schoolboy had a good chance of traveling there as long as he had an *Ausweis* approved by the German security service. After all, Dorsal reasoned, schoolchildren regularly visited the area for the summer holidays.

R must have hesitated to propose such a dangerous mission to

Toquette. Everyone knew that Gen. Karl von Stulpnagel, military governor of France, had decreed death for any man caught helping the Allies, and deportation to a concentration camp in Germany for any woman. By allowing Phillip to undertake this mission, the Jacksons would consent to him risking his life. And *R* understood the implications of Phillip's being arrested and exposed. He knew the teenager would be eager for the job and a vacation away from Paris. But if he were arrested and talked, the operation at Avenue Foch would be in peril.

So *R* stated his case to Toquette: "London needs help." He must have also presented the outlines of the plan: Phillip would go by train to Nantes with "Verdier," an agent who regularly appeared at the Jackson apartment to deliver and pick up mail, and whom Toquette knew and trusted. In Nantes, Dorsal would figure out a way to get Phillip safely into Saint-Nazaire for a "schoolboy" visit.

To everyone's astonishment, Toquette announced that the Jacksons had friends who lived at Pontchateau, a town only a few kilometers from Saint-Nazaire, but outside the forbidden zone. As former Nazairiens, Marcelle Le Bagousse and her family had left the city when the bombing started. Marcelle's husband was a railroad worker, and like most Frenchmen, Toquette assumed he despised the Nazis. What's more, Phillip had stayed with them in Saint-Nazaire a few years back before the Occupation. Phillip got on well with their daughter, a young girl he called Rosie. Her name was actually Rosewita but everyone called her Erika—except Phillip, who named her Rosie. Toquette thought that the family would welcome Phillip to their home again. Sumner had no objections to the plan.

When *R* came to the Foch apartment a few days later, he explained how Phillip would go to Nantes with Verdier, meet Dorsal, and pick up the camera. Dorsal would take him by car to the train station at Pontchateau, where he would be met by Marcelle or her husband. *R* showed Phillip how to stand away from a window so as to avoid being seen when using the Kodak. On a map of Saint-Nazaire, *R* pointed out the likely places to photograph submarine pens, the harbor, and where antiaircraft batteries were believed to be installed. (Goélette had some information about this, but it was over a year old.) *R* urged Phillip to try to get up to the bell tower of the

Church of Saint-Nazaire. It overlooked the docks and the locks where the U-boats were moored and laid up. He showed the boy how to hide a roll of 120 film in the false bottom of a suitcase he would carry, and he instructed him not to take the camera with him on his return to Paris. Phillip was to destroy it or leave it at Saint-Nazaire or Pontchateau after removing the exposed film. *R* agreed to meet with Phillip on his return to Avenue Foch and pick up the exposed roll of film. In the meantime, Verdier would arrange their travel, including securing a special German *Ausweis* for Phillip.

Thus, a great adventure began for Phillip—an event years later he would dismiss as nothing, but which earned him merit and distinction. First, he traveled overnight to Nantes with Verdier at his side. Upon leaving the Gare Montparnasse, there was a routine security check. The train was packed with Parisians trying to get away from the stifling heat of summer. Phillip remembers quickly wearying of the trip. But he was grateful to have Verdier with him. His companion was always in good spirits and carried sandwiches and a thermos of water mixed with wine. Phillip slept fitfully on and off. He thought of the job before him. It scared him. And he remembered Rosie—a skinny, spoiled, and playful only child.

At Nantes early the next morning, there was no security check at all. Verdier took Phillip to Dorsal's home, where he spent the night. Dorsal gave him a simple Kodak box camera and hid a roll of 120 film in the false bottom of one of *R*'s cases. There was nothing to manipulate on the camera. The lens was fixed-focus, set at infinity.

The morning trip to Pontchateau was hair-raising. Dorsal drove the *traction-avant* Citroën like a maniac, taking the curves in the hills above Pontchateau like a racing driver. Phillip nearly threw up a number of times. His stomach churned as the car whipped around the tight curves. Verdier sat in the front with a machine pistol between his knees just in case they were stopped at some improvised checkpoint set up by the Feldgendarmerie.

As arranged, they delivered Phillip to the rail station at Pontchateau and drove away after they were assured that Mme. Le Bagousse had met him.

When Phillip entered the vast kitchen of the family's farmhouse, he was greeted by Monsieur Le Bagousse. He remembers the big *che-*

minot putting his arms around him and calling him *Mon petit Phillipe*. Marcelle looked on, beaming. Rosie shook his hand. Then Marcelle embarrassed her daughter by saying something like, "Erika, you're not going to embrace Monsieur Phillip? Look how handsome he is. He's all you've talked about for two days." Indeed, Phillip at fifteen was nearly six feet tall with broad shoulders. He had left puberty behind.

Phillip opened his suitcase with ceremony to reveal, item by item, the gifts Toquette had prepared: a sausage, one of Sumner's last bottles of a good Bordeaux, a few yards of a precious wool gabardine that Toquette had been saving, and an illustrated book of the stories of *La Fontaine* for Erika. Mother and father were clearly pleased at the gifts from Paris. Erika put her hand on Phillip's shoulder, pecked his cheek, and whispered something like, "*Merci.*"

Phillip then remembers he picked up the lunch sack and removed the hidden camera. Later, he would ask himself, "How could I have been so stupid?"

Monsieur Le Bagousse froze and said something like: "Are you mad? We are near an excluded zone! You can get shot here for having a camera. Is there film?" Le Bagousse opened the back of the camera and then examined the contents of the lunch sack and suitcase. He came up empty.

"*Zut!*" he exclaimed, finding nothing and adding words to the effect that he better not see any film around. He confiscated the Kodak.

That afternoon, Erika took Phillip into Saint-Nazaire using her father's railway pass. On the train and at both rail stations, she was greeted by her father's friends, who had known her since childhood and watched her grow to become a beautiful teenager. Phillip was shocked as he walked from the station and down the Rue Jaures. The town was as rumored: only half-standing. He remembers seeing German sailors—submariners, from the badges they wore—sitting at a local café drinking coffee and schnapps. Otherwise, the town was deserted.

The Church of Saint-Nazaire was almost empty and no one seemed to care where they went. He and Erika climbed to the bell tower. From on high they looked out over the Loire River and the sea, and before their eyes, a German submarine with the flag of the

Kreigsmarine fixed to its conning tower entered the Saint-Nazaire basin. *"Mon dieu,"* Phillip exclaimed. "If I only had the camera." Erika must have realized then that there was more to Phillip's visit to the bell tower, and that the confiscated camera was essential in some way.

The night was particularly warm. Phillip had the shutters of his room open, and moonlight streamed in from a cloudless sky. The door opened and Erika slipped soundlessly into his room.

"Shh!" she whispered, and sat on the side of the bed. Phillip remembers being bewildered. Then Erika whispered, "Take this," as she handed him the Kodak. She had discovered her father's hiding place in the linen closet. Phillip took the camera and stashed it away, and he and Rosie talked until late into the night.[19] Despite her curiosity, Phillip would say nothing to her other than something like, "It would be fun to show my pals at school pictures of a German submarine."

The next day, Erika accompanied Phillip back into Saint-Nazaire. He took photographs of the town and the German submarine pens from the church bell tower. (If there were antiaircraft [AA] batteries around, he never saw them.) In the face of obvious peril, as Phillip described the incident, he was once again "playing a game." At the time, he was amazed how easy it was to take the pictures and to get in and out of the town. Despite their reputation, the Germans could be lax, and in Phillip's case, never even suspected the two young people. Once they arrived at home, Erika returned the camera to the linen closet, never raising the suspicions of her father.

When Phillip returned to Paris with Verdier, *R* was waiting for the film at the Gare de Montparnasse. The exposed film eventually arrived in London, making one more contribution to the cause of the Resistance.

6

FLYING FORTRESSES— SECRET AGENTS

On the morning of Bastille Day, July 14, 1943, Toquette insisted that Phillip visit his father at the hospital. Phillip thought that meant Toquette was preparing for a visit from "them." (His mother was always thinking up reasons to get him out of the house when "they" came.) The Jacksons agreed they would all meet later at the lake and celebrate what they hoped would be the last Bastille Day under the German Occupation.

Since the Saint-Nazaire escapade, from time to time Phillip had seen *R* and other unnamed men sitting in the parlor of the Foch apartment where his father's patients waited. Once, late in the evening, he caught a man filling a small suitcase with banknotes. Phillip was urged to stay in his room, as Sumner kept repeating, "Pete, what you don't know can't hurt us or our friends!"

While his parents tried to limit his involvement in their undercover work, Phillip had in fact recently spirited another unknown man with a suitcase to the staircase leading down to a metro station. He never spoke to the man but made sure he didn't lose him. At the station Phillip signaled his contact—a man he knew only by sight—and the two strangers disappeared down the stairs.

Louise, the maid, wrapped up some hard-boiled eggs for Phillip to carry to Sumner at his office. She was always fussing over Dr. Jackson, worried that he didn't eat well—but then no one did in those days. Toquette trusted Louise, who was a key figure in their secret work. Louise knew the warning signals she must make in case the police came around: hang the gray floor mop from the windowsill that gave onto the garden, and move the plant in front of the window that gave onto Rue Traktir, a side street off of Avenue Foch.

On this day, however, no warning signals were needed as Phillip Jackson walked his bike slowly along Avenue Foch in the direction of l'Arc de Triomphe. There, twelve boulevards met like spokes in a wheel. And it was there, every day at noon, that an elite unit of the Wehrmacht marched down the Avenue des Champs Elysées to the Place de la Concorde. A mounted officer, saber in hand, led the troop astride a marvelous chestnut horse with double bridles and white hooves. They strutted along to the Rue Rivoli and the Hotel Meurice, where Gen. Hans von Boineburg-Lengsfeld, the Paris military governor, had his headquarters. (Many believed that the parading officer's horse was actually of French stock, adding to the disgrace.)

Few Parisians were perverse enough to watch the two hundred fifty elite Wehrmacht troops parade. Most shopkeepers bolted their iron shutters and deserted the streets. If caught out, many turned their backs in defiance. At the Coudert Frères law firm at 52, avenue Champs Elysées, staff members pushed their chairs away from their desks and stood with their backs turned ostentatiously to the windows as the Germans paraded on the street below at the same hour each day.[1] The workers stood silently until the Germans had passed. Then they resumed their seats and went back to work.[2]

The night before, the BBC had announced the Allied invasion of Sicily. And on this July 14, Phillip wondered if there would be a popular demonstration like the year before. If one took place, he had been ordered to stay away. He knew too much.

Phillip couldn't see the Place de L'Etoile from where he walked. The last building on Avenue Foch hid his view, but he could hear the martial music resounding off the walls of the nineteenth-century Haussmann buildings. So he waited until he heard the troops march away and then he wheeled his bike down the Avenue Foch. He might have taken Rue Piccini, where Toquette and Sumner had worked in World War I, but he was forbidden to go anywhere near the west end of Avenue Foch. General Oberg's men and various SS chiefs and German security units had their headquarters there. The area was teeming with SS and Gestapo in their brown leather coats. Only a few days

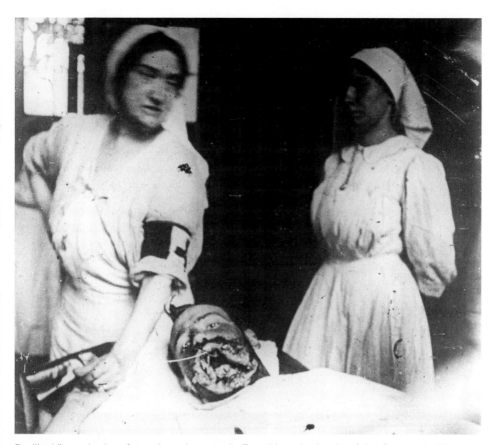

Dr. "Jack" saw broken faces (*gueule casse* in French) at the battle of the Somme in WW I, and later in Paris hospitals. Here, a nurse holds the hand of French trooper whose face has been blasted away by shrapnel. Amazingly, troopers' faces were repaired by surgery perfected in World War I. (Photo courtesy of Editions Tallandier Phototheque.)

Dr. Jackson probably outbound to join the British Army in 1916. (Photo courtesy of Massachusetts General Hospital, Archives and Special Collections.)

Sporting a cane, Lt. Sumner Waldron Jackson of The Harvard Unit (left) in the uniform of a British Officer when he served as a medical officer at the Battle of the Somme in France, circa 1916. The man on the right is unidentified. (Photo courtesy of Massachusetts General Hospital, Archives and Special Collections.)

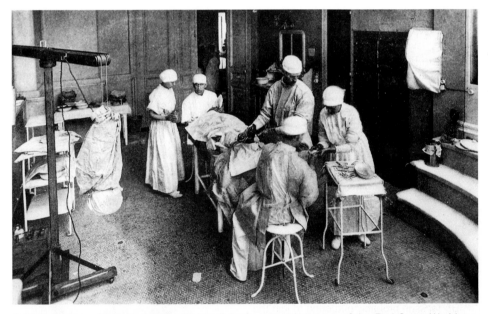

Captain Jackson (seated at patient's head) in the operating room of the Red Cross World War I Hospital, Rue Piccini, Paris, sometime after 1917. He is administering anesthesia to a wounded soldier while another surgeon operates. Toquette is very likely the nurse standing next to him, holding a can of anesthetic. (Photo courtesy of Massachusetts General Hospital, Archives and Special Collections.)

Toquette and Sumner Jackson in happier times, circa 1917–1918, possibly on a honeymoon visit to Cote d'Azur. Sumner wears the uniform of a U.S. Army officer and the two silver bars of a captain on his cap. (Photo courtesy of Phillip Jackson.)

Sumner and Toquette Jackson, circa 1930, when Dr. Jack was the chief urologist at the American Hospital of Paris. (Photo courtesy of Phillip Jackson.)

Phillip and Sumner Jackson in the garden of their Avenue Foch apartment, circa 1930. From this spot French Gestapo police took the Jackson family to a Vichy prison in 1944. (Photo courtesy Phillip Jackson.)

Sumner (center) towers over Dr. Thierry de Martel (profile) and Toquette (third nurse from right). Her head is slightly tilted forward in her typical pose. The photo was taken in the garden of the American Hospital at Neuilly just before the German Occupation of Paris. A few weeks later Dr. de Martel would commit suicide over the defeat of France and the Occupation. (Photo courtesy of Phillip Jackson.)

L'Hôpital Américain de Paris
Pendant la Deuxième Guerre Mondiale

American Hospital of Paris

The cover of a pamphlet heralding the American Hospital of Paris' efforts during World War II.
The photo shows an ambulance with attendant-drivers and a nurse, circa 1939–1940.
(Photo courtesy of the American Hospital of Paris Archives.)

A group of volunteer women ambulance attendant-drivers with their vehicles, before going to the battlefront to pick up wounded British and French soldiers, March 1940. From left: Mme. Vongoetschen, Mme. Fabius, and Princess Therese de Caraman-Chimay. Their chief-of-service was Mme. Robert Thion de la Chaume. (Photo courtesy of the American Hospital of Paris Archives.)

RÉPUBLIQUE FRANÇAISE

Guerre 1939 - 1945

CITATION

COPIE DE L'ORDRE GENERAL N° 329/C

Le Général d'Armée HUNTZIGER
Commandant en Chef les Forces Terrestres, Ministre, Secrétaire d'Etat à la Guerre

CITE A L'ORDRE DE L'ARMEE

L'HOPITAL AMERICAIN DE NEUILLY

"Sous l'impulsion de son médecin-chef le Docteur E.L. GROS, et grâce à la collaboration de :
Dr. L.C. BAILLEUL,
Dr. BESSON WALTER
Dr. S.W. JAKSON
Dr. A. CHERON
Dr. A.BISSON
Dr. N.C. ROGERS
Mr E.B. CLOSE
Melle E. COMTE

l'Hôpital Américain de Neuilly, expression de la générosité bienfaisante américaine, a fourni un magnifique effort pendant la période des hostilités, soignant et opérant bénévolement, de jour et de nuit, les blessés affluant de tous côtés, sauvant ainsi un grand nombre de vies humaines.

Au contact immédiat de l'ennemi, puis en zone occupée, a continué avec une activité inlassable, non seulement à soigner les blessés, mais encore à porter son aide aux prisonniers."

Cette citation comporte l'attribution de la Croix de Guerre 1939-1945 avec palme

A Vichy, le 9 octobre 1940
Signé : HUNTZIGER

Citation homologuée par inscription publiée
au Journal Officiel du 10.10.1941 page 680 CG

- EXTRAIT CERTIFIE CONFORME
À Pau, le 8 avril 1999
Le Lieutenant-Colonel J.P. BOUQUET
Commandant le Bureau Central
d'Archives Administratives Militaires

This citation carries the award of the Croix de Guerre 1939–1945 with Palm. (Dr. Jackson's name is spelled "Jakson.") It reads in part: "for a magnificent effort in face of the enemy while voluntarily caring and operating on wounded day and night during the hostilities, saving thus a great number of human lives ... and in the occupied zone a never-ending effort to care for wounded and prisoners." (Photo courtesy of the French Ministry of Defense.)

The Jackson home facing the lake at Enghien was a refuge for the family during their secret work for de Gaulle's Resistance movement in Paris. (Photo courtesy of Phillip Jackson.)

Flying Fortress gunner, Sergeant "Joe," escaped the Gestapo thanks to the efforts of the Jackson family and the French Resistance. (Photo circa December 1943, from *Nostalgic Notes*, March 1991, publication of the 94th Bomb Group Memorial Association.)

Sergeant Joe, a Flying Fortress gunner who had parachuted into a Paris suburb, came through this garden of the Memorial Building of the American Hospital of Paris to be treated by Dr. Jackson. The physician later hid Joe from the Gestapo on an upper floor of the building and later at the Jackson home. (Photo courtesy of the American Hospital of Paris Archives.)

The "Butcher of Paris," General Carl-Albrecht Oberg, Higher SS and police leader in Paris from 1942–1944, played a sinister role in the life of the Jacksons. Oberg ordered the killing and deportation of the Jackson family and countless Jews and French Resistance agents. (Press Association photograph courtesy of National Archives and Records Administration, College Park, MD.)

As Higher SS and police leader in Paris, General Carl-Albrecht Oberg, right, ordered the deportation of the Jackson family. His colleague, Helmut Knochen (left) was head of the SS security service headquartered at 31 and 77, avenue Foch, Paris. Leon Degreele, center, was head of the Belgian Nazi Wallonie Legion. The three pose on the steps of the Trocadero in Paris, sometime after 1942. (Photo courtesy of Editions Tallandier, Phototheque, Paris.)

Neuengamme concentration camp prisoners, circa 1943–1944. The second prisoner from the right is French general Henri Brunet who was arrested and sentenced to death by the Nazis in 1943 for his daring work in the French Resistance. Brunet was at the camp at the same time as Sumner and Phillip, and Dr. Jackson probably cared for him at the infirmary. (Photo courtesy of Editions Tallandier Phototheque)

Toquette, June 1945, in Sweden following her release from Ravensbrück concentration camp. Toquette's face was permanently scarred from being bittten by vermin at the concentration camp. (Photo courtesy of Phillip Jackson.)

JACKSON
charlotte

REPUBLIQUE FRANCAISE

LAISSEZ – PASSER
(valable jusqu'au 31 Décembre 1945)

N° 374

NOM : *JACKSON*

PRENOMS : *Charlotte*

LIEU ET DATE DE *3 Aout 1889*
NAISSANCE : *Colombier (Suisse)*

PROFESSION : *infirmière*

DOMICILE (enFrance)/
11 Avenue Foch

Taille :
Cheveux :
Yeux :

Signature du titulaire:

Ce laissez-passer est délivré sur
la foi des déclarations faites
par le titulaire à son arrivée
en Suède

STOCKHOLM, le   1945

A *Laissez-Passer* issued to Toquette by the French Foreign Legation in Sweden, days after she was freed from Ravensbrück. (Photo courtesy of Phillip Jackson.)

The SS prison ship *Thielbeck* show here under steam after WW II when she was refitted and named the *Reinbek*. Phillip escaped from the ship when British typhoons bombed the freighter shortly after Adolf Hitler's suicide. Of the 2,800 prisoners held in the ship's holds, only 50 were saved. (Photo courtesy of Editions Tallandier Phototheque.)

Phillip "Pete" Jackson in the uniform of the Royal Ambulance Corps, soon after he escaped death on the SS *Thielbek*. (Photo courtesy of Phillip Jackson.)

From left: General de Grancey, head of a group of army resistants, and Mr. Le Druillemec, a schoolteacher and resistant from the island of Jersey. Like Phillip (on right), they were arrested by the Gestapo for their underground work against the Nazis and sent to Neuengamme. Here they stand in front of the War Crimes Tribunal in Hamburg, where they testified at the trial of their SS captors. (Photo courtesy of Phillip Jackson.)

The only known photo of SS Hauptsturm-führer Dr. Heinrich Illers, chief of the Gestapo in Paris during the German Occupation of France. Under General Oberg, Illers sent thousands, including the Jacksons, to concentration camps. This photo was taken from a distance by a telephoto lens while Illers was in the garden of his villa at Gretseel, circa 1971. (Photo courtesy of Serge Klarsfeld.)

Phillip Jackson was a hero of the French Resistance at the age of 15. At age 75 in the garden of the Institute (hospital) des Invalides, Paris, he wears on his left breast the French decorations: Officer of the Legion d'Honneur and the Croix de Guerre with Bronze Star. The day this photograph was taken, Phillip couldn't find the medal awarded to him as a Resistance fighter deported to a Nazi concentration camp. (Photo by Antoine de Roux, Paris.)

earlier, on the 1,119th day of the German Occupation, Charles de Gaulle's representative in France, the titular head of the French Resistance, Jean Moulin (alias "Max") was arrested in Lyon and brought to Paris. He lay in agony in a cell at 84, avenue Foch.[3] The SS tortured him there and at Neuilly in a villa near the hospital for weeks until he finally died on a train destined for Germany. But Phillip couldn't have known this.

Phillip steered his bike past the guard at Place de L'Etoile and past the monument draped with the Nazi swastika. Across the way the Germans had ripped out a bronze statue and installed a small pillbox guarding the axes of the gracious boulevards MacMahon, Wagram, and Hoche. Albert Speer's Todt organization had melted down bronze statues throughout Paris to make artillery shells.

At first, the Wehrmacht frightened Phillip. But the more he observed them, looking at their faces under their steel pots, the more he realized they were just kids or dumb thugs in fancy uniforms. It was their helmets and bayonets that frightened people.

On the Avenue Wagram, he pedaled at full speed. The road was empty except for an occasional German vehicle or a wood-burning *gazogen* Citroën. After the Port Champerret, he whizzed past the brick Octroi de Neuilly and an empty black, white, and red German sentry box marking the entrance to Neuilly. He never ceased to be struck by the marks of conquest and occupation all over the city—the forest of German road signs: Der Militarbefehlshaber im Frankreich, Hauptverkehrsdirektion Paris. It disgusted him.

As he cycled past a billboard, he saw a poster advertising "Baby Cadum" soap. Someone had painted a Hitler-style mustache on Baby Cadum. Phillip grinned. The Germans would immediately remove these "works of art." (If caught in the act of defacing property with anti-German graffiti, you could be shot.)

Phillip entered the hospital through the emergency room entrance. He unlocked the wire-mesh cage that held the bikes of the hospital staff, hung his on a hook, and went inside.

Everyone knew Phillip Jackson. He had been born there some fifteen years earlier. A group of smiling nurses greeted him, and he spent a moment with Mademoiselle Comte, the power behind the hospital. He handed over the package of eggs while gently kissing her on each cheek. She told him his father was in the operating theater and would be tied up for most of the day. He then took the elevator reserved for personnel only. At the fourth floor, he exited and turned past his father's apartment to a flight of stairs that led to an emergency exit and the terrace of the hospital.

It was a day made for Paris. The sky was an azure blue, the sun a brilliant diamond in the sky. He shaded his eyes. To the west, to his left, he could see Mont Valerien and its wooded hill some 54 feet above sea level at Suresnes, a Paris suburb. It was there that Wehrmacht and SS units murdered men and women of the Resistance. Below him, a patchwork of luxurious villas bordered the tree-lined boulevards of Neuilly. After almost three years of occupation, most of Neuilly had been turned into a village for the Nazis and their Vichy collaborators.

Suddenly Phillip heard the sound of antiaircraft fire coming from the AA battery located nearby at Nanterre, less than a mile from where he stood. A massive air raid was in progress. Against the blue of the sky, white contrails streaked behind B-17 bombers. He knew they were U.S. Flying Fortresses. What a Bastille Day, he thought, as gray puffs burst and blackened the sky and antiaircraft shells began exploding all around. Then he heard the bombers.

———◆———

Earlier that same morning at Bury Saint Edmonds near Cambridge, England, Master Sgt. Buck Moro had entered a broken-down U.S. Eighth Air Force quonset hut to wake his airmen for the day's mission. It was 4:30 A.M. and the hut stank of coal soot from the pot-bellied stoves that had burned most of the night.

The typical wakeup morning drill, according to Sergeant Moro, was:

> I'd walk into the Quonset hut at the edge of the airfield and flip the light switch on the wall. They woke, huddled under covers, in rows and rows of steel cots, head to foot. I'd walk among them and stifle their groans, bellowing something like, "Troops, drop your cocks and grab your socks. Mess call in ten minutes, mission briefing at Zero Five-Thirty, Zero Five-Thirty! Up and out, troops! Take no papers with you, troops!"

Then I'd walk into the damp and chilly early morning of the English countryside. It smelled clean and fresh. Dawn was minutes away. Twenty percent, twenty percent won't be here tomorrow. And I would have to collect their things. Some of them were only 19. And I'd wonder: who'll I lose? Lose a few and forget 'em. You had to survive.[4]

Indeed, by May 1943, the casualty rate for the Eighth Air Force in England was 82 percent. From May to October—when the following episode took place—the pool of airmen was diminished by a third each month, for a total turnover of 200 percent. In actual numbers, sixty-three hundred airmen were killed or captured during this short time. On any given day, twenty planes might take off across the English Channel and only twelve or so would make it back.[5]

One of the men that Sergeant Moro had awakened that morning was Eleftherios Gregos,[6] from Columbus Avenue in New York City. Now dressed and shaven, he plodded into the crowded, steamy mess hall with its smell of powdered eggs, bacon grease, and boiling coffee. He sat with his crew. Everybody called the nineteen-year-old tail gunner "Joe," and he was never without a piece of chewing gum in his mouth.

Joe sat next to his pal, Charles Huguenot, a Fortress mechanic. Charlie came from Brooklyn, and everyone called him "Huge-nuts"—but not to his face. They joked with each other in the chow line, Charlie whispering a joke about a password. Joe took a seat and stirred his coffee. He remembers asking Charlie: "What password?"

Charlie answered: "When youse comes down in France and meets an underground fighter, mainly goils . . . youse gotta give a password."

"OK, I think I understand. What's the password? Tell me, you bastard," Joe laughed.

Charlie Huguenot, alias Huge-nuts, leaned over and whispered hoarsely in Joe's ear: " 'Frenchie kiss me,' then you stick your tongue out!" And Charlie stuck out his tongue—and did a 'raspberry' near Joe's ear. The raspy sound jolted Joe and he jumped up, spilling his coffee on the table.

Later, Joe sat on the bicycle seat of the tail position of his B-17

Flying Fortress. He methodically checked the ammunition belts for the mounted flexible .50-caliber guns. The other gunners on his ship were doing the same. (Joe should have been in the waist of the plane that day, but he had switched positions with one of the waist gunners.)[7] All around him he could see the other Flying Fortresses' rudders moving slowly as the pilots went through their one-hour checkout before takeoff.

Joe was over six feet tall—extraordinary for a tail gunner in such a cramped space. B-17 Flying Fortresses flew with a crew of ten very uncomfortable men. The nose of the plane had barely enough room to contain the navigator and the bombardier in sitting positions. The pilot and copilot sat above them looking out over the ship's nose. Behind them was the top turret gunner, who also served as an engineer. He had a 360-degree field of fire for his .50-caliber guns. An upright bulkhead separated him from the bomb bay. Another bulkhead closed off the bomb bay from the tiny compartment of the radio operator and the left and right waist gunners.

The ball turret gunner, encased in a "Plexiglas" sphere that protruded from the ship's belly, moved his two guns with foot pedals. His position had the clearest view on the ship and was the most vulnerable. It was known as the suicide position. Joe's station in the tail of the B-17 was the most isolated and cramped space in the plane. His job was to guard against enemy fighters that attempted to creep up on the bomb-group formation from behind for an easy kill.[8]

That morning the crews had been briefed for a maximum mission. They were to go against the French airport at Le Bourget a few miles from Paris. This would be the 94th Group's fifteenth mission.

Major Hopkins, the briefing officer of the 331, Joe's squadron, reminded everyone that Le Bourget was the airport where Charles Lindbergh landed in his historic New York-to-Paris flight in 1927. The airport had been converted to a maintenance repair depot for the Luftwaffe. Hopkins told the men that there was an intelligence report of some forty enemy training aircraft in the area. But, he reassured them, "This one should be a breather. You'll pick up fighter escort—Spitfires—over the French coast and on the return from target." Hopkins ended the briefing with, "You can drop one for Colonel Lindbergh."

From the rear of the small auditorium, some wit yelled, "Fuck Lindbergh and gimme pizza!"[9]

Joe slipped into his Blue Devil heated suit, pulled on coveralls over his long-john underwear, and donned an A-2 leather jacket. He wore wool socks over summer socks with his GI shoes. He wound a silk scarf around his neck to keep noise from interfering with talking on his throat mike. As Joe's B-17 taxied in trail for takeoff, Joe put on his sheepskin flying boots and gloves. He checked his oxygen mask and line and verified that the plug was connected to his heated suit. Above 10,000 feet, they would need oxygen and warmth. Frostbite and the loss of oxygen were real threats: if you ran out of air, you were out. At minus 42 degrees, if you took a glove off to fix something, your finger froze and you risked amputation from serious frostbite.

Joe put on his Mae West life jacket and checked the parachute pack that lay next to him. "You ain't gonna need it," he said out loud to himself and snickered. He was that superstitious.

Lt. Floyd B. "Ben" Watts, pilot, along with 2nd Lt. Joe Bieger, copilot,[10] gunned the heavy Fortress loaded with bombs, munitions, and fuel down the bumpy airstrip to the very end until Bieger pulled up the wheels and they got off the ground. They nearly clipped the base utility poles. When all five bombers were in the air, they assembled, climbed to altitude, and headed for the departure point in southeast England. Joe looked out to see streamers of vapor trails—contrails—that were signposts for the Kraut fighters. Joe had not made his bed. He would do it when he got back.

There were two hundred Allied aircraft in the sky on that Bastille Day, 1943; their contrails crossed and crisscrossed. Fifty of the planes were dedicated to bomb Le Bourget, including Joe's squadron that was flying in the low position—tail-end Charlie in the Purple Heart corner. Squadron Leader Maj. Ralph Saltsman led the 331st that morning over the English Channel. The squadron was short one plane, grounded for mechanical reasons.

Pilot Ben Watts spoke over the intercom. "OK, guys! Lovely morning and check oxygen. Gunners test-fire!"[11] The guns made the ship vibrate as they went off, the spent shells littering the deck.

As they approached the French coast at Normandy, Joe cranked his head around, looking for the Spitfire escort. "I never saw one. They never got too far past the Channel."[12] Then they crossed the Seine and headed for the target. Minutes later, "Someone up front called out: 'FW 190s' and then they were sailing through our formation."[13]

The planes bore distinctive black-and-yellow checkered patterns and stripes on their vertical tails and engine cowlings. The spinners were done in yellow. Joe thought the German pilots had plenty of nerve, attacking the B-17 formation head-on:

> The first aircraft through passed on our right side. I couldn't believe how close he was. But I could see the pilot was dead, slumped forward in the cockpit—he hit the right aircraft of a two-ship element that was directly behind us. Our plane vibrated from nose to tail, and there was a steady staccato as our crew gunners pumped .50-caliber machine-gun shells into the oncoming enemy, shell casings spewing everywhere.

All around the aircraft were the black puffs of steel death as the German antiaircraft batteries followed the Fortresses over the target. Joe's aircraft took multiple hits in the nose; number 3 engine caught fire. The plane was going down rapidly.

> Two of the FWs that went through the formation were sitting about a few thousand feet below and behind us. I called Shorty Carpenter [S/Sgt. John L. Carpenter] on the intercom in the ball turret to keep an eye on them. Then someone came on the intercom and said 'Okay, let's cut out the chatter.' That's the last I heard on the intercom. We had either an oxygen or hydraulic fire on the flight deck. Beiger [*sic*] told the crew the entire instrument panel had disintegrated in front of him from cannon fire.[14]

Twenty-thousand feet above and to the northeast of where Phillip stood transfixed on the roof of the hospital, the big Fortresses entered their bomb runs. The pilots of 331 Squadron were holding formation as the German FWs pressed their attack. Maj. Ralph Saltsman was trying to save his ship and crew. A wave of 190s dove at his B-17, and 20mm shells tore into the skin of his aircraft like a series of hot rivets.

He felt a part of the rear of the plane explode. The Fortress vibrated, rattling its frame. A gunner on the intercom described the damage calmly: "Skipper, the horizontal stabilizer and dorsal fin's been hit. Fabric's gone on control surfaces."

Saltsman could barely control the plane's movement. To his left he watched his pal, Ed Daily, piloting another B-17 wave good-bye and rejoin the formation. To his right he saw a Fortress fall out of line, loose fabric flapping from its tail section. Still he tried to hold formation.

On Joe's plane, pilot Floyd Watts took evasive action to avoid oncoming enemy aircraft. The abrupt maneuver tore the covers off Joe's ammo cans, and the belts spewed out on the deck of the ship. Joe watched an FW-190 come directly at him in front of his gun. He got off a few bursts before the ammunition belts jammed. Then Joe tried to pull the tail escape-hatch release as a precaution, but only one pin came loose.

Twenty-millimeter shells were tearing through the cockpit of Saltsman's B-17. Oxygen bottles exploded into bright orange flames. The ball turret gunner was giving a wounded waist gunner first aid when Saltsman decided that saving the aircraft was futile. "Bailout! Bailout now!" Saltsman ordered. But because of the flames in the cockpit, he couldn't hit the alarm bell. The cabin was ablaze, the fire intense. "Bailout!" he screamed. His radioman relayed the message.

Lt. Ben Watts never reached his assigned target. The enemy attacks on Joe's plane never let up; 20mm gunfire wracked the vessel. Two engines were out and the right wing was on fire. Sergeants Reppert and Phillips, the waist gunners, strained to open the escape hatch. It wouldn't come open and they tried to jettison a gun in the hatch to clear the window for escape. The exploding shells killed them. Joe reported their deaths to Watts on the intercom. Another 20mm shell exploded between Lieutenants Eastman and Manning, the bombardier and navigator, respectively, wounding them. It was then that pilot Watts rang the bailout bell.

Isolated in the tail of the aircraft, Joe could feel the plane peel off. He knew they were in trouble. When he heard the bailout bell he snapped on his chest chute.

The flight deck was on fire, destroying the intercom. After helping Eastman and Manning out, Ben Watts watched as the two men dived out of the aircraft and pulled their ripcords. He saw two chutes open. Next, copilot John Bieger, turret gunner John Buice, and Sam Potvin, the radio operator, bailed out the waist window. Ben Watts "dumped" out of the bomb-bay doors into a spinning sky.

John Carpenter, the ball-turret gunner, came to the tail of the aircraft. "We gotta get out, Joe!" But the tail-hatch escape door was still jammed. Joe sat on it, forcing his way through. At about 16,000 feet he pulled the ripcord. The chute opened immediately and Joe looked to see three other chutes below him, the aircraft shuddering above. It peeled off on its left wing and careened toward the ground. In seconds, the B-17 burst into flames and slammed into a green field.

Looking into the sky above him, Joe watched as Squadron Leader Saltsman's crew bailed out—eight chutes billowing in the wind. And then Joe watched in horror as "Five-by-Five," Lt. Kee Harrison's Fortress, fell behind the formation. Instantly, droves of enemy fighters lined up and attacked the crippled bomber. Twenty-millimeter shells entered Harrison's flight deck. The oxygen bottles burst. The cockpit filled with smoke. Harrison held on and put his 250 pounds of weight behind the wheel. What was left of the formation was pulling away fast. He firewalled the throttles but nothing happened.

When the smoke cleared, Harrison saw that no. 2 and 4 engines were out—the latter trailing black smoke. The propeller on no. 2 windmilled badly. Dave Turner, Harrison's copilot, was out of his seat fighting the fire. A voice came over the intercom: "Fighters at twelve o'clock high." Suddenly, Harrison was staring into the guns of six ME-109s coming directly at him. He thrust the wheel forward. The lead fighter came at him head-on. Harrison's Fortress abruptly lost altitude, avoiding disaster. As he drifted to earth, the last thing Joe saw of Harrison's plane was the tail of Five-by-Five being shot away.

By some miracle, Harrison maintained control of his aircraft. With all power shut off, doing 350 miles an hour, losing 2,000 feet a minute, he headed for a cloud bank some 50 miles away. The crew's ears throbbed. Dixie, one of the gunners, had a cold and his eardrums burst. At 2,000 feet below the base of the clouds the six fighters pressed the attack. Harrison ordered, "Bailout!" At 1,000 feet he put the ship into a tight turn, and ordered copilot Dave Turner to give the recognized surrender signal by lowering the landing gear. Then he sent Turner to the rear to inspect the damage. The ME-109s kept coming and kept firing. The bombardier, his face the color of ashes, looked up from below, his eyes questioning. Harrison ordered him to jump. He nodded and went out the hatch. The copilot returned to his seat to report to Harrison that the engineer's parachute had burned. The man couldn't jump. Harrison realized he would now have to crash-land to save the soldier's life.

Spotting a flat grain field appearing to his left, Harrison ordered landing gear up and set the plane to crash-land. Copilot Turner could hardly manage to raise the gear—his hands were so badly burned. Both pilots struggled to maintain control as the plane sliced through some trees near the edge of a clearing. The field was short and they still had speed. Harrison murmured between tight lips, "Please God, no stumps," as he pushed the aircraft onto the ground. Though the wheels were up, he applied the brakes from reflex. The Fortress skidded sideways and came to a stop just short of a line of trees.

Turner and the engineer went out of the right-side window. Harrison went out of the left window headfirst. He got to his feet, paused, and then ran around the aircraft to check on the other crew members. They all were safe. It was beyond Harrison's comprehension. "God lubricated me!" he shouted to his crew. "Pushed me out of the side cockpit!"[15]

Five-by-Five's crew gathered up their chutes and headed for a nearby wood. Later, with the help of the French Resistance, Harrison and two of his crew spent weeks hiding and walking across the Pyrenees through France to Spain. On the march, Harrison lost 50 pounds before he rejoined his unit in England. His other crew members were interned until the end of the war.[16]

Joe floated to earth, held in a backward angle because of a faulty chute. He saw a tiny village coming at him from below. Men on the ground watched intently as he floated by. He played with his shroud lines to avoid the telephone wire coming at him, but stopped when the chute began to swing. Then he landed in the soft earth of a beet field.[17]

On the terrace roof of the American Hospital at Neuilly, Phillip, breathless, his heart pounding, stood shielding his eyes. He had just watched a Luftwaffe fighter plane break apart, falling to earth in three sections. Then a Fortress seemed to fall lazily from the sky until it spun, then stabilized, fell again, and disappeared. Phillip was mesmerized as a ball of fire rose in the distance. The rail line would be out for three days where the B-17 had crashed. He continued to study the sky, watching the hunters and the hunted turn within a triangle made by Neuilly, Le Bourget to the northeast, and the town of Bondy to the south. The distant landscape was marked with explosions as more Fortresses released their loads on Le Bourget. The bursting black "ack-ack" around the aircraft was intense. He could hear the firing of the German guns at Nanterre.

Suddenly, the door leading to the terrace flew open. Phillip spun around to see his father standing in the stairwell, wearing a blood-spattered apron over a white gown. Phillip's heart skipped a beat.

"Damn, Pete!" Sumner screamed. "Get the hell out of here. Shrapnel's falling all around!" They walked to the doctor's apartment. Sumner changed clothes and managed to produce a pint of whisky. Phillip remembers trying to describe the dogfights he'd witnessed between the German FWs and U.S. B-17 Flying Fortresses.[18]

Sitting in the middle of a beet field bordered by a ditch and a road, Joe's chute stretched out behind him. He unbuckled the straps and pulled all the silk into a bundle. He buried the chute, harness, boots, and Mae West. He peeled off his blue suit and covered everything with dirt and stalks from the beets in the furrows of the field. It was only then that he realized he had taken shrapnel in his right arm. Stripped down to his olive drab shirt and pants, and wearing his GI ankle-high shoes, he ran across the road and down a steep embankment into another field. He saw no one. Joe figured he could reach the area where the other chutes had come down and maybe join his crew to begin their evasion together. He began following a line of hedges leading to a nearby wood. Suddenly, just before the wood, he saw two men on a road trying to start a motor-bicycle. They saw him at the same moment. "Boches!" one yelled in warning, and pointed excitedly down

the road. Joe dove into the bushes. A few seconds later a German soldier on a bicycle pedaled lazily by. Joe crawled into an adjacent wheat
field, slowly, inch by inch, making minimum movement to get out of
the area.

"Comrade!" A Frenchman came into the field shouting. He
rushed Joe back to the road where a car was waiting. With barely a
word, the man gestured nervously for Joe to get into the backseat as
another man opened the door. It was all very rushed and confused.
Joe remembers sliding into the Citroën four-door sedan and watching
the man who'd shouted at him cover his body with wood logs while
the driver started the car. The vehicle bumped along for a while. Then
it seemed to Joe that they had come upon a paved road; but it felt like
forever until they reached a house.[19]

At that same moment, Sumner and Phillip were on the opposite
side of Paris biking toward the lake at Enghien where Toquette was
waiting. It was, after all, Bastille Day. Not far from the lake house,
Colonel Saltsman was hiding behind a tree when a squad of Wehrmacht appeared at the other end of a thicket of woods. The Germans
took him to a nearby farmhouse while their unit continued searching
for downed Americans. Saltsman was brought before the Wehrmacht
captain in command. The man spoke good English. He clicked his
heels and saluted, saying, "For you, sir, luck! The war is over!"[20]

Not so lucky were Joe's fellow gunners S/Sgt. Burton H. Reppert,
the left-side waist gunner and S/Sgt. Lawrence B. Phillips, the right-
side waist gunner. (Were it not for a last-minute switch, Joe would
have been manning one of those guns.) The two men went down with
their plane, killed while trying to open the main escape hatch. Radio
Operator Potvin reported that when last seen, "both gunners were
lying on the deck of the aircraft with their heads blown off by a 20mm
shell that exploded between them."[21]

Along with Joe, seven crew members did succeed in bailing out of
the crippled B-17. Potvin left through the right waist window and
landed near Bondy. Despite his being wounded in the arms and legs
by shell fragments, he evaded capture and returned to England.[22]
(Neither Joe nor Potvin ran into the other six crew that bailed out of

the B-17.) Lieutenants Eastman and Manning were captured near
Paris, and were treated in a Luftwaffe hospital at Cliché before being
deported to Stalag VII, an infamous German prisoner-of-war camp.[23]

The balance of Joe's crew were lucky: First Lieutenant Watts, Second Lieutenant Bieger with S/Sergeants Buice and Carpenter landed
not far from where Joe came down. With the help of the French Resistance, all managed to evade the German patrols desperately seeking
the crew. The men slowly made their way through France into Spain
and eventually to England. They were hidden, given civilian clothes
and false documents, and passed along an established route managed
by various French Resistance groups who specialized in aircrew eva-
sions. As we shall see, the networks were incredibly efficient in the
face of the determined German Security Services' efforts to penetrate
the Resistance and capture airmen. Many flyers didn't make it, and
when arrested in civilian clothes—with or without their identification
"dog tags"—they were often sent to concentration camps in Germany where survival was doubtful. French Resistance workers who
were captured rarely survived. They were jailed in Gestapo prisons,
often tortured, and deported. In Thomas Childers's book, *The Shadows of War*, the author tells of an American pilot's odyssey through
Occupied France in 1944, his arrest by the Gestapo, and deportation.
The pilot, Roy Allen, ended up in Büchenwald KZ, was transferred
to Stalag III, and survived the war.[24]

When they reached the lake house, Phillip told Toquette about
his morning adventure on the terrace of the hospital. It frightened his
mother, and Phillip promised his parents he'd stay off the hospital
roof.

Toquette had news from Paris. She had learned from *R* that the
Gestapo had penetrated some of the Resistance groups in Paris and
was offering 50,000 francs for any Allied airman, dead or alive. In fact,
R told Toquette that a member of a Resistance group in Paris had
given a family 20,000 francs to cover their expenses for hiding an English flyer. Then the agent took the man away, promising that he
would get the airman to Spain. The flyer disappeared. *R* said the Englishman was sold to the Gestapo, and the agent was "taken care of."

He stressed that Toquette should warn Sumner and Phillip to be on guard, closemouthed, and to take no chances.

At about the same time that nineteen-year-old Joe, the B-17 gunner, was making his escape, an English girl being treated at the hospital, a refugee from a German prison camp, pinned the following Bastille Day salute to Dr. Jackson on the American Hospital's bulletin board:

> *Portrait of an American:*
> *We all agree he's a perfect dear*
> *Altho at times he inspires fear*
> *And we quake in our beds when he draws near*
> *Oh, so severe!*
> *But those eyes so stern and steel blue*
> *Can gleam with humour and laughter, too*
> *And life takes on a brighter hue*
> *When he smiles at you*
> *What he says goes and there's no appeal*
> *Against a will as strong as steel*
> *So you may as well just come to heel*
> *However you feel.*
> *From prison camp we drifted here*
> *And he cured our bodies and calmed our fear*
> *So let's give him a rousing cheer*
> *For he's rather a dear.*

A copy of the patient's tribute reached Enghien, addressed to Toquette. Phillip remembers reading the sonnet as Toquette teased Sumner about his many female admirers. Sumner admitted that the poem had been pinned to the main bulletin board of the Memorial Building, but he had taken it down. It reappeared the next day.

It was now mid-August 1943. The Allies had taken Sicily from the Germans, whose forces were retreating on the Russian front, and in Italy Mussolini was replaced as head of the Italian government. But in France, the Gestapo and SS had made big gains against the French underground, arresting Jean Moulin and other leaders of General de Gaulle's Free French Resistance.

Sumner's daily rounds at the hospital involved seeing critical cases morning and night and dealing with newly admitted sick and wounded railroad workers and refugees from camps near Paris. Elisabeth Comte, his chief of nursing, invariably accompanied him. She had learned to close her eyes and lips to the "goings on" in the hospital. (It was Mont Valerien and the firing squad if caught.)

As Sumner was rigidly secretive, he never revealed to his wife and son any details of his hiding fugitives from the Germans or the nature of the Resistance work he carried out at the hospital. It is impossible to guess how many "illegals" he and his colleagues sheltered there. The best witness we have is Otto Gresser, the hospital director, who reported after the war, "Dr. Jackson's work was very serious and went on for a long time."[25] Even after their arrests, Phillip says that his father refused to talk about what he had done for fear that German spies in the camps would inform the SS.[26]

His workload at this time was such that he could only come home to Avenue Foch on weekends—though he tried to make quick visits early in the morning. Every day, he telephoned Toquette and Phillip, who were frequent visitors to the hospital.[27]

Thus Sumner was on hand in mid-August 1943 to greet an exceptional guest: a swarthy southern "Frenchman" standing over six feet and dressed in an ill-fitting suit.[28] His head was topped with a French beret; but he wore U.S. Army–issued, low-cut, brown GI shoes. Odd as that may seem, Joe was escorted by Gladys Marchal, an English Resistance agent and switchboard operator from Paris. She brought him to Dr. Jackson in desperation, almost as a last resort, because Joe's agent handlers couldn't manage to get him falsified papers. It was a dangerous business helping Allied flyers. From the time Joe parachuted onto French soil, the German military police and Gestapo were desperately trying to locate the crew of his plane. They knew that six of the American flyers were hiding in the region and trying to evade them—and they had ordered the French police to capture them.

The weeks leading up to his trip to the American Hospital were terrifying. After escaping the German patrol, Joe was driven to the home of Louis Legay at Pavillon-sur-Bois, a Paris suburb. A friend of Legay's gave Joe a suit of clothes, and Joe offered his hosts chocolate, a tube of milk, and matches from his "aids box." (He had given away his chewing gum to the truck driver who picked him up.) He then burned the aids box in the kitchen stove at the Legay house. One of the things that tickled Joe, who somehow found humor in many of the nerve-racking events of his escape, was the insistence of his hosts to see his "fly-button compass." Since Joe didn't speak French, one can imagine the farcical behavior of his Gallic-Latin benefactors as they gestured to make themselves understood.

During this waiting period, Joe was hidden in no fewer than three French homes as the Resistance sought to arrange his escape route.

I was taken to various places to be shown off or to make contact with the people who would be able to get me false papers. . . . I recall being taken to a bar where there was a statue of Joan of Arc outside. . . . I wasn't much of a drinker, only beer. And they were always putting a drink in front of me, and it was always wine or hard stuff. More than once I was driven in a small car and the driver drove like he was half-crazy. I was worried and asked if they were concerned, and one of the men sort of nodded to the back seat and the fellow back there flashed one of those small machine guns that the Allies had made up for cheap and fast use by the troops.[29]

Joe wrote in a report that "the first few times you walked by or was [sic] near a German soldier, it was fairly scary. But, being a Greek, Polish American, with a beret and a tan, as olive skinned as I was I could pass for a Frenchman from southern France, easily."[30]

And so it was in this disguise that the French-looking American flyer first met Sumner, as he later recalled: "An English girl, Gladys Marshall [sic] . . . took me to the American Hospital at Neuilly and I met Dr. S. Jackson of Bangor, Maine."[31] Sumner's office was "a nice place, well furnished. A citation framed on the wall caught my eye and I believe it was the French Legion of Honor."[32] (It was the Croix de Guerre with Palm.)

Sumner examined Joe, treated his wounds, and had Mlle. Comte put him in a hospital bed. "Everything, bed and linens were spotlessly white. . . . I had a good night's sleep."[33]

At first, the Jacksons considered placing Joe in the Neuilly home of a Canadian former general "who had a boardinghouse filled with old men, mostly English, let out of a concentration camp. . . . The aged Englishmen had to report to their German keepers, whom they called, 'Jerry,' every day." But, "Dr. Jackson said it was a crazy idea." Joe eventually stayed at the Jacksons' apartment on Avenue Foch for a few days while they worked to obtain forged identity papers, work papers, and a ration book that would allow him to travel in France.[34]

Joe's escapades, as we shall see, seem almost comical at times, partly because of his distinct personality and New York grit. However, he and those who aided his escape were engaged in a deadly, life-threatening business. Wartime Paris was no place of rest and recreation for a downed American flyer trying to escape the Gestapo. In fact, by the time of Joe's visit, the Jacksons were living in conditions of near starvation, appealing through the Red Cross for warm clothing from Switzerland. Food supplies were precarious: Parisians were raising guinea pigs for meat, trying to digest rutabaga turnips,[35] making cake from potato flour, and drinking homemade alcohol. Joe lived under the constant threat of capture, in cramped quarters, and never sure if a "friend" might betray him.

Toquette finally arranged for Gilbert ("Gil") Asselin of the Resistance group Libération to convey Joe to southern France. But first Joe was hidden for three weeks in the Paris apartment of Lise Russ, Gil's mistress. (Gil made Joe believe it was *his* apartment.) Gil then delivered him to a safe house near Ste.-Foy-la-Grande. From there Joe was taken to Toulouse, which was a jump-off point to cross the Pyrenees to Spain—then a neutral country—and on to England.

Phillip knew nothing of Joe or his visits to the hospital and Avenue Foch until much later. (He had been sent to Enghien so that he wouldn't run into Joe.) Today Phillip says, "I suppose my mother thought that at 15, being with an American B-17 gunner was a bit too much for me." Then he laughs, "I think my father brought Joe to the apartment on the back of his bike."[36]

While Joe wandered about France having what Col. Frank Halm of the 94th Bomb Group Memorial Association calls "a unique experience," many miles away in Switzerland a certain Mr. Victor Brunier was undertaking an extraordinary journey.

Brunier's identity card claimed he was a thirty-five-year-old French architect from the lakeside town of Annecy. In reality, he was

Flight Commander Frank Griffiths, who had been flying missions on the continent: parachuting agents—called "Joes"—and supplies to Resistance groups in France. His Halifax "O" for Orange had crashed in the town of Meythet near the French city of Annecy in the Haute Savoie a month after Joe had parachuted from his burning Fortress. In his book *Winged Hours*, Griffiths describes his narrow escape from France and the odyssey that led to his arrival in Switzerland under Brunier's assumed identity.

He had left England on a mission over France to supply guns to the French Resistance at 9:40 P.M. on August 14, 1943. At one o'clock the next morning, he circled above Annecy, a few miles from the Swiss border town of Geneva, and peered out to see the color of the outer port motor's exhaust flames turn to white. Then the engine died. He trimmed the aircraft and gave full throttle to the other three engines. The plane stabilized, and he banked to remain over the lake in case he had to ditch. He told his crew to "take up crash stations" but got no reply. Then the inner port side engine gave off white flames. He ordered the dispatcher to jettison the cargo (small arms, ammunition, sardines, money, chocolates, and cigarettes) destined for the Resistance in the Annecy area.

The flight engineer finally came on the intercom: "Skipper, we have to change fuel tanks." "O" for Orange was losing altitude, descending in a permanent left-hand turn at about 110 miles per hour. Nothing, Griffiths thought, is more utterly useless than a Halifax with two dead motors at the bottom of an alpine valley in the middle of the night.

Then the flight engineer announced, "OK, Skipper, you're on number one and three tanks now." There was a call from the dispatcher: "We're at crash stations."[37]

Griffiths engaged his shoulder-strap tension lever as the aircraft touched the tops of some trees at about 90 miles per hour. He thought he still had some control. Then the plane's left wing took a terrible shock. They had hit a house in the village of Meythet—a few miles from Annecy.[38]

The residents of Meythet witnessed the crash of "O" for Orange.[39] One of the village folk wrote:

The plane's wing hit the Villa du Fier, lost a motor implanted in the frame of a villa, and broke into the Rey-Grange house—the highest building in Meythet. The plane continued across the road and crashed into the small house of the village shoemaker.

It was a scene from Dante's *Inferno:* The plane's munitions and fuel had exploded, and liquid fire ran into the small stream traversing the village. The town was in flames: houses, the streets, and the stream. A sinister light lit-up the night as the fire radiated everywhere.[40]

Sylvain Donzel remembers how

[a]n enormous airplane flew by so low it scraped the treetops. One could see the motor on fire as the plane made a series of great circles around Annecy before coming down in the middle of our village. Before my eyes the plane struck a house in a geyser of flame and burning metal.[41]

Raymond Astier:

I saw the plane lose a motor in the roof of the Villa du Fier. When it exploded I threw myself down. My mother was woken [up] by the noise and then the two of us fled with others in the village. We were terrified of the bombs exploding. Then I saw the flames devour four neighbors: Ermina and her two children and Ernest. . . . I saw a crewman with a red bandana around his neck that hadn't burned, laying dead in the shoemaker's cottage.[42]

"O" for Orange spread destruction and death everywhere in Meythet: eleven villagers died and Griffiths's five crewmen perished. After the crash, Griffiths says he lost consciousness. Then:

When I came to, I was hanging in my straps and I became aware that there was a fire raging behind me. . . . I was in terrible fear of burning. . . . I made two or three panic attempts to get out of my seat with the straps still on. . . . Then I pulled out the pin and seemed to fall a great distance. I hit the ground with such force that my right arm broke.

I became unconscious again. When I woke I scrambled to my

feet and started to run away. After a few yards I was grabbed by two men who spoke excitedly, Italian, I think. . . . Suddenly there was a terrific explosion as one of the petrol tanks went up. Sheets of flame and rubbish went over my head and the two yelled something and ran. I turned away and ran as far as I could to get away from the fire. (That fire will haunt me for the rest of my life.) It was very hot when we left England, and in consequence, I was not wearing my uniform tunic. The two Italians had removed my parachute harness and Mae West, so, as I ran away I think that I was taken for a Frenchman. As my back was on fire I don't think the crowd could see the blood on my face.

I started up a village street and a youth on a bicycle came towards me. He looked at me very closely as he passed, stopped immediately and chased after me. I could see right away that he was friendly.

He said in a hushed whisper in French, "You are English?" To which I replied, "Yes, where are the Boches?"

He said, "There aren't any, they are all Italians."

I told him I wanted to get to Spain and he helped me to sit across the crossbar of the bike, sidesaddle. My arms were useless. I could see that my right wrist was broken. I had such pain that I couldn't hang onto the handlebars properly. Finally another lad came to help us and they pushed me on the bike to a house. They led me upstairs to a kitchen and shrieks went up from the woman inside when they saw me. I must have looked a lot worse than I felt.

I was given a glass of Marc. It was good and it brought me around.[43]

Griffiths was incredibly lucky to have survived the crash and even luckier to have landed in the hands of the French Resistance at Meythet. They arranged for a doctor, a member of the Resistance, to set his broken arm and treat his wounds. Later, agents hid him in the nearby mountains for over a month before finally conveying him across the French-Swiss border into the hands of the British secret services in Geneva.

Griffiths remained in Switzerland for almost two months. Though he could have accepted internment with other Allied aircrews at Arosa, Switzerland—a kind of Alpine paradise—he insisted on passing back through France in order to escape to England and return to duty. (The only way to escape to England in 1943 was by an RAF airplane pickup, or to walk out through France to Spain.) He had been in the business of transporting "Joes" and supplying Resistance operations by parachute in Norway, Poland, and Holland. He knew the dangers of trying to pass through France to reach Spain: torture and certain death if caught in civilian clothes by the Gestapo. Griffiths says he felt "it was my duty to get back to England . . . and to carry on with the war. But there was another reason which far transcended the call of duty and that was the strongest force in man: the desire to get back to a certain woman . . . and she was in England."[44]

Joe, too, was driven by the thought of a woman—his mother Mary, a widow living on 77th Street off Amsterdam Avenue in Manhattan. Her welfare was of paramount concern to him, as Joe's brother, Theodore, suffered from infantile paralysis. Another brother, Nicholas, was a B-26 bombardier. He had his own motivation to escape:

> (I) had no time for romance (while trying to evade capture). How do you make a pass at someone whose family is laying their life [*sic*] on the line to get you out? All I wanted was my (forged) ID and papers and then "let's get going!" My mother was a widow with three grown boys. I could see her worrying her heart out, worrying herself to death. Luckily my brother kept her spirits up by saying, "Don't worry Mom, Joe can take care of himself—he'll be back."[45]

While Griffiths was being hidden in Switzerland, tail gunner Joe followed Toquette's strict itinerary. After leaving Paris with Gil, Joe arrived at Ste.-Foy-la-Grande in the south of France. He spent some time there picking grapes at a farm while arrangements were being made to move him to Toulouse from where he could depart for Spain.

In Switzerland, arrangements were being finalized to smuggle Griffiths into France. In mid-October 1943, he presented himself to the British Consulate in Geneva. There he was told that he would be guided to a secret place near Paris where a Lysander[46] plane would pick him up and deliver him somewhere in England. He was to pretend to be "Victor Brunier" while he was escorted to the Swiss border just outside Geneva. From there he would cross into France and meet a guide near the Annemasse railroad station in France. Griffiths was told that his guide would take him part of the way and then hand him over to another Resistance group. They would lead him to a secret airfield somewhere near Paris where the aircraft would make the pickup.

Before leaving Geneva for the French-Swiss border, Griffiths received a final briefing from Victor Farrell, who worked under the pseudonym of "Passport Control Agent" and handled SOE affairs in Geneva. Farrell told his pupil:

> The less you know, Squadron Leader, the less you can give away under interrogation. But just take it that we are very well organized and in constant contact with London. The chaps back there have these things planned out to a 'T'. You've got two white handkerchiefs in your pockets. Carry one in your hand and keep blowing your nose—it's a signal to our people and has the advantage of hiding the scars on your face. Our chaps will pick you up. With your smart looks, you'll have no problem.[47]

Griffiths was handed a French identity card, work card, and ration card all made out to Victor Brunier's name.

As it turned out, everything went wrong.

First, instead of traveling alone, Farrell (the SOE agent in Geneva) introduced Griffiths to two "Joes" and insisted that Griffiths cross the French-Swiss border with them. That meant the possible risk of delay, missing his train and the connection from Annemasse to Paris. Then he learned that the Gestapo in Annemasse had been warned that the French *maquis* were to stage a show of arms in the region that very week. The French police and the German security forces were on full alert.

It was a foggy evening when they set out. Griffiths and his two companions followed instructions. They walked alongside the frontier wire in the twilight, a heavy fog forming here and there, until they came to the grounds of a house surrounded by a high brick wall. There they entered through a gate and saw two poplar trees standing against the inner wall of the garden. The top of the wall was, in fact, the border; on the other side lay France. Both Joes went over first, and Griffiths followed. He climbed the wall with no trouble, but the roadway on the French side was considerably lower than the garden lawn on the Swiss side. He looked down at what was quite a drop onto a packed dirt road. Still not fully healed from his plane crash injuries, the vertical leap caused a terrible shock. He cried out and nearly fainted.

After a pause, he recovered and set off down the road, walking some way until he caught up with the Joes, his handkerchief in his hand. As they turned a corner they encountered a French gendarme standing in front of a sentry box. Griffiths's knees began to buckle. His mouth went dry. No one had told him of this possibility. He felt sure the sentry must have heard him as he landed on the road.

The gendarme stepped forward and asked to see their papers. After the guard had examined Griffiths's documents carefully he handed them back without a word. Then he nodded, and with typical French politeness wished them, *"Bon soir."*

They continued walking in the gathering darkness toward what they hoped was the Annemasse railroad station. With curfew only a half-hour away, they worried about the guide who was supposed to lead them to the train station and beyond.

Suddenly, Griffiths heard the wheels of a bicycle crunching into the dirt roadway and he felt the air stir behind him. His heart began to pound. A man came up parallel to him and dismounted. He tipped his beret with two fingers. *"Suivez-moi,"* he ordered, smiling from ear to ear. The man walked his bicycle beside them. After a couple of blocks they entered a row of apartment buildings where the stranger jettisoned his bike in the basement, and led the men to the door of a fourth-floor apartment. He rang the doorbell twice followed by an additional short ring. Griffiths breathed a sigh of relief when the door was opened by Mme. Roche, a vivacious, petite Frenchwoman. "It was the enthusiasm on the woman's face," he said later. "It's something you can't explain but you just know that the people are all right and on your side." Indeed, he and the two "Joes" had arrived at the home of their guide, Monsieur Roche, a gendarme and member of the French Resistance in the region. Roche had been sent to find them after the guides who were to take them to the Annemasse train station had to flee after a run-in with the French police. Everyone in town was very tense.

A few hours later Griffiths stood before one of the icons of the French Resistance—a woman known to him only as "Françoise." From the beginning, Madame Françoise Dissart, a member of Libération-sud—a major Resistance group allied with Goélette—had her doubts about the man she interrogated in the Roche family apartment. Griffiths tells how

> . . . her manner was not friendly. I noticed she didn't shake hands with me when she came in. Her cross-examination was fast and fierce; she wanted to know all my particulars and fairly screamed at me when I wouldn't give her my base and squadron number. She knew that RAF aircrew had been briefed to give *only* their name, rank, and number. It was assumed that anyone giving more information was working for the Gestapo, attempting to infiltrate the Resistance.[48]

Françoise continued the interrogation while a hulking, equally unfriendly man stood by her side. Griffiths started to sweat. In desperation he opened his shirt and showed her his identity discs.

"All she said was, 'Who gave them to you?' She obviously didn't trust me." His companions who accompanied Griffiths across the border tried to intervene. "But he came out of Switzerland with us," they offered.

Françoise snorted as if to say, "That proves nothing." Then she took a cigarette out of her mouth, looked piercingly at Griffiths, and asked, "Are you married?"

Griffiths relates how he weakened and nodded his head. Like a flash Françoise spat back, "What was the date of your marriage?"

It wasn't a military question so Griffiths answered, "Thirtieth August 1941."

A smile spread across Françoise's face and she offered her hand. All the tension evaporated. Obviously Françoise and her organization were very well informed. They had been in touch with England and had asked for some personal information about Griffiths so that they could be assured that he wasn't a Gestapo agent posing as a flight commander. (Later Griffiths would learn a lot about Françoise, including the fact that the unfriendly thug by her side was there to kill him had he not given satisfactory answers.)

Finally, Mme. Roche came into the room with a bottle of Marc. There were drinks all around.

Françoise Dissart turned out to be an angel.[49] She conveyed Griffiths on the long and perilous road south, helping him to pass through the many German checkpoints on the rail journey from Annemasse to Toulouse. Before she turned back, she led him to the home of Therese Baudot de Rouville, outside Toulouse, a Frenchwoman who spoke English with an Irish brogue (as her mother was Irish). Griffiths describes Therese's hideout and how he met Joe:

> It was an Irish house. Everything was topsy-turvy. But it was a warm place and it smelled of fresh bread baking in the oven.
>
> I was eating my *petit dejeuner* in the dining room when a weird figure walked in; a swarthy-looking southern Frenchman standing over six feet. He wore a zip-fastened golf jacket and at first, I thought he was the gardener or a handyman. He came into the kitchen, grabbed me by the hand, and said, "How! [Using the Indian greeting, a New York wisecrack that Joe typically used.] You're the first Englishman I've spoken to in months!" Then he went on, "I bailed out over Le Bourget on Bastille Day. Been having a great time visiting France. Just call me Joe, I've been picking grapes, you know."

Griffiths said that Joe, the B-17 gunner,

> looked the perfect French farm worker, so completely did he blend in . . . that he was trusted to go out shooting rabbits. He was popular with everyone despite his complete lack of French. Then one day, disaster struck. His hosts were informed that Joe was being held in the village gendarmerie. Scouts were sent out to investigate the situation. They returned to report that Joe was playing chess with a gendarme! Apparently, Joe had chatted him up in English one day when he was out of uniform. The gendarme had known of Joe's identity all along, but the local residents were never too sure of where the man's sympathies lay. In fact, until Joe came along the people in the

region thought he was a Pétainist. Joe was an amazingly relaxed person, nothing ever disturbed him: Germans, the Milice, gendarmes worried him not at all. He was supremely confident in their company and was thoroughly enjoying his "tour" of Europe![50]

A few days after arriving at Therese's house, as autumn came to southern France, Griffiths and Joe set out together, once again accompanied by Françoise Dissart. Their route took them down the Carcassone Valley to Perpignan and the snowcapped Pyrenees. There they were handed over to Antoine, a Catalan Resistance fighter. Françoise vanished. Antoine with his cousin, Paul, would lead the two airmen over the Pyrenees Mountains into Spain, from where they would eventually reach Gibraltar and freedom in England.

While Griffiths and Joe were escaping across France to Spain, Italy declared war on Germany.[51] And D-Day, the Allied invasion of France, was just eight months away. But in Germany and Occupied France, the Germans were working on a surprise for the Allies: a long-studied assault on England by unmanned missiles, known as V-1 rockets.

Michael Hollard was chief of the French Resistance group, Agir, and the first agent in France to report the existence and deployment of these infernal machines in the autumn of 1943. He later wrote: "I had no idea of the crucial importance which was attached in London to the plans [of the V-1 rockets]. It was just another job to be done—one more mission."[52]

The reports from Resistance groups in France and along the Atlantic coast described a liquid-fueled, pulse-jet drone aircraft (primitive by today's standards) that could carry a 2,000-pound warhead. These V-1 rockets (the Germans called them "hell hounds" and "fire dragons") needed only to be pointed in the right direction from launching sites to reach London. Hitler's scientists had conceived them to be the first of a series of terror weapons that the Nazis boasted would crush Britain and prevent the invasion of Germany.

At about the same time, a peculiar and uncommon event occurred in Niort near La Rochelle, France. A Wehrmacht security officer working at a Franco-German arms factory told his hotelkeeper, Madame Missant, about his hatred for the Nazis. Missant, who was a val-

ued Goélette agent, quickly reported to Goélette leader Renaudot
("*R*") in Paris that the security officer might be amenable to spying
on his fellow Germans. The officer in question turned out to be the
Austrian Baron Eric Posch-Pastor. He joined Goélette under the
pseudonym "CLAYREC—RJ 4570" in mid-1943, about the same
time as the Jackson family was formally introduced to *R*.[53] Posch-
Pastor also used the name "Etienne Paul Pruvost" because it matched
the initials (EPP) on his civilian dress shirts.

The recruitment of Posch-Pastor was an incredible bit of luck for
the Goélette group. This intrepid anti-Nazi Catholic was not only au-
dacious but also very well connected in German circles in France. He
became the center of a group of Austrian Catholics serving in the
German bureaucracy and military in France and Italy, prepared to
spy for the French Resistance.[54] In a major coup he managed to get
his cousin, one Major Guillaume headquartered at the Wehrmacht
arms and munitions service, located at the Hotel Astoria in Paris, to
steal the technical drawings, specifications, and launch site locations
of V-1 rockets from his office. These purloined, top-secret documents
further corroborated Michael Hollard's information about the V-1
threat.

Now British intelligence in London ordered up a major effort in
France and elsewhere to collect information that would allow Allied
bombers to destroy the flying bombs. Hollard was able to send more
materials to London via Switzerland by the same route Flight Commander Frank Griffiths used to cross the French border into neutral
Switzerland. From Geneva, Hollard's documents were dispatched by
radio and courier to London.

The Goélette group, however, had no access to Switzerland, so *R*
devised a way of copying Posch-Pastor's documents and using couri-
ers to bring the materials to London.

R could not risk having Posch-Pastor visit Goélette's mail drops
in Paris—and he certainly didn't want his agent to come to the Jackson home on Avenue Foch. But as a German official, Posch-Pastor
could visit the American Hospital without arousing suspicion. Thus
Sumner Jackson's office at the hospital became another mail drop for
Goélette. Though Sumner met Posch-Pastor at the hospital, the doctor never knew his German visitor's real identity. In fact, Toquette

and Phillip learned the truth about Posch-Pastor only after the war—at a conference of Goélette agents organized by Renaudot.[55]

The Goélette files at the Château de Vincennes tell of a courier—and it may have been Toquette—going from Paris to Brest and then to the town of Lannils to deliver documents to the town's parish priest, the Père Lucq.[56] Father Lucq delivered the papers to the home of a Madame Pallier, where the priest found two stranded British seamen: Harold Pickles and Roger Bartley. It was Christmas 1943 and a neighbor, Amédée Rolland, brought a number of British sailors and airmen he had been hiding on his nearby farm to the Pallier home. The report tells that they all drank a good deal and sang the "Marseillaise" and "Tipperary," despite the fact that a German unit was installed in a shed close by. Then the airmen and sailors, with a vast quantity of "mail" including the Goélette documents about the V-1 rockets, were put aboard an SOE-run boat, *MGB 318*, bound for Falmouth Harbor.

When it reached London, the boat's mother lode earned high marks from General Eisenhower—particularly the Posch-Pastor materials that revealed some of the first details of the V-1 rocket.[57]

The V-1 pilotless flying bombs were launched from ski-jump–like ramps at speeds of 350 miles per hour. Each rocket carried a one-ton warhead, and four of the first deadly engines reached London on June 13, 1944, a week after D-Day. In all, the Germans sent more than eight thousand V-1 terror weapons against London. Around twenty-four hundred landed on London targets, killing 6,184 and seriously wounding 17,981 civilians.[58] That the British knew about these weapons and were able to take defensive measures was thanks to the work of Goélette agents such as Baron Erich Posch-Pastor von Camperfeld, Michael Hollard and his underground group Agir, and other brave men and women.

Later Winston Churchill paid a personal tribute to those who risked their lives to save England from the perils of the V-1:

> Our Intelligence enabled our fighters [planes] to be made ready. The launching sites were found enabling our bombers to delay the attack and mitigate its violence. To all our sources, many of who worked among deadly danger, and some of whom will be for ever unknown to us, I pay tribute.[59]

Dwight D. Eisenhower, in *Crusade in Europe,* reckoned that "[h]ad the Germans succeeded in perfecting and using these weapons six months earlier . . . Overlord [the Allied invasion of France at Normandy] might have been written off."[60]

By the winter and spring of 1944, the tempo of Gestapo arrests had reached a sickening crescendo throughout France.[61] Michael Hollard and three of his agents were arrested in Paris on February 5, 1944. Hollard was tortured by the French security police and the Gestapo. He was condemned to death for espionage but his sentence was never carried out and he was deported to Neuengamme, the SS-run concentration camp located south of Hamburg, Germany.

In early May, Gilbert Asselin, who had helped Joe escape to Southern France, was arrested in Paris and questioned about his activities. The Gestapo then picked up four of his associates.[62] Gladys Marchal, the Englishwoman who had initially brought Joe to the American Hospital, was arrested shortly thereafter. She was released after twenty-four hours. At some point during the interrogations, one of the suspects (and no one knows who), mentioned Dr. Jackson's name.

Around the same time, the Goélette network in Vichy was betrayed by someone whose identity is also unknown. The Milice raided Goélette's secret station at La Bourboule, a hamlet of Vichy, and found uncoded correspondence, including "compromising letters addressed to Mrs. Jackson."[63] The Milice turned over what they found to the chief of the Gestapo at Vichy, George Geissler. As Dr. Jackson's connections with the American Hospital, the French Red Cross, and with Pierre Laval were known to the Gestapo, the case was treated as a sensitive matter. Geissler informed his colleague in Paris, Heinrich Illers, who took the matter up with SS general Oberg.[64]

At some level of the Vichy Milice and/or the Gestapo, orders were issued to arrest the Jacksons, and a trap was laid around the Avenue Foch apartment in the hope of catching other Goélette members.[65]

The Resistance agent "knows that sooner or later [his work] must end in disaster. It was more than a risk—almost a certainty." Working underground, they "were constantly reminded [of this], not only by the daily toll of arrests, but by the very circumstances of their existence."[66] Sumner knew that the danger of being caught and arrested grew with each day, but he was adamant that liberation by the Allies—which for him meant American boys landing in France—was imminent.

Time had run out for the Jackson family.[67]

7

BETRAYAL, ARREST, DEPORTATION

Paris was a cold, damp place that spring of 1944. The City of Lights seemed "blacked out" to many—crushed by the weight of the Nazi Occupation. Parisians were worn thin from cumulative deprivations, hunger, and stress. Even those who collaborated with the Nazi powers were depressed, for they knew the end of the Occupation was near, and that liberation would lead to retribution for them. As the tide of war changed to the Allied side, there was good news: the Red Army was winning on the Eastern Front, and Allied armies were pushing the Germans up the boot of Italy.

Elizabeth Ravina, a former operating room nurse-supervisor at the American Hospital, was in the United States when she received a letter from Sumner "telling of starvation and of his family's dire need of clothing."[1]

Clemence recalls in her memorial to Sumner that he had had pneumonia that winter and suffered from fits of coughing.

> He was drawn and careworn and went about in an old army sweater with a hole that showed his elbow when he took off his long surgical coat.[2] He went back and forth to Neuilly on a bicycle . . . he made me think of Don Quixote during that winter, with him balanced on the high frame of the bicycle, wearing an aviator helmet, his hands in heavy fur gloves, one holding the steering bar [and] the other waving goodbye.[3]

Clemence saw Toquette for the last time that spring on Monday, May 15, 1944.

"I [had] picked lilies of the valley in the small garden at Foch; but [Toquette] gave me the impression that she was happy when I left; of course I didn't linger."[4]

A few days later, Clemence received an unsigned letter in the mail. It read: "Clemence: If you pass by avenue Foch don't visit the people you know there." She thought she recognized the handwriting as that of Toquette, and so took the warning very seriously.[5]

According to Clemence, the police at the local precinct serving the Jackson family's sector—Ave. Foch/Rue Traktir—had warned Sumner: "Look out, Sir, you're being watched."[6] But Sumner, she says, was so confident that the Americans would soon land in France that he ignored all warnings and didn't fear being arrested. He thought his arrest would be just like his 1942 internment: a joke.

In the spring of the year 2000, Phillip Jackson, six-feet-two with his father's imposing physique, sat on the edge of his hospital bed at the Institute des Invalides, the great hospital-cum-monument that is the Hôtel des Invalides built by King Louis XIV for his war wounded.[7] As a wounded veteran, the seventy-three-year-old Phillip had a reserved room there. On this day, the fifty-sixth anniversary of the Jackson family's arrest by the Nazis, Phillip repeated Clemence's words: "We thought it was all a joke," he said, and began to sob as he told his story.

Phillip was about to leave for school the morning of Wednesday, May 24, 1944. At the first ring of the doorbell, he opened the door, not bothering to look through the peephole. Kiki, the family's Belgian shepherd, barked. From the kitchen, Louise Heile saw three men push past Phillip and enter. She slammed the kitchen door, holding Kiki by his collar. The dog went wild, barking and scratching at the door.

With great presence of mind, Toquette received the intruders with a smile and ushered them into the living room.[8] Phillip stood facing the men, who identified themselves as Milice—French police who by

1944 were controlled by the Gestapo. The men wanted to see Dr. Jackson. Toquette explained that Sumner was at the hospital doing his morning rounds. Two of the officers left immediately in their car to find him.

Toquette had hidden secret Resistance documents among Sumner's pharmaceuticals. She called Louise to serve coffee and offered the remaining Milice guard an aperitif while making light talk. When the man—distracted—made a telephone call, Toquette seized the opportunity to hand documents to Louise with orders to "go ahead and deliver these to Mr. Petit." Louise slipped out of the house through the kitchen door.

Minutes later Sumner arrived in the Milice's automobile. The Jacksons were ordered into the garden while their apartment was searched. The contents of closets and cabinets were emptied and strewn everywhere. But the police found nothing compromising. They then ordered the Jacksons to prepare for a road trip that would take place the following day, but the Milice wouldn't specify the nature of their business or their destination. Phillip packed his history notes and homework, expecting to study for examinations to be held the following week. Then Toquette arranged a lunch for their "guests," after which Sumner offered a cigar to the chief and retired with him to "chairs" in the garden for a smoke and amiable conversation.

Phillip went to water a plant standing in the window facing onto Rue Traktir. He carefully arranged the drapes and in so doing, saved many Goélette agents from arrest and possibly death. This signal alerted the agents, including *R*, not to visit the Avenue Foch apartment for a meeting, as planned, and for others not to pick up their "mail."⁹

Meanwhile, the hospital staff continued frantically to call Dr. Jackson at the apartment. But the Milice prohibited all contact with the outside world.

We don't know how Sumner and Toquette passed their last night of freedom under guard. Phillip was confined to his room. In the morning, the chief of the Milice made another telephone call and apparently talked to his superior. Nothing was said to the Jacksons. They were simply taken away in automobiles. Louise, who had returned from her "errand," stayed in the apartment with Kiki and some Milice agents who were left behind in order to trap visiting members of the Goélette group. Keeping vigil in the Jackson apartment, the police managed to ensnare one hapless man named Stolz, a Paris broker and neighbor of the family and a known admirer of Vichy and Marshal Pétain. The Jacksons didn't like Stolz, but they befriended him for appearance's sake. Stolz passed by the garden entrance to Avenue Foch on Wednesday of that week and thought he saw Dr. Jackson sitting in a chair. He hailed him and was greeted by: "Why, come in and talk to Dr. Jackson." The poor fellow was arrested on the spot and ended up in the Gestapo prison at Vichy and later at Compiègne. He was nearly deported to "nowhere."[10]

After a long and trying car journey—250 miles crammed into the back of a black Citroën *traction-avant*—Sumner and Toquette landed at the headquarters of the Milice at the Château des Brosses. Phillip, who was then almost 16-and-a-half years old, was dropped off at the Milice prison, a former casino in the town of Vichy. Separated from his parents, he says today that he was hungry, thirsty, and frightened. A prisoner in the casino's cellar, he had nothing to eat or drink for three days. He became delirious and dreamed he was on the lake at Enghien, rowing, the sky a crystal blue. He rowed and rowed. Then it rained, and the water foamed, and the waves threatened his little boat.

The Château des Brosses is located a few minutes' drive south of Vichy at Bellerive-sur-Allier, where the Sarmon River branches off the Allier. It's an evil place, or it was in Sumner's time. Even today the locals talk about how the French security police under the Gestapo behaved at the château. Everyone knew that prisoners were tortured in the cellars.[11] But the police did not torture Sumner or Toquette—perhaps because the Jacksons were Americans and the French feared the coming invasion. The couple was put up in two small separate rooms, not quite cells but nearly as spare and barren. Amazingly, Sumner treated some of the guards who needed medical care.[12]

The next day, the chief of the Milice at the château arranged for the Jacksons to dine together. They were served at a table on the terrace while a Milice guard watched over them. No one stopped them from conversing in English, and they were able to agree on what they would say when questioned so as not to contradict one another. At one point, the chief reassured the Jacksons with words like: "You'll see, this will be cleared up and you'll be free to return to Paris."[13]

Sumner and Toquette were then taken from the Château des Brosses to rejoin Phillip at the Milice prison at the Vichy casino. Toquette was placed in a cell alone and Sumner and Phillip shared one. They were interrogated separately. Phillip says, "My father told me later that he admitted nothing, but we did not know what my mother said."[14]

On May 31, 1944, Toquette was able to write to Tat from her Milice prison cell in Vichy.[15] (Phillip Jackson agrees with the author that the text contains hidden meanings.)

Wednesday, 31 May

My Sister:

The weather continues to be good here but cooler following a storm. This is the third letter I have written you at intervals of two days. I have nothing new to say as far as we are concerned. Today is the day Pete should have taken his examination for the Baccalaureate and I haven't seen him since Friday [26 May 1944].

I am beginning to feel really very dirty. I haven't undressed since the same day [day of arrest?] and even if I could undress it would be to put back on the same clothes and I have nothing to clean myself with. Happily, I am wearing practical clothes: my Scots skirt[16] that doesn't get crumpled and a gray sweater, flexible and comfortable.

Above all take Desjars[17] as often as possible to work in the vegetable garden and hoe the vegetables, water, etc. . . . If you pass by my place take the eggs, wine, and anything else you may need. If the strawberries are ripe and Madame Duhil can send Alain to pick them up he can at the same time bring you two bottles of wine and send the strawberries to my friend Madame Heinmann at 9 Boulevard Cachet. This seems complicated and I don't want you to tire yourself with all that you have to do. I hope Aunt Mimi[18] is better, tell her that I think of her and also my dear Rosalie.[19] Jack [Sumner] is still here but on the first floor whereas I am housed on the second floor, better off [than] him, the poor fellow. If you get my letters you could telephone to LUADI[20]—Miss Comte, the director of the hospital, to give her news of us.[21]

If someone has sugar to exchange for soybean[22] at equal weight do it from your [stock] and take from our stock in the sack when you run out.[23]

My courage is being tested to the extreme not so much for me as for Pete and also for Jack; if I knew that he was free my particular fate would be less painful.

One comes to see that there are two sides to a question and [that there are] good people everywhere, people should mind their own business and leave decisions to those in charge.[24]

> My sister, I hug you.
> Your Sister

Nine days had now passed since the family was arrested in Paris. Allied armies would enter Rome on June 5, and American paratroopers would land in Normandy on French beaches and parachute into French towns the night of June 5–6, 1944. But it might as well have been a century away.

The Jacksons had disappeared from the outside world, but questions were being asked. Telegrams between the State Department in Washington and the Swiss Consulate in Paris found by the author tell the following story.

As early as May 31, 1944, an anonymous letter reached the Swiss Consulate in Paris, reporting that the Jacksons had been arrested on May 26 [*sic*]. In one of the Swiss telegrams to the State Department, the American authorities were advised that the Jacksons were in possession of Swiss identity certificates. Apparently, through Toquette's family, Sumner and Phillip obtained what amounted to Swiss passports. (We do not know if the Jacksons ever used their Swiss status to help their situation, or if this would have helped with the German authorities. Throughout this time they claimed American nationality.) The same cable from the Swiss reports that the family had been arrested by the French Milice and "probably" taken to Vichy. The Swiss asked French officials in Vichy and the German military court in Paris for more information.[25] French authorities replied that German officials had arrested the family but that the Jacksons had not been taken to Vichy. (Later, a letter from Phillip to a friend in Paris confirmed that the Milice in Vichy were indeed detaining the family.)[26]

Then, in a dramatic turn of events, the Gestapo became aware that the Jacksons were held by the Milice at the casino in Vichy. They ordered the family transferred to the Gestapo prison located in the Hôtel du Portugal on the Boulevard des Etats-Unis across from the closed American Embassy in Vichy. A far cry from the Château des Brosses, this prison reeked of fear, sweat, and blood.[27]

Phillip says:

I was in a very small cell with three other men. There was no daylight or air, but electricity from about 07:00 hrs till 21:00 daily. There was a plank of wood about the size of a door fixed against the wall, and we were given three blankets for four men.

There I remained for thirteen days and was taken out only once into the daylight and air for questioning. As I was an American citizen they treated my family and me decently during questioning, which in my case was extremely summary. I told them I knew nothing and I was informed I should be released in a very short time. The man who questioned me was a French inspector of the Gestapo whose name or nickname was Nerou. He was of average height, very dark hair, about 25 years old. The jailers were uniformed members of the German SD: Sichereitsdienst (German security service under the SS). My cell was in the Portuguese Embassy, Boulevard des Etats Unis, Vichy. (Boulevard of the United States.)

I knew and spoke to people, particularly those in my cell, who were whipped and tortured during questioning, and I saw a jailer whip one of my fellow prisoners about 25 times in my cell. I was also whipped by jailers if I was not standing to attention or for any other minor pretext.

One man in my cell, a Frenchman whose name I have forgotten, he came from Clermont-Ferrant,[28] told me he had been whipped and beaten by . . . Nerou. I saw evidence of this beating, as the man's back was covered with different colors and bleeding. (I tried to look after him as best as I could.)

Our rations consisted of three small pieces of black bread per day, and one flat plate of a so-called soup.

We were taken out once to get a wash near the cell and were given about a minute to wash without soap or towel. There was a bucket in the cell for urinating, and once every evening we were taken to a toilet near the cell. We were given about 30 seconds to do this. The guard was standing at the open door with his whip in his hand.

SS chief Helmut Knochen may have been in Vichy when the Jacksons were taken by the Gestapo. Knochen was a regular visitor who coordinated the deportation of Jews with Vichy authorities. He was famous for having lured two British intelligence agents to Venlo and capturing them. This feat earned him the Iron Cross first and second class. As General Oberg's deputy, Knochen certainly knew of the Jacksons' arrest—as did Oberg and Heinrich Illers. The fact that an American family had been arrested could not have gone unnoticed. Still, the Gestapo hid the family's arrest and transfer to their Vichy headquarters from the Swiss authorities who were bombarding Berlin for information about the Jacksons at the request of the U.S. State Department.

Swiss agents must have known unofficially that the Jacksons had been transferred from the Milice to the Gestapo. Vichy was a small village; diplomats and intelligence agents lived in close proximity, eating in the same restaurants and enjoying the same limited pleasures. There was even a popular bar in downtown Vichy that was named "The International Spy House," where stray bits of information were picked up and exchanged by embassy attachés. The German intelligence services read all Vichy embassy communications and tapped all telephones. In November 1942, both the American communications systems and the American Embassy were shut down.[29]

The Gestapo prison at the Hôtel du Portugal and in surrounding villas where Sumner, Toquette, and Phillip were held were terrible, malodorous places. A fellow prisoner attests:

> There were sinister noises: cars screeching to a halt, the cries of the tortured in the basement of the Hôtel du Portugal. When one heard a car stopping suddenly, and four doors slamming, one knew it was the Gestapo. One could hear people crying out from the basement . . . of the hotel.[30]

The Germans had arrested a Resistance leader a few months before the Jacksons' incarceration. They had come for him on February

10, 1944, taken him to the basement of a pink villa across from the Hôtel Portugal, and beaten him bloody. "These were professionals. They knew what they were doing," says another witness named "Saurou."[31] Years later, a Vichyssoise said of the houses occupied by the Gestapo, "I would never live in one of those houses."[32]

Phillip tells about how he and his parents were transferred from the Gestapo prison at Vichy to Moulins:

> I was with my father and mother and other prisoners [when we were] transferred to the German military prison of Moulins, north of Vichy. Once we arrived at Moulins, we were enclosed in an old medieval dungeon where we had to go up 118 steps to our cell. My father and I were in the same cell, my mother in another part of the building. We remained 21 days at Moulins, conditions not bad, but we suffered from hunger. We were examined once more, my father, my mother, and myself, this time by a German of the Gestapo. Declaration null for my father and myself—for my mother I do not know.

Toquette managed to send a postcard to Tat from Moulins dated June 22, 1944:

> My Sister,
>   You can write to me two pages written very clearly. . . . I am well and my morale is good. . . . I saw my son and husband the other day during an inspection. They are together and that makes me happy. I have nothing: toothbrush, etc. . . . My comrades try to help but they have very little, too. Please try to send a few things but no food. Kisses. Your Sister.

Toquette was able to send another note to Tat on July 14, 1944. She wrote on a piece of brown wrapping paper headed with Tat's name and address. It is believed that she must have thrown the note from a train at the railway station of Angoulême (447 km southeast of Paris). A covering letter from an anonymous benefactor with Toquette's note enclosed reached Tat on July 20, 1944. The letter explained that Toquette's note was discovered after a convoy of women, escorted by Germans, had passed through Angoulême—destination unknown. The forwarding letter was unsigned but ended with: "Have courage, a friend." Inside, Toquette wrote:

My Sister,
I am headed for Paris. Jack and Pete left here (Moulins) a week ago. . . . I got your package with the small checked dress. . . . Your Sister.

Then on July 19 she wrote a final message from France, in pencil on a scrap of wrapping paper. How it reached Tat is a mystery:

My Sister,
Since the 14th, I am at Romainville camp. I hope to stay here . . . forbidden to write, have visits but I can have a package a month. If you send something be sure I am still here by giving [the prison gate guards] each package. . . . Jack and Pete must be together at Compiègne since July 7, they left Moulins a week before me. My health and morale are excellent. People leave here frequently for Bitche in Alsace Lorraine[33] and no one is sure of their tomorrow.[34]

Phillip continues the story of his odyssey with his father:

At Moulins prison I saw my mother for the last time.[35] Then my father and myself (hereinafter referred to as "we") were transferred to the concentration camp of Compiègne. We traveled by bus—very trying without water, in a burning sun. We had left Moulins at 7 A.M. and reached Compiègne the next day at 3 A.M. We were handcuffed from the start at Moulins till the arrival the next day at Compiègne. (However, this is nothing compared with those who were handcuffed for weeks and weeks in their cells.)

We were allowed to get off the bus during the night to urinate; we walked into a field and for a moment, thought we might escape in the darkness but my father said we hadn't a chance handcuffed together. We spent one week in Compiègne, a wonderful week—Red Cross parcels—no work; the only trouble was vermin, fleas and lice en masse.

At last, July 15, 1944, a fatal day, we marched in a long file, 2,000 prisoners, to the Compiègne rail station. We had to cross a bridge

over the Oise River to get to the station and I almost jumped into
the water until I saw the river wasn't deep enough. At the station we
were packed into cattle wagons for Germany: 60 in one carriage
built for 40—everything closed. They gave us quite a large loaf of
black bread and a sausage for the trip but we had three days practi-
cally without water . . . a pint three times a day. Yet we were privi-
leged in the preceding trips, 80 to 100 traveled in each carriage.

We were escorted by German gendarmes in trench-green uniforms, incredibly brutal. In another wagon, 17 men escaped and the
balance of 43 men was put into another wagon which already contained 60 men. The 103 men were deprived of their clothes and did
not receive water for the remaining two days and nights of the
trip. . . . During the passage through a tunnel the *Schupo* guards
fired a clip of ammunition into those men and one man was killed.
I saw him being carried and dumped by the track.

These were terrible moments.

Our convoy was, I believe, to go to Dachaü, but on July 18 we
arrived at Neuengamme in the curve of the river Elbe. At the station,
we were taken over by the SS, whips in hand and holding their enormous fierce dogs. We were horsewhipped out of our carriages by the
SS [guards] and marched to the camp in batches of 100 guarded by
the SS with machine guns under their arms. About 1,500 of us were
put into a very large cellar.

We were then taken out in batches of a hundred and taken to
some showers, where we were deprived of our clothes and everything else we wore or carried, such as hernia belts, rings, watches,
and everything. Our heads and the remainder of our bodies were
shaved. Then we had a bath, after which a most minute search was
made of our naked bodies with lamps. Then we received a most miscellaneous collection of old clothes, not even fit for a beggar to wear,
and a pair of wooden shoes.

We were then sent into our barrack blocks in the camp.[36]

The circumstances related to the Jacksons' arrest are puzzling. It
may have been the confusion of the moment, for in the spring of 1944
in France there was chaos and a gnawing anticipation: almost everyone believed the Allies would soon cross the English Channel, invade
France, and eventually defeat the Axis armies. The German security

service knew it better than anyone, and their units were preparing to flee France.

We don't know what Gilbert Asselin, the Libération Resistance member who was arrested in early May 1944, told the Gestapo. Did he discuss how the Jacksons had helped Allied flyers at the American Hospital and at their apartment? His ex-mistress, Louise (Lise) Russ, thought him a traitor.

Did Gladys Marchal, who brought tail gunner Joe to Sumner at the American Hospital, talk when she was arrested by the Gestapo at the same time as Gil? She knew all about Dr. Jackson's Resistance work at the hospital. Did the Gestapo release her after questioning because she "cooperated?"

What motivated the French police at the Jackson family's local precinct to warn Sumner of his imminent arrest? The Milice were definitely infiltrated by the Gestapo and Reich security service. Why didn't a unit of the Paris-based Gestapo, headquartered a few yards from the Jackson apartment, arrest the family instead of leaving the task to the French Milice at Vichy some 250 kilometers (155 miles) away?[37]

And finally, who addressed the letter warning Clemence to keep away from the Avenue Foch apartment? If it truly was Toquette, did she have a premonition of what was to come?[38]

As to the Milice's involvement, one finds a clue in a U.S. State Department cable dated August 7, 1944. It reports that the Swiss Legation at Vichy had information from "Milice authorities . . . who confirmed the Jacksons [were] arrested for participation in [an] espionage organization, allegedly confirmed by compromising letters found by the Milice at Vichy and addressed [to] *Mrs. Jackson*" [author's italics].[39] This somewhat contradicts a citation written by *R* and found in Phillip's Goélette file. *R* wrote: "The Central of our Group was betrayed to the Milice 24 May 1944. A document being coded gave the name and address of *Phillip Jackson* [author's italics]. He was arrested the next day with his mother and father."[40]

It is possible that the Milice intentionally withheld the Jacksons from the Gestapo in hopes of trading off an American family to the coming Americans. But the Milice may have participated in a charade—serving as a cover for their Gestapo masters—to shield the fact that Gilbert Asselin had betrayed his comrades and was working as a Gestapo agent in Paris and later in the Büchenwald concentration camp. (There are a number of documented cases of Gestapo agents "planted" in prisons. And no prisoner could refuse to participate in the treachery.[41] This is chiefly why the Jacksons never talked about their work as Resistance agents.)[42]

The Jackson family's arrest was eventually handled by the highest levels of the SS security organization. Dr. Heinrich Illers[43] and SS general Carl-Albrecht Oberg must have approved the family's transfers to various prisons in France and their deportations to concentration camps in Germany.[44] Sumner was too well known and respected in French medical and Red Cross circles for his case *not* to have attracted attention—and Red Cross officials must have been alarmed by his disappearance.[45]

Immediately following their arrest, the Jacksons' friends and colleagues began frantically searching for them.

In Washington, the U.S. State Department had learned that the family had been sent to the German military prison at Moulins. The department cabled the American Legation at Bern, asking for the "exact location of Moulins and request[ing] Swiss to report urgently the latest known whereabouts of Jackson family." Bern replied later, as if they had no maps of France, "Inquiry of Swiss Foreign Office reveals nothing (repeat nothing) in files [that] indicates exact location of Moulins; Swiss foreign official formerly stationed [at] Vichy assumes Moulins mentioned is town due North Vichy on former demarcation line where located German Army control station. Further inquiry impossible as all (repeat all) communications [with] France cut."[46]

On July 24, 1944, the American Legation at Bern sent an airmail pouch message to Washington (received on August 22, 1944). The message reported that "the Legation has been informed on June 6, 1944, by Mr. Barrelet de Ricou, a Swiss national, former general manager of Lloyds and National Provincial Bank of Paris, now residing in Montreux, Switzerland, that his sister, Mrs. Charlotte Sylvie B. JACKSON, bearer of replacement passport No. 3533 issued in Paris on February 26, 1941 [nine months after Paris was occupied], her husband, Dr. Sumner Waldron JACKSON, bearer of replacement passport No. 3537 issued at Paris on February 27, 1941 and their minor son had been arrested on May 26, 1944 by the French authorities and transferred to Vichy."[47]

Washington sent a "secret" telegram back to Bern on August 31, 1944: "Since Germans may have removed Jackson family and may be holding them as hostages . . . Swiss authorities should request of German Government information regarding their whereabouts. Signed: Cordell Hull."[48] (Hull was U.S. secretary of state from 1933 to 1944.)

On November 1, 1944, Toquette's sister-in-law, Julia Barrelet de Ricou, wrote to Mrs. Franklin Delano Roosevelt at the White House, asking for her intervention. The letter was forwarded to the State Department, which replied that no information was available about the Jackson family's whereabouts. Albert E. Clattenburg, assistant chief, Special War Problems Division, U.S. Department of State, responded to a second appeal by Julia, in which she asked that the Jacksons be exchanged for German prisoners being held in the United States. Clattenburg explained that:

> The German Government has indicated that it will not permit the departure of Americans from areas under its control except in pursuance of agreements providing for the exchange of nationals. As the United States Government, for security reasons, has found it necessary in previous exchanges to withhold certain Germans whose return was specifically requested by the German Government, the Department has not been in a position to insist upon the inclusion of specific Americans in the exchange. We cannot, therefore, encourage the hope that arrangements may be made with the German Government for the exchange of any designated individual.[49]

A dispatch in the *Waldoboro Press Herald* from September 6, 1944, reported that:

> scores of Waldoboro residents, especially [Sumner's] brother, Daniel Jackson, were keenly interested in the Associated Press dispatch from Paris [no date given] telling of the efforts to trace Dr. Sumner Waldron Jackson, noted surgeon, Spruce Head native and Bowdoin graduate who has disappeared after he and his wife were interned on

the grounds that he and his wife had harbored American fliers. . . .
Dr. Jackson, 58, who had resided for several years in Paris, was interned for a shot [*sic*] time at the beginning of the German Occupation, and last May 26, he was taken in custody again.[50]

But what of the American Hospital? General de Chambrun could
not have failed to notice that his resident physician in charge, a man
with whom he was in daily contact for almost four years, one who
had received the Croix de Guerre through the general's own offices,
had disappeared—taken from the hospital by Vichy police. Nevertheless, there is no record of de Chambrun having tried to intervene with
Vichy or German authorities to obtain the Jackson family's release,
even though he had connections in Vichy political circles through his
son, René[51] But it may have been too late for any appeal. After June 6,
when the Allies landed in France, Vichy officials were powerless and
their German masters were packing to leave France. Marshal Pétain
and Minister Laval would soon be arrested by German security forces
and taken to Germany.

Then on July 20, a group of German generals tried to assassinate
Hitler at his command post at Rastenberg. And in Paris the same day,
General Karl von Stulpnagel, commander, Militarbefehlshaber, Paris
region, arrested twelve hundred members of the German security service (SD, Sipo, and Gestapo).[52] Those rounded up included General
Carl-Albrecht Oberg, higher SS and police leader, and his right-hand
men: SS chiefs Helmut Knochen, Herbert-Martin Hagen, and Kurt
Lischka with Gestapo chiefs Heinrich Muller and Dr. Heinrich Illers,
chief of department, Gestapo: IV C and later IV 6, Paris.[53] Each of
these men was responsible for the arrest, murder, or deportation of
résistant fighters: men, women, and adolescents who wouldn't swal-
low the bitter pill of Nazi Occupation.[54] (They were all eventually arrested by the Allies after the war as we shall see.)

Alas, at 10:30 in the evening of July 20, Hitler's voice came on
the radio. It was all over. *Der Führer* had survived a bomb blast in a
conference room at Rastenberg.[55] As soon as the news reached Paris,
Oberg ordered his security police to arrest General von Stulpnagel
and other Wehrmacht officers suspected of conspiring to assassinate
Hitler. They were sent to Germany under guard. General von Stulp-

nagel was hanged on a butcher's hook along with others whom Hitler believed to have participated in the plot.[56]

On August 7, Hitler appointed Gen. Dietrich von Choltitz commander of Gross-Paris. A week later, French and Allied troops landed at St. Tropez and Provence in southern France.

Then on August 19, 1944, General Oberg and his senior officers, including all of the aforementioned Sipo-SD staff, fled Paris for Germany. By then Sumner and Phillip had reached the Nazi concentration camp at Neuengamme and Toquette was in Ravensbrück camp.

On that same day, August 19, what Sumner had tried so hard to prevent finally happened: armed and wounded German troops were brought to the American Hospital of Paris for treatment. The Wehrmacht began taking over the Memorial Building.

Earlier the same morning, Wehrmacht troopers had been fired upon by Resistance fighters in front of the mayor's office at the Hôtel de Ville at Neuilly, about 750 yards from the American Hospital. This incident—a major uprising against the German Occupation of the city—marked the beginning of street fighting in and around Paris. In retaliation, the Germans staged a battle at the Hôtel de Ville. Two Panther tanks fired on French Resistance fighters hiding in the building, slamming shells into the elegant nineteenth-century structure. The building was awash in blood and gore, its interior walls pitted with rifle slugs, grenade fragments, and exploded munitions. The survivors used their neckties to bind their wounds. When it was over, four Resistance members were dead, forty were gravely wounded, and those who were eventually captured were shot at Mont Valerien. A handful escaped that day through the city sewers.[57]

The staff of the American Hospital had no doubt that they would be caught up in the coming battle between the German forces and the advancing Free French and American units sent to liberate Paris. All along the surrounding tree-lined boulevards, the German high command for Paris, Oberbefehlshaber West, had bivouacked over a thousand troops with their tanks, cannons, trucks, and scout cars. Indeed one of the routes chosen by General Leclerc's Second Armored unit led through Neuilly.

Paris erupted in chaos! On Hitler's direct orders, the German high command had mined the city: its monuments, buildings, and bridges.

Suddenly, on the morning of August 24, an Austrian officer commanding the troops at Neuilly, a Colonel Bernhuber, asked General de Chambrun to arrange the surrender of the German command. The next day, at 9 A.M., troops of French general Leclerc's division took the surrender of the German troops at Neuilly lined up under a white flag on the Boulevard Inkelmann.[58]

That same day, at the Hôtel Meurice on the Rue Rivoli, overlooking le Jardin des Tuileries, General von Choltitz surrendered Paris— *"Le jour de gloire est arrivé."*

Once again, as in World War I when Sumner had served in Paris as a captain in the U.S. Medical Corps, the Memorial Building of the American Hospital of Paris became a U.S. military hospital—the 365th Station Hospital of the U.S. Army. Old Glory and the French tricolor were again raised on the roof of the Memorial Building near where Phillip had watched U.S. Air Force Flying Fortresses battle German planes.

There were still many chapters to write about the hospital. One is worth mentioning here. James Grier Miller was a physician and an OSS officer working in Paris after the Occupation. He tells the following story:

> One day a French medical officer told me that there was an epidemic of meningitis among the children of Paris. I went with him to the Necker Polyclinique Hospital and there saw over a hundred very ill young children and babies in a long, gloomy ward that looked like a dark cathedral. Many of the children had the characteristic rigidity of the neck and back seen in meningitis. The sisters caring for the patients had neither sulfa drugs nor penicillin. The children were dying every hour and it was an appalling sight.
>
> I went over to the American Hospital in Neuilly and told the Commanding Officer about the dying French children. Although we were not supposed to give American Army medicine to the French, he himself helped me load cartons of penicillin into a truck and told the driver to take me and the medicines to the Necker Hospital. I showed the nursing sisters how to do lumbar punctures and drip the penicillin intrathecally into the childrens' spinal fluid.

A week later I returned to the hospital to see how the children were doing. The sisters came running to me with tears of happiness in their eyes. They took me into the long, gloomy ward and there— where a week ago every hour babies were dying—now they were all cured and had gone home. There was a long row of empty cribs.[59]

But the war to defeat Germany was not over, and the Jackson family was still suffering the hardships of internment.

8

RAVENSBRÜCK—NEUENGAMME

August 15 is the Feast of the Assumption in France, and for
Catholics in 1944 the day is sacred, commemorating the belief
in a miraculous event: the taking of Mary, the mother of Jesus, into
heaven. The German commander of the Romainville prison fort,
where Toquette was now held, had earlier authorized the French
prison chaplain to hold an Assumption mass to celebrate the holiday.
But it was not to be.

The chief guard at Romainville was an immense German named
Kratz who shouted the news early in the morning of August 15,
laughing and rattling his collection of keys: *Nicht Messe, Nicht Messe!*
Morgen, Alles transport Deutschland, tous mourir (no mass, no mass,
tomorrow, all to Germany, all die). Over Kratz's laughter came the
sound of cannon. The Allies were near. Toquette and her comrades
had lived for this moment.

Cannon sounded again. There would be no mass, but the prison
grapevine whispered that the Allies were at Rambouillet, only 32
miles away. There were sounds of laughter mixed with cries of joy:
"Soon! Soon!" These women who had suffered so much—arrest, imprisonment, some torture—dared hope. This, too, was not to be.

Toquette had come to the Romainville prison on July 14 from the
Moulins camp, where she had seen Sumner and Phillip in passing as
they left handcuffed for Compiègne. The Gestapo may have trans-
ferred Toquette to Romainville so she could be "examined" again in
Paris. Somehow, the Swiss Consul—because of Toquette's dual
American and Swiss nationalities—found her there and arranged for

126

her sister, Tat, to visit with her for thirty minutes on August 10.[1] Tat found Toquette "full of courage"—and Toquette even reproached her for crying during the visit.[2]

Toquette was among those who were forced out of their cells and lined up outside the blockhouses of the fort, where they waited for buses to take them to trains destined for "nowhere." Again the sound of cannon; the German guards were visibly nervous. The women sang.

Fearing separation, friends locked arms, hoping to stay together. They cried out to their comrades in the cells above: "Hello up there! Listen: prisoners are being taken away. . . . Tell the Resistance. . . . Stop the train, do you hear? Stop the train!" A woman waved a white handkerchief. They yelled again and again: "Tell the Resistance. . . . Stop the train!" A young Hungarian prisoner sang *Ave Maria*, her voice clear as crystal.[3]

At the prison gate, Toquette and others were herded by German guards onto buses while at that very moment, Raoul Nordling, the Swedish consul general, was meeting at the Hôtel Meurice in Paris with General von Choltitz, head of German forces in Greater Paris. They were negotiating the final arrangements to turn over political prisoners destined for deportation to the protection of the Swedish Red Cross. A few weeks earlier, Nordling assigned Eric Posch-Pastor (the Goélette agent known as "Clayrec–RJ 4570") to visit Romainville and other prisons under false papers. His mission was to help open the negotiations for transferring prisoners. But the Goélette agent could not have known where Toquette was being held captive.[4] So, tragically, the Swedish Red Cross was never able to stop Toquette's deportation.

Toquette's American friend, Virginia d'Albert-Lake, was one of the prisoners to board the buses that morning. She had been arrested, imprisoned, and was about to be deported with Toquette. A member of the French Resistance group Comet, she and her husband, Philippe, had helped some sixty-five Allied flyers to escape from France before she was caught and imprisoned. Virginia describes how she was put aboard a bus at the Romainville prison gate:

> I arranged to be one of the last to board a bus, hoping to land near the driver, a Frenchman, so I might give him a handful of messages.

With great care, watching the SS guard over my shoulder, I showed the messages to the driver. He signaled his agreement with a nod.

Others pass messages to me: the last words of wives, mothers, and girls about to be sent to Germany. The guard wandered away for an instant. I passed the driver the messages. He whispered: "Filthy work. Since this morning, I've driven prisoners from Fresnes and Cherche Midi without stop to the station at Pantin."

"So they're emptying the prisons?"

"Right!"

"The Allies, are they coming?"

"Yes, Madame, they're barely 40 kilometers away!"[5]

The bus convoy wound its way through the Paris suburbs to the railroad station at Pantin. There, Toquette met Maisie Renault, the sister of Colonel Rémy (Gilbert Renault-Roulier), one of General de Gaulle's top-secret agents inside France. Maisie and her sister, Isabelle, worked with her brother's Resistance group, Confrérie Nôtre-Dame. After the war, Colonel Rémy wrote how he had prayed his sisters would escape arrest by the Gestapo. But, sadly, they were seized and locked up with a group of Communist Resistance fighters. Rémy wrote:

> Life had not prepared these two young girls to live among such a tough bunch . . . who during the few seconds they were allowed into a toilet, talked to them using the language of the gutter.
>
> The girls still said their morning and evening prayers and visited the prison chaplain. My sisters made friends with these patriots. And I believe that certain of those hard-bitten "Reds" found Christ in the simple faith of the two young women.[6]

Toquette, Virginia Lake, and Lucienne Dixon, another American who had fought in the Resistance along with Maisie Renault, ended up in cattle cars destined for Ravensbrück KZ on August 15, 1944. Maisie Renault describes Toquette at that time:

> Toquette was short and light, very gentle, of joyful appearance and striking bravery. She was very secretive concerning the reasons leading to her arrest. When we left Romainville, the atmosphere was

rather relaxed. We could hear the Allied forces' guns and, according to the news, they had reached Rambouillet. The end of the war seemed very close.[7]

The four women, among hundreds of prisoners transported that day in one of the last SS deportation convoys, arrived at Ravensbrück on August 21, half-starved and dying of thirst in the summer heat.

Geneviève de Gaulle, the niece of Gen. Charles de Gaulle, was a prisoner with Toquette at Ravensbrück. Her poignant words say much about what that death camp was like:

> Suddenly, there is a beam of light and the terrible hoarse voice of our jailer, the shadows of two SS.
>
> *Raus*! Nightmare or reality? Baty and Félicité, who share my mattress of straw, are awake. They reach for our things and bring down my mess tin; help me down, too. I fear what awaits us. Executions more often take place in the night.
>
> I am in the bunker at Ravensbrück. There are no blankets, only straw mattresses. Bread is given every three days, soup every five days. In the bunker they flog prisoners twenty-five, fifty, or seventy-five times—few survive. We all know about this and we know that Professor Gebhardt[7] is using the younger women as human guinea pigs for experiments.[8]

In the end, Mlle. De Gaulle's life was spared on the orders of Heinrich Himmler, the head of German Reich security. She, along with Virginia Lake, was later transferred to a Red Cross facility in Germany that handled the exchange of prisoners.[9]

Toquette spent a couple of weeks in quarantine at Ravensbrück. Then, she and Lucienne Dixon were among prisoners sent on a work detail to Torgau KZ, where life was somewhat better.

Toquette's last message was sent from the Torgau concentration camp. It was written on a 4x4-inch square slip of paper and addressed to her brother, Touvet, at his home in Switzerland:

> Madame Jackson, No 57 855, American, would be grateful if you would write to Touvet Barrelet de Ricou [address in Switzerland] to say to him that she is well and has been here for a week after 15 days

at Ravensbrück. Tell him simply that the message is from "Toquette." Many thanks.

Her note arrived through the aegis of the International Committee of the Red Cross (ICRC). It was enclosed in an ICRC cover letter, dated October 13, 1944, which advised:

> We have been able to pass a message from Mrs. Jackson to you. [Toquette] is interned at Torgau (Germany) and works at the Muna factory. We advise you not to write to her. The message was transmitted to us in a confidential manner.[10]

Unfortunately, after a few months Toquette and Lucienne Dixon were sent back to Ravensbrück, After a brief stay at Ravensbrück, Toquette was transferred to Petit-Köenigsberg with Virginia Lake. For Toquette and Virginia Lake, Petit-Köenigsberg was a brutal place where French, Polish, Russian, and a handful of other women (Toquette and Virginia were the only Americans) were forced to clear a road in the forest. They toiled in the cold and snow in lightweight garments, felling trees and pulling tree stubs out of cold mud and frozen ground. Virginia Lake says:

> We women had never done hard labor. Clad in scanty summer clothes we were near dead with cold and hunger. [We got] a piece of bread and a cup of a kind of coffee in the morning, a thin soup at noon, many couldn't make it.
> Worse than the work was the "line-up." The cold was unbearable. The women fell unconscious in the snow and if no one was able to pick them up and take them to the infirmary they just laid there. Each minute demanded an extraordinary effort. When someone fell [to the ground] our first thought was, "I won't move. I'm too weak. I can't possibly help to carry someone." Then we would hear: "Who is it? Who is it?" If it were a friend we would force ourselves out of our stupor to get hold of the dead weight that was a fellow human being in distress. There was barely a morning that passed without having to carry someone to the infirmary.[11]

Many women didn't make it. When they were useless as slave labor for the Nazis, their lives ended in the gas chambers of Ravensbrück. Toquette was saved from this fate when she fell seriously ill. As an American citizen, she received special treatment and was sent back to Ravensbrück and placed in the camp's infirmary. Usually, after returning to Ravensbrück, most of the prisoners from Petit-Köenigsberg died of exhaustion.[12] It is a miracle that Toquette survived.

Glen Whisler of the American Red Cross who was stationed at Malmo wrote to U.S. minister Hershel V. Johnson of the U.S. Legation at Stockholm on April 30, 1945. He tells about what he found after interviewing many ex-prisoners of Ravensbrück:

On arrival at Ravensbrück the women were completely disrobed, even to shoes, and told to bathe in cold water. Then, in the presence of leering and jeering soldiers (German) they were given superficial medical examinations . . . tests for venereal disease, which included vaginal examinations. Since infected persons were given no treatment, and since the instruments used were not cleaned or sterilized between patients, there is reason to believe that the process was done simply to humiliate the prisoners. Following the process the women were marched, nude, into an open courtyard where they waited in all weather. . . .

The prisoners were issued clothing consisting of anything from a one-piece dress (nothing else), to a fairly complete outfit including shoes, but seldom including underwear and never including an overcoat or warm outer garment. Those not getting shoes tried to steal or buy them from other prisoners. . . .

Normal rations were "coffee" for breakfast. It was at least hot and dark. For lunch a bowl of hot soup, sometimes with vegetables, almost never with meat. For dinner the same soup. One kilo of bread was distributed daily for each eight persons. . . .

Beds were bunks built into the walls in tiers of three. On the wood was a thin pad of straw. One blanket was furnished for each bed. From three to five women occupied each bed. The blankets could not be washed, and everything quickly became louse-infested. Roaches and other insects abounded. . . .

Each barrack had a pit-type toilet. There was a washhouse. . . . The women used sand to scrub themselves. Clothing could not be washed there. Most women washed clothing and put it on wet. This was done at the Siemens plant although it was strictly forbidden and severely punished.

Admission to the hospital could be had only when the patient had a fever of 39 degrees centigrade (102.2 degrees Fahrenheit). The hospital had fair equipment but almost no medicines according to Mrs. Lindell and Mrs. Jackson. . . .

Patients lay naked two to three to a bed; nursing was done by other prisoners and was sympathetic but inept. . . .

The head doctor ordered his assistants to pass through the tuberculosis ward and [select] various patients saying, "Give me that one and that one." Those patients were carried out by soldiers and dumped into carts. Then, according to Mrs. Lindell they were taken to a crematorium where they were shot in the back of the head and then cremated.

Other persons were put to death in a gas chamber or were given injections of lethal drugs. The ashes from the crematorium were carried out by the prisoners and used to fertilise the farms or for road building. Mrs. Lindell estimated that at least 5,000 women were cremated between December, 1944 and mid February, 1945. Miss Rarusyn added that they were not all dead when cremated. This camp (Ravensbrück) is one of the "good" camps as distinguished from the "extermination" camps, which have few survivors.

Prisoners tried hard to get assigned to the desirable jobs in the kitchens and as nurses. Some of the women did outside work . . . most did inside work at the Siemens plant, which had been set up inside the camp area after they were bombed out at Metz and Paris. Women worked a ten-hour shift and they had two hours of "hard labour" at the camp after that.

Each morning between three and four o'clock, the Germans held "Appel" or roll call. Each woman not in a hospital bed was required to line up in the open yard and wait for as long as two hours while the presence of each person was determined. This took place in all kinds of weather and without any warm clothing. From the rain and cold many women got heavy colds, and many deaths from pneumonia were attributed to the *Appel*.

Punishment for minor offences included suspension of bread rations for one or several days and/or standing on the street corner on Sundays in one of the German villages. When in the villages the prisoners were jeered at and abused by the civilians. More grave offences were punished by hair-shaving, beatings, solitary confinement without food and in some cases death.

While Ravensbrück was not an extermination camp, it handled its prisoners in the most callous way possible. Mrs. Bolyos said that she and her mother had to watch her younger sister raped en route to Ravensbrück. The girl died from her injuries and the mother died later at Ravensbrück.

It is difficult to write such a report as this in a factual and objective way. The gross inhumanity of German cruelty practiced on these women makes one regret at times the United Nations' principles. . . . There is no need to comment further on the beatings with weighted rubber truncheons and wooden clubs, the slugging and slapping, the grinding hard work and the loss of sleep. Nor have I much information about the ugly rumor that there are women kept at Ravensbrück whose bodies have been distorted and deformed by sadistic operations in the name of pseudo scientific research. Properly qualified intelligence officers might well check that possible page in the German atrocity dossier.

One looks at the wispy bodies and spindly arms of these women with wonder that the human body and will to live can endure so much. And one is shocked to learn that only prisoners in the best condition are allowed to be evacuated. In one case described by Mrs. Lindell, the head doctor ordered three French women removed from an evacuation line because they looked too bad. They, or their ashes, are still there.[13]

Under Hitler's *Nacht und Nebel* (Night and Fog) decree, the Third Reich's enemies were deported or systematically exterminated.[14] In France most people didn't know the destination of prisoners who were sent east to *Pitchi Poi*,[15] nowhere. But the German people knew by 1933; eight years before the Occupation of Paris, they nicknamed them Konzertlager (concert camp), giving the name a harmless ring instead of its real purpose: Konzentrationslager (KZ) concentration camp (for political prisoners and Jews).[16]

Neuengamme KZ, where Sumner and sixteen-year-old Phillip were interned, was located in the marshy Elbe country southeast of Hamburg. It had been set up in 1939–1940 to supply cheap prison labor for the armaments factories of northwest Germany. At the time, it was composed of a great concrete space surrounded by electrified barbed-wire fences and watchtowers. Prisoners were housed in wood blocks. Camp services were in brick barracks. A separate part of the camp was reserved for medical experiments on adults and children. Of the ninety thousand prisoners sent to Neuengamme between 1939 and 1945, nearly half died in the camp.[17]

The arbitrator of punishment at Hitler's camps was Theodor Eicke, described by a fellow Nazi as an "aggressive, reckless, and dangerous lunatic."[18] Eicke had been detained for three months in a psychiatric clinic in 1933 until Heinrich Himmler, himself the diabolically skillful organizer of rationalized modern extermination methods, discovered him and appointed him as chief of concentration camps: Inspekteur der Konzentrationslager. Himmler then promoted Eicke to the rank of SS Gruppenführer (major general). Eicke replaced the guards at Dachaü camp with SS Death's Head formations—the very name sent shivers down the spines of ordinary Germans. He outlined exact instructions on corporal punishment, beatings, solitary confinement, and the shooting of "enemies of the state" who were to be treated with "no pity and maximum personal severity."[19]

The SS motto, "Tolerance is a sign of weakness," became a model for the German concentration camp system. The SS and the camps they managed did not fall under the regular German administration. The SS were free to inflict whatever punishment they thought suitable. A Swiss jurist stationed in Berlin in 1945 wrote:

> As proper guardians of Germany's security [the SS] did not consider themselves bound to the rules of criminal procedure, especially in view of the increasing power of their chief (Heinrich Himmler, Reichsführer-SS and the Waffen-SS), who was simultaneously Minister of the Interior. The SS could not tolerate that the *Volksschadling* (vermin of the German population) might escape from the mesh of the law. Indeed, accused persons, non-Jews and Jews, having been acquitted by a regular German court and set free were very often arrested again by the SS immediately after the trial and sent to a concentration camp for some reason of national security.[20]

Neuengamme was a profitable business for the SS, with trading, manufacturing, and industrial works owned and run by the SS and somehow connected to the camp. The SS owned the businesses, and their officers were shareholders. In one report dated 1939, senior managers complained about a lack of business acumen among SS officers in charge of certain works. Legitimate German industrial firms and banks such as the Dresdner Bank in the town of Bergedorf managed and financed the operations of the factories attached to the slave labor camps. The prisoners were employed at places like the Walter Werke, an ammunition factory; the Klinker Werke, a ceramic and brick factory; Jastram Motor Werke; and Messap Werke, manufacturing time fuses for shells. Amazingly, the German Red Cross financed some of these factories.[21]

Prisoners were trucked or marched to their workplaces, and the vehicles returned at night with the dead bodies of those who had collapsed at their jobs. In the evening the prisoners attended political lectures or were made to witness hangings of fellow inmates. This treatment was deliberate, for deportation had a double objective: remove enemies of the Third Reich and obtain slave labor. Those who were strong enough to survive the journey to the camps and the first weeks of grueling labor were good for at least several months of work.[22] Workers who fell ill were selected for liquidation. They were killed in batches of fifty to one hundred—injected with petrol, gassed, or hanged. Women were brought to the camp to be hanged to the sound of music.[23] The camp cremated some fifteen hundred bodies each month—the two ovens worked full time, every day.

On November 29, 1944, a group of twenty Jewish boys and girls between the ages of five and twelve who had been deported from France arrived at Neuengamme from Auschwitz to be used as laboratory animals. They were inoculated with tubercle bacilli. In April 1945 the children were taken away to a school building in the nearby town of Bullenhuser Damm. All of the children were hanged there after being injected with morphine.[24] Earlier, in February 1945, a number of boys between the ages of nine and fourteen were seen to have entered the *Revier* (the camp's infirmary). Few left alive. It was learned afterward that the children had been subjected to a series of biological experiments; most of the children were exterminated by lethal injection. Three French doctors who tried to prevent the experiments were hanged.[25]

Jews and political prisoners of various nationalities—Russians, Poles, Germans, Danes, Norwegians, and French—were regularly put to death in Neuengamme's gas chambers, which were built to accommodate a thousand inmates at a time.

Ravenous dogs were set upon prisoners who tried to escape. There were five hundred dogs in the camp used for guard duty and punishment. When a prisoner had been torn to pieces, the other inmates were made to walk around the camp singing.

After a revolt in the punishment cells on the night of April 28, 1945, the SS sealed the cells and lobbed hand grenades and fired machine guns through the windows. The guards stripped twelve women naked, shaved their heads, and hanged them in the prison corridor.

SS major Max Pauly, thirty-three years old and the father of five children, led the SS staff and guard detail—some six hundred strong. They all belonged to the SS Division Totenkopf. Prisoners designated as guards and administrative workers assisted them in their work.[26]

During the first month at Neuengamme, Sumner and Phillip were together in one block. Even after the weeks spent in German prison camps in France, father and son must have been shocked by the daily atrocities that took place at Neuengamme. They wore "ignoble attire"—rags branded with two paint strokes on the back in the shape of a cross, two vertical stripes on the front of the jacket and two more on the legs of the trousers. Father and son were marked with numbers printed with a wooden type on pieces of canvas sewn to the jacket and the trousers. Phillip's number was 36.461; Sumner's was 36.462.

They were forced to take part in the camp's routine "welcome ceremony," when prisoners were made to form a square with an empty space in the middle. In the center, the conductor of a brass band stood on a stool, the band in front of him with their instruments at the ready. When prisoners were formed up, the band played a military march. In one such "ceremony," as the band played, four men appeared carrying a heavy scaffold with a crossbeam of wood, from which hung a noose. The band continued to play. The scaffold was set down. On this particular day, the music stopped abruptly as a painfully thin young man with hollow features appeared, hands tied behind his back, dressed in the convict's striped garments. He looked to be in his teens and deathly pale as he climbed the scaffold. A powerful guard (the Lageraltester) wearing a sailor's cap, his badge of office, followed the young man up the scaffold and adjusted the rope around his neck.

The guard shouted the man's crime to the assembled: attempting to escape and stealing food. "Does he not deserve to be hanged?" he yelled. "Yes," someone called back, which was greeted with shouts of approval from the crowd. The condemned youth waited. Then the trap was released and he dropped, his body jerking as the rope became taut. He revolved slowly, stopped, swung the other way, circled about, and then came to rest. Then his corpse was lowered to the ground and removed.

A second victim appeared. He was a powerfully built man in his thirties with a neck like a bull. He was not pushed but mounted the stand with his hands tied behind his back. The noose was adjusted, the shouted speech was repeated, and again hundreds of voices joined in to condemn him. When the voices had died the guard pulled the lanyard—but the trap failed to function. The guard tried again. On his third attempt, the trap fell away. The prisoner dropped and hung by the rope, but he was far from dead. Kicking and twisting he could be seen fighting for his life as his body violently convulsed. The struggle went on for a long time as the assembled prisoners looked on. Finally the man's movements grew weaker until he hanged still, swinging gently.

Night fell and the column of prisoners moved off. Their evening meal of a thin gruel was waiting. But hungry as they were, few new arrivals could touch it.

Older men were hardened to such horrors. They knew that every day someone in the camp died: hanged in private in a "death cell" from a rope fixed to a ring; or in the hospital, the result of a flogging; or in the night, simply from exhaustion and starvation. Each day prisoners could see the yellow smoke coming from the twin chimneys of the crematorium.[27]

Sumner was known as the "big American" who wasn't afraid of work and stood head-and-shoulders above his fellow prisoners. According to Clemence Bock, one of the foremen in the factory where Sumner worked for a time "had spent 18 years in America. He took a liking to Sumner and tried to make his life easier."[28] Sumner worked at the factory forge and then at an electric soldering machine until the heavy sparks burned his eyes. He was sent to the hospital and later served there unofficially under an SS physician and a Czech prisoner-physician who acted as a surgeon. But Sumner fell ill with an infected middle finger, and after three operations the Czech doctor had to remove it under abominable conditions.[29]

Phillip, meanwhile, performed odd jobs: moving heavy barrels, repairing machinery, and finally, thanks to his father's intervention, working in the camp's kitchen. There were twenty-eight cook-helpers for 13,000 prisoners. His shift was from midnight to two in the afternoon. Working in the kitchen probably saved Phillip from starvation or some type of life-threatening assignment. But it nearly killed him when he spilled boiling soup on his feet, causing third-degree burns. He spent five weeks in the infirmary under his father's care.[30]

The story of the odyssey of father and son continues in Phillip Jackson's words:

> I was in the camp from July 18 [1944] to April 21 [1945], at which time the camp was already being evacuated. My father was not often with me, but I saw him every second day. In the camp itself, there were about 10,000 men, and they worked either in or in the neighborhood of the camp. In addition, there were about 20,000 men attached to the camp, but who worked in *Kommandos* of varying sizes dispersed in the north part of Germany.
>
> Our daily food consisted of about one quarter of a three-pound loaf of black bread and one liter of cabbage soup per person. This food was, should I say, only enough for those who were not doing physical or muscular work. Those who were doing the latter died in about three months.[31]
>
> The morning meal consisted of one-twelfth part of a loaf of bread, a 1,500-gram loaf, with half a liter of coffee usually—some sort of brown powder cooked in a 50-liter container. (I suppose it contained acorns.) Lunch was one-and-a-quarter liters of soup, and in the evening, one-sixth part of a loaf of bread, always the same 1,400- or 1,500-gram loaf. Sometimes, we would have margarine and a sort of paste with it. The soup was either cabbage or turnips. We did not get other vegetables. There was considerably more water than vegetables.

Normally we had 500 men sleeping in one block, two to three to a plank-bed, but often this would increase to 700 and then to 1,100. A block was about 80 yards long and 10 yards wide and about 7- or 8-feet high.

There was a blackboard at the entrance of each block with the number of prisoners living in the block written on it. Conditions of living were absolutely foul—the stench was awful at night when all the windows were closed. We never had soap or towels to wash with, and we were given a very short time to use water on ourselves.

In the summer, we did twelve hours work a day.

Major Pauly was responsible for all the brutality, deaths, and foul conditions of living within the camp.

In my estimate during the period I was in the camp, namely July 18, 1944 to April 21, 1945, 35,000 persons were killed or died. I calculate this from the fact that when I arrived, I was given the official number of 36,461, but the official notice board at the camp's office indicated approximately 20,000 persons living in or attached to the camp. Just before the evacuation of the camp, I had seen a prisoner wearing the official number of 81,000, but the official notice board showed approximately 30,000 as living in or attached to the camp. Therefore there was an increase of 10,000 living persons, and an increase of arrivals of 45,000—the difference being 35,000 killed or died.

My father was working in the camp infirmary (Revier No. 3) as an unofficial surgeon. I was a patient there along with 400 other prisoners, the whole month of March 1945. There were six rooms containing about 42 beds each. That would be a total of 240 or 250 beds, approximately.

It was very common and indeed quite normal that two prisoners should be in the same bed. The explanation for that is that on the doors of each room there was a small blackboard on which "beds" was written, with the number of beds actually in the room, followed by the word "occupied." The number standing after "occupied" was almost always superior to the number of beds.

The staff of the camp was normally about 20 SS men, most of whose names I did not know, but which I could easily recognize.

I knew the following names:

SS Captain ANTON THUMANN. He was the *Lagerführer* [assistant to the camp commander]. He was constantly going around camp beating and whipping the prisoners and letting his large and unmuz-zled police dogs loose on the prisoners. I saw this happen many times. One day when we were marching back to the camp I saw him punch my capo [prisoner designated to supervise work details], namely 7083 Fritz Schon, a German political prisoner, several times in the face, because Thumann said our column was not marching in step. Thumann never used a whip; he had the habit of punching peo-ple or knocking them down and kicking them in the face and body. I witnessed him doing this many times. He always attended the hanging of the people and read the sentences and gave the order to hang.

SS Sergeant WILLY DREIMANN. He was *Rapport-Führer;* that is to say senior NCO of the *Blockführers* [SS NCO in charge of one or more blocks of prisoners]. His hobby was riding around the camp on a bicycle with a leather whip, beating the prisoners as he went his way. He was a sadist in every respect. He always attended the hangings. On these occasions, the prisoners were made to take their clothes off before they were hanged, and he used to shout, "Get a move on—the quicker you are, the quicker you will be dead" or words to that effect. I heard that sometimes these people were not killed outright, and afterwards Dreimann would go to the mor-tuary and strangle the bodies with his own hands.

SS NCO HANS SPECK was one of the *Blockführers*. His favorite hobby was whipping people in the face with a riding whip. I saw him do this on several occasions. He was a terror in the camp and when he was about, everyone worked much harder for fear of his brutal punishments.

Major Max PAULY and the guards enjoyed terrorizing the pris-oners. In February, for example, when I washed a pair of trousers covered with filth and lice and hung them outside the block to dry, Pauly saw them. He ordered the block guard to take the "thing" in. These were Pauly's words to the guard about me: "Bash him in the bloody face."[32]

As British forces approached Neuengamme toward the end of April 1945, Heinrich Himmler issued a secret order: "To the Com-manders of Concentration Camps. Surrender is out of the question. Camps are to be evacuated immediately. No prisoner is to be allowed to fall into the hands of the enemy alive."[33] Major Pauly ordered the camp evacuated. Forty thousand prisoners were sent south and east. The seriously ill went to die in Belsen, while 1,038 walking sick were herded onto freight trains. At Gardelegen, the SS shut them in a barn, set it afire, and shot those who survived; 22 escaped. Obersturmführer Tamann ordered 35 prisoners shot immediately before Neuengamme was emptied.[34]

About fourteen thousand prisoners—mostly French, Belgians, and Czechs—traveled north from Neuengamme on foot and in cattle cars to the port city of Lübeck. Andre Migdal, KZ no. 30655, was a young Resistance fighter who was deported to Neuengamme via Buchenwald in 1944 (see chapter 11). He tells how he and others evacuated the camp:

> We left by foot in the morning and arrived at a train station—just an ordinary train station in Germany. There we were forced to dig a mass grave for 600 of our fellow prisoners who had left the camp the day before. They had all been killed. I don't know who killed them; their bodies lay between two cattle cars. We were ordered to dig a big hole and throw their bodies into it. Then we were made to board the same cattle cars.[35]

On April 21, 1945, Sumner and Phillip were crammed into a cattle car bound for Lübeck with sick prisoners from the infirmary; many were terminal typhus cases. An SS guard beat Sumner when he demanded water for his patients. While in the wagon, Sumner removed an abscess in Phillip's groin, and his health greatly improved a few days later. Neither father nor son knew the whereabouts of Toquette. Later, Phillip would say that they just assumed she had died a prisoner in some camp. Still, arriving at the port of Lübeck gave them hope. Rumors abounded that the city would be liberated by advancing British troops. Prisoners for the first time could breathe sea air far from the confines of Neuengamme camp.

Here is what Phillip Jackson told the War Crimes Tribunal:

> We (my father and I) with a few hundred other prisoners, including the hospital sick, left Neuengamme by train. We passed through Hamburg and arrived at Lübeck on the afternoon of 22 April 1945.

Our train stopped alongside the quay, where the SS prison ships—
the SS Athen, SS Thielbek, and SS Elmenhorst lay at anchor. The
ships were then loaded with prisoners from other convoys. We remained there a week at a railroad siding, tending the sick and dying
such as we were able to in that train. The prisoners were in a terrible
condition. They were starved, could not move, and performed their
acts of nature on the floor of the wagon, unable to go to the barrel
provided for that purpose. It must be remembered that there was
overcrowding and the stench was unbelievable.[36]

Michael Hollard was part of a group of some three thousand
Neuengamme prisoners held below decks on the *SS Thielbek* moored
at the quay of Lübeck. They had lost all track of time—no light or
air; watery soup and bread of sawdust lowered into what had become
a cesspool.

"All French-speaking prisoners on deck!" A guttural voice ordered. Hollard heard the shriek of the grate being lifted above him.
At first the prisoners didn't understand. Again the shout: "French
speakers up!" One at a time some ninety men, so weak each had to
be pushed up by the man below, climbed the single metal ladder out
of the abyss.

On deck their eyes watered and stung in the daylight. They lined
up before a table, and one at a time an SS female clerk, her peroxide-
blonde tresses stuffed under a cap, her fingers stained with ink, entered their names and places of birth in a registry. Hollard avoided
eye contact; something was happening. After all the rumors of the
war's end, was there to be a miracle? Then a hose was turned on and
they were allowed to wash the filth and grime from their bodies.

Later, one by one, they were ordered down a gangway to the
dockside. As the prisoners assembled on the quay, Hollard saw a man
he knew standing in front of a cattle wagon at a railroad siding. It was
his friend and camp-mate from Neuengamme, the American doctor,
Sumner Waldron Jackson: tall, emaciated, a mass of white hair—
imposing even in the black-and-white pajamas. They embraced.

"Come on, come quickly!" Hollard urged. "We're getting out."

Dr. Jackson shrugged his shoulders in despair and turned to the
prostrate figures covering the floor of the wagon. They were the bodies of his sick and dying patients—including his son, Phillip.

The column of prisoners moved off and began to disappear. Hollard hesitated, then staggered ahead to join the others. He looked back to see Dr. Jackson following him with his eyes.[37]

It was Hollard's last glimpse of this "devoted" American. A few hours later, SS guards forced Sumner and Phillip to leave the dying men. With a handful of sick prisoners from the cattle wagon, father and son went into the hold of the *SS Thielbek*, where Hollard had been held. It was crammed with thousands of other prisoners, mostly Poles, Russians, and Germans. On April 30, 1945, the day Adolf Hitler committed suicide, the boat left the quay and sailed out into the Bay of Neustadt.

Michael Hollard and ninety-eight others were put aboard the Swedish rescue ship *Magdalena*, saved by the intervention of Swedish Count Bernadotte. Thanks to a series of talks with Himmler, Bernadotte successfully saved thousands of his fellow citizens and a handful of other nationals including French and American prisoners at Ravensbrück and Neuengamme concentration camps. In an incredible twist of fate, Toquette sailed to freedom aboard the *Magdalena*'s sister ship, the *Lily Mathessen*. Both Swedish ships lay side by side at Lübeck quay, flying the blue flag with a gold cross.

Once on board, Toquette passed through the Bay of Lübeck and may even have seen the Nazi prison ship *Thielbek*. She landed at Malmo, Sweden, on April 28, 1945. In a letter dated the following day and addressed to Tat in pencil and in a shaky hand, Toquette wrote:

Malmo, 29 April 45

My Sister,
I know nothing about you since we saw each other at Romainville. Do you have any news of Jack or Pete? If my handwriting seems to tremble it is because I have open wounds on three fingers and no eyeglasses. I also have otitis and my ears run—I can't hear on one side, my feet are swollen and I have terrible dysentery. But after all that my morale is good. It is a miracle I am not dead; and to think that I will see you soon. No time for more. Kisses, Your Sister.[38]

Glen Whisler of the American Red Cross stationed at Malmo saw Toquette there on April 29, 1945. He reported that "Mrs Jackson is being hospitalized today for draining ears and ulcerated sores on her hands and legs. She is little more than a skeleton."

Toquette, safe in Sweden, was quarantined by the Red Cross. On May 7, 1945, she received a note from a friend in the United States through the American Consul in Malmo. It read: "Your husband and son in Germany [are] safe and free and looking for you/Paris relations all well/will attend money matters Monday." It was not until the tenth of June that Toquette learned the truth.[39]

9

SS DEATH SHIPS

North of Hamburg, where 54 degrees sweeps across the Baltic Sea, lies Lübeck, a twelfth-century imperial German city whose bay gives out to the city of Neustadt. Here in late April 1945 the Nazis assembled a small fleet: the liners *Cap Arcona* and *Deutschland* and the steamers *Thielbek* and *Athen*. By the end of the month, these ships and a number of barges held more than ten thousand prisoners from Neuengamme and other nearby concentration camps.[1]

The order to move prisoners from the camps around Hamburg to prison ships came from Hamburg Gauleiter Karl Kaufmann, the Reich commissioner for overseas shipping, acting on orders from Berlin. Kaufmann would later tell a War Crimes Tribunal that the prisoners were destined for Sweden. But at the same trial on the same day, the head of the Hamburg Gestapo, Count Bassewitz-Behr, testified that "In compliance with [Himmler's] order the prisoners were to be killed."[2]

The *Athen*, a damaged but sailable motor vessel, would be used to transfer prisoners from Lübeck to ships lying off Neustadt and from ship to ship. Her master, Captain Nobmann, at first refused to allow prisoners to board. He argued that the *Athen* was too small, the trip too dangerous, and that there was no lifesaving equipment on board. He relented when the SS threatened to execute him. When crammed full of prisoners, the *Athen* would sail out into the Bay of Lübeck and tie up to the *Cap Arcona* lying off Neustadt Harbor.

Neuengamme prisoners vividly recall the events surrounding their transfer from Lübeck to SS prison ships. As Maurice Choquet,

KZ no. 40422, waited on dockside to board the *Athen*, he realized, "I had never seen a ship before, nor the sea." He was startled when he saw the black-bordered headline on the front page of a sailor's newspaper. It read: "*Unser Führer Ist Gefallen* (Our Führer has fallen)".

> All around me prisoners cried, "Hitler is dead! The war is over. We'll be free." Then when we reached the *Thielbek*, the capos . . . whipped us onto the ship like beasts. We climbed down two metal ladders. When I got down it was dark, stinking, full of prisoners. The metal floor was covered with straw. There were no toilets.[3]

The Polish prisoner Tadeusz Kwapinski recalls boarding the *Athen* at Lübeck:

> Shouting and beating, the SS drove us onto the ship. Over iron ladders we climbed down into the holds. Because of the rush some prisoners tripped and fell from great heights, severely injuring themselves. At the bottom of the hold we could hardly move. It was dark, cold, and damp. There were no toilets and no water; soon it began to stink.[4]

Pierre Billaux, KZ no. 39359, a French prisoner transferred on the *Athen*, says:

> We were in total darkness, then the SS would remove the hatch cover and in the shaft of light lower down a rope. No care was taken for the dead. Prisoners would attach the rope to a foot, a leg, or around the neck. As the guards hauled up the rope the body would swing left to right, in and out of the shaft of light.[5]

The *Cap Arcona* was one of the most beautiful ships of the Hamburg-Sud fleet. The slender, twin-propeller, three-funneled luxury liner built in the Hamburg shipyard of Blohm and Voss was registered at 27,571 tons. Launched on May 14, 1927, she regularly sailed between Hamburg and Rio de Janeiro under the name *Queen* until commandeered for war service. Following the invasion of Poland, she was docked at Gdynia and used as a floating barracks. When the Russians advanced on the Baltic ports, *Cap Arcona* was used to transport civilians, Nazi personnel, and troops to Denmark.

When she anchored at Lübeck Bay, the *Cap Arcona* was no longer maneuverable, with damaged boilers and no fuel reserves. Her captain, Heinrich Bertram, refused to take prisoners aboard. He relented like Captain Nobmann when an SS major from Lübeck boarded his ship and showed him an SS order: comply or be shot. On April 26, an SS commando made the ship "escape-proof" by removing or locking away all the lifesaving equipment.[6]

The *Thielbek*, lying at the quay at Lübeck, was a 2,815-ton freighter that had been damaged in an air raid on the Elbe River in 1944. She was being repaired at the Lübecker Maschunenbau-Gesellschaft shipyard when Kaufmann commandeered her and ordered *Thielbek* to move to Lübeck before repairs were completed.[7]

Phillip Jackson remembers that soon after Michael Hollard left them at the rail siding of the quay at Lübeck, he and Sumner, with a few of Dr. Jackson's walking sick, were forced onto the *Thielbek*:

> We weighed anchor one hour before the arrival of the first English reconnaissance forces. Then we sailed [the ship was probably towed] to Neustadt Harbor in the Bay of Lübeck. We anchored there one night—three steamers in all: the *Thielbek*, with some 2,000 prisoners; the *Cap Arcona*, with some 5,000 prisoners; and the *Athen*, with some 2,000 prisoners.
>
> Sumner and I with other prisoners were packed into the holds of the ship without permission to get on deck. We had 200 grams of bread and a half-liter of very bad soup per day. The conditions were in fact appalling. [As] the prisoners died, their bodies were piled at one end of the hold and then hauled up by the SS and thrown overboard.[8]

Not far from the *Cap Arcona* and *Thielbek* lay the *Deutschland*, a 21 thousand-ton passenger liner also built by Blohm and Voss in 1923 and rebuilt in 1934. During the war she was used as a troop ship and carried German soldiers destined for Norway. Then, on April 28, 1945, work began to convert the *Deutschland* to a hospital ship. The soldiers disembarked and a naval surgeon and twenty-five nurses came aboard. An attempt was made to paint the ship white, but there was insufficient paint. Steincke, the ship's captain, had a single red cross painted on the side of one of the ship's funnels. [The *Deutschland* may have held 2,000 women prisoners.][9]

There were also three large river barges in Lübeck Bay that day, each containing about a thousand men, women, and children from the Stutthof concentration camp near Danzig, Poland. One barge vanished during the night and the other two remained tied up to the *SS Thielbek*.[10]

What was the Germans' plan? Waffen SS major K. Rickert, who worked for SS officer Gen. Count Bassewitz-Behr, testified at the Hamburg War Crimes Trial that he believed that the ships were to be sunk by Nazi submarines or aircraft. (A British War Crimes Commission would later conclude that it was the intention of the SS to murder the prisoners by sinking the ships with the prisoners locked in their holds.)[11]

At Lüneburg, south of Hamburg, Adm. Karl Donitz, Hitler's successor, was to begin negotiating the surrender of German forces with Allied plenipotentiaries. But the Allied high command was convinced that the Nazi elite were planning to escape by ship to a redoubt in the mountains and fjords of Norway. From there, they could continue their fight in natural protective barriers where small armies of men could hide and preserve the Nazi ideal.

As night fell on May 2, 1945, the *Thielbek* was anchored not far from the *Cap Arcona* in Neustadt Bay. The *Deutschland* lay some distance away, and the *Athen* was about to head for Neustadt port to get her water tanks filled. During the night, the two remaining barges crammed with prisoners were cut loose from the *Thielbek* and drifted to shore.

The next day, May 3, the RAF command called for a maximum effort. They ordered their "ultimate" weapon: low-level attack squadrons of Typhoons belonging to the Second Tactical Air Force and based at airfields in northwest Germany to stop what the RAF command believed to be fleeing Nazis. The planes carried four 20mm cannons armed with high-explosive, armor-piercing shells and eight rockets tipped with warheads that exploded on impact. Some of the Typhoons carried 500-pound bombs. The Germans called them *schreckliche Jabos*, and their attacks were devastating.

British military commanders failed to heed warnings from the International Committee of the Red Cross (ICRC) that the SS prison ships anchored off Neustadt in Lübeck Bay actually held as many as ten thousand concentration camp prisoners.[12] Instead, preparations began for what would be one of history's greatest maritime disasters.

The RAF pilots of squadrons 263 and 197 at Ahlhorn air base—a former Luftwaffe airfield in northern Germany—were awakened before dawn. "Morning tea, Sir," said the military policeman charged with the duty. With tea in hand, twenty-three-year-old squadron leader Martin Rumbold got the day's operations order for his 263 Squadron flying Typhoon attack aircraft. Target for the day, May 3, 1945: "Destroy a great number of ships assembled in the Baltic Sea."

While Rumbold was having tea, squadron ground crews were mounting eight rockets on the underside of the aircrafts' wings and loading 20mm cannon shells. Rumbold informed his men of their target and route. Then he and his seven other pilots got into jeeps and were driven to their planes, whose engines had been warmed up by their crew chiefs. The Typhoons took off one after the other, soaring north into the overhanging cloud.

On this day, all across northwestern Germany, RAF units were sent aloft "to shoot up everything that moved." German soldiers loathed the Typhoons as Allied troops despised the German Stuka dive-bombers—no place to hide, no time to get away. And RAF pilots believed they would be shot if caught by the Germans.

At 11:35 A.M., Rumbold's 263 Squadron flew over a number of ships lying in the Bay of Lübeck. But poor visibility forced them to break off the attack and return to base.

Indeed, what Rumbold saw that morning were the SS prison ships *Cap Arcona*, *Thielbek*, and *Deutschland*. The motor vessel *Athen* was making her way to the nearby harbor of Neustadt to take on water and new prisoners. Had Rumbold been equipped with telescopic vision on his fly-over that morning, he would have witnessed hundreds of prisoners in 'queer garb' on the decks of the ships, some waving bed sheets and joyously motioning above to the pilots they thought had come to save them.

The weather soon improved and Rumbold and other squadron leaders of the RAF Second Tactical Air Force were briefed on a new mission: "Destruction of enemy naval formations." RAF reconnais-

sance had shown "a heavy concentration of ships in the Bay of Lübeck moving in the general direction of Norway. . . . There are none
of His Majesty's ships in the area to block the enemy's way."

Four RAF squadrons took off on the afternoon of May 3rd: the
184 at Husedt, Rumbold's 263, 197 at Ahlhorn, and 198 at Plantlunne.

The 184 Squadron made the first attack. At 12:05 P.M., four Typhoons led by Flight Lt. D. L. Stevens dived on what pilots later described as "[a] two-funnel cargo liner of 10,000 tons with steam up."
In reality, it was the 21,000-ton passenger liner *Deutschland*, dead in
the water, with a red cross painted on one funnel. The Typhoons fired
thirty-two rockets; four hit the ship and one failed to explode. One
of the rockets caused a fire that was soon extinguished. No one was
hurt. The *Deutschland*'s Captain Steincke ordered white sheets flown
from the ship's masts to signal surrender. Then he demanded lifeboats
be prepared for a quick departure. Steincke was a wise man.[13]

Miraculously that morning, Captain Nobmann on the MV *Athen*
disarmed his SS guards while ferrying prisoners into Neustadt. As the
Athen approached a jetty, a 17-pound artillery round hit the ship. The
guards and seamen jumped overboard and some prisoners escaped (or
Nobmann told them to flee). Then a British unit advancing on Neustadt entered the town and boarded the *Athen*. The unit's leader, Colonel H.G. Sheen, describes how they found

> charts which contained valuable operational intelligence. The cargo
> of the ship consisted of thousands of prisoners who were being
> transported to Norway. They were packed in so tightly into the
> holds that it was difficult for them to lie down, and they had been
> without food and water for a week. There were no latrines and they
> had not been allowed to leave the holds. When the hatches were
> taken off, the majority of them were too weak to climb out. Those
> that did, emancipated and half-naked, were hardly human in appear-
> ance. They were of every nationality: Jews and political prisoners,
> and one group who strove to maintain military order . . . were survi-
> vors of the maquis [anti-Nazi underground fighters] from the Occu-
> pied countries, many from Norway. The German guards had fled
> but had shot prisoners who had been stowed on deck. Their bodies
> were floating in the harbor when we arrived.[14]

Aboard the *Cap Arcona*, prisoner Jean Langlet, KZ no. 30344, and his comrades had just finished downing a small can of thin soup which Langlet thought was "especially fatty that day and whose defining quality was warmth." He and his pals then stretched out on cabin mattresses and discussed the predictable evening meal: an eighth of a loaf of bread. The bread, a can of weak ersatz coffee, and a tin of watery soup had been their daily meal for some two weeks after leaving Neuengamme. Still, they did have a black market aboard, whose coin was cigarettes and remnants of Red Cross packages. A morsel of bread cost forty to eighty cigarettes. A tin of bully-beef could be had for thirty-five cigarettes.

Apparently, Langlet and others aboard *Cap Arcona* didn't hear the noon explosions on the neighboring *Deutschland* and remained in their cabin. Then around 3 P.M. "muffled explosions" were heard, followed by an ear-shattering burst and machine-gun fire. Acrid smoke poured into their cabin and the surrounding corridors. In a general panic, the prisoners ran about wildly; some hid under their cots. Langlet threw himself on a tin of bully-beef that he and his pal, Fourgassier, had bought that morning with their last cigarettes. He emptied the can into the cabin sink while Fourgassier screamed, "What are you doing? Are you crazy?"

"I don't know," replied Langlet, explaining that in the heat of the moment, "I went about gathering the bits of meat from the sink, swallowing them peacefully, thinking that this would constitute a solid meal, giving me strength."[15]

It was RAF "Ace" Johnny Baldwin's 198 Squadron that rocketed the *Cap Arcona* and terrified Langlet and his comrades.[16] At 3 P.M., five of Baldwin's Typhoons attacked the ship, firing forty rockets with 60-pound high explosive heads and 20mm cannon. One rocket failed to explode. The rest penetrated between the ship's funnels and along the hull, igniting the cabins and along the entire length of the liner. Flames swept through the ship.

The remaining four Typhoons of 198 attacked the *Thielbek*, lying 750 yards from *Cap Arcona*, with cannon and thirty-two rockets. Though she absorbed every hit, the *Thielbek* did not burst into flames.

Sumner and Phillip were below the decks of the *Thielbek* with

thousands of other prisoners. Some were sick with typhoid and typhus. Sumner did what he could to help them. Phillip tells what happened:

> At about 3 P.M. I was able to go on deck because I spoke Ger-
> man and persuaded a *Volkstung* guard—not an SS—on duty to let
> me out of the hold. Suddenly we were attacked; I was not hit by
> the projectiles. Thank God our ship didn't burn. All was confusion:
> screams of men below, sounds of antiaircraft fire. *Thielbek* began to
> list to starboard. Water flooded below decks, a man screamed:
> "What's to become of me? I can't swim!"
>
> I opened a hatch and yelled for my father. I waited a few min-
> utes [but] could not see him. I stripped, but remained on the deck
> for another five minutes to try and see my father to jump together
> in the sea. At last, unable to see him and the boat listing and sinking,
> I got down into the sea through a trap in the side of the ship without
> having to jump. I swam like never before.[17]
>
> Andre Migdal was also in the hold of the *Thielbek* when the
> ship was attacked:
>
> [W]e move about in our new "camp." A fearful stink lacerates
> our throats. The deck is covered with straw; it's dark and there are
> terrible screams. I try to find our buddies. . . . We gather around the
> steel ladder: Phillip Renaud, Jean Delalez, George Laurenge, Yves
> Bodiguel, "the colonel," Andre, the young Parisian, Jackson and
> me. . . . Sitting on the straw we wait. In the morning we get a pint of
> hot water. It was not as hot as the pushing and shoving around the
> ladder. We talk of escape.
>
> Later, we hear the [overhead] motors of flying aircraft, the
> sound of antiaircraft fire. What is happening? Then a violent shock.
> Something fell into the straw . . . burst into flames . . . water flooded
> in. Here in the hold people went mad: cry out; more water floods in
> and puts out the fire. I fight to get to one of the two vertical lad-
> ders—there are 1,200 of us that want to get up that ladder. I man-
> aged to get a leg up and foot by foot . . . then I'm knocked down
> into the water, it saves me but holds me. My pants are tied at the
> ankles with a cord; I have to lift kilos of water. I strip. The prisoners
> had torn planks from the wall and they float. The men grab them. I
> leap to the ladder again. . . . I know not how I made it up that ladder.
>
> On deck the ship starts to list; an SS guard grabs his pistol and
> blows his brains out.

The prisoners throw themselves in the water. I don't know how to swim and I watch them. . . . Near us two big ships are in flames. Hundreds of heads bob in the water. Planks of wood float everywhere. The *Thielbek* keels over; an empty boat drifts by. . . . With others I throw myself onto it and the boat turns over, its keel in the air. We hang onto that slippery keel, our hands grip for life. I have to kick a man away; he sinks, drowns. I can't hold on. A plank drifts by and I dive for it. The boat drifts away. I lay alone on my plank.[18]

Phillip continues:

I managed to board one of the three salvage boats the Germans had launched from shore. I was saved before they knew we were prisoners. They saved only their sailors and soldiers and let over a thousand prisoners drown. Others were hit by cannon fire from the Typhoons. I sat huddled, freezing, near the ship's antiaircraft guns that were firing at the attacking Typhoons. By the time the craft reached shore I was near frozen and deaf from the noise of the guns. The SS shot the first 150 who landed on the shore. About 200 of us were saved out of thousands.

At the port they put me and other prisoners against a wall. We had a narrow escape. The SS set up machine guns to get rid of us. Then a British tank arrived. That was our liberation.

One of the few Frenchmen who was saved saw my father about a hundred yards from the ship, swimming with a plank, "already in difficulties." I could not find my father among the survivors.[19]

Forty-five minutes after the first attack, the *Thielbek* settled in the water, overturned, and sank carrying more than twenty-six hundred prisoners to their deaths.

Aboard the *Cap Arcona*, Jean Langlet finished eating the bully-beef he had dumped into the sink and then dove into a corridor:

A man was lying in his own blood, his legs severed above the knee. He begged us, "Don't leave me." We got him on deck in the fresh air when a guy from Neuengamme, a former Belgian attaché at the Paris Embassy, came up. He bent over the wounded man and kissed him. "It's over!" he said. On deck: total chaos! Thank God the wounded man had a breath of fresh air. I hope he blacked out before he died.

We were pushed to another deck, a fire raged about us. I saw the *Thielbek* about 150 meters away on her side. Some lifeboats loaded with prisoners pulled away. Sailors, some German prisoners, and some Poles had life preservers; they would kill to keep them. Some had wood doors and planks. A man who cut hair at Neuengamme went crazy in front of me. The shore was about three kilometers away. A Russian near me was swallowing gobs of powdered milk from a can. He gave me a mouthful. A German craft went by. I pushed my way down the deck, felt bodies underfoot, and reached a bulkhead. It was 20 meters to the sea. I hesitated. The craft, a patrol boat, returned. A guy next to me jumped. He bobbed up, and I went over feet first—I think someone pushed me. It was about 100 meters to the boat and I reached it somehow. There was a ladder. I managed to pull myself on deck and found a corner to hide in, shivering like a wounded animal. The planes came back over us, firing their cannon: tac, tac, tac, tac. Finally, we reached a jetty and I jumped. When my feet touched wood I ran for cover. There was a warehouse with about fifty guys lined up against the wall. A German sailor with a machine gun watched over us. Thank God the SS had left. We tried to warm ourselves. Russian prisoners standing shoulder to shoulder were pounding each other to get warm. I ran into the American brought up in France—Phillip Jackson, son of the head of the American Hospital at Neuilly. I had seen him at Neuengamme. He had escaped from the *Thielbek*. He was desperate to find his father. I couldn't help him.[20]

There were forty-five hundred prisoners trapped belowdecks on the *Cap Arcona* with some SS and crew. With her superstructure ablaze, the crew tried to pump water but failed because her equipment was damaged. When they attempted to lower lifeboats, the manila rope caught fire and the boats crashed into the sea. On D-deck, seven hundred gravely ill and dying men burned to death. The SS had stuffed Russian prisoners of war into banana coolers deep inside the ship. Most suffocated or died in the flames.

Equipped with life jackets taken from locked compartments, most of the SS guards were able to jump overboard from the *Cap Arcona*. They shot any prisoner who tried to escape. Neuengamme prisoner Heinrich Mehringer, on deck below, saw an SS man with two guns shooting at prisoners trying to climb out of a stairwell. When his guns failed he was knocked down and trampled to death by the onrushing mob. Other SS were beaten with iron bars or clubs. Mehringer's back and head were on fire but he felt cold rather than hot because he was so agitated. He saved himself at the last possible moment by reaching for an iron pipe:

> I was just able to grab it with one arm and with superhuman effort pulled myself up. I had to stand on the heads of the mass of men. Ten others were lucky enough to follow me before the flames sealed the rest into one great fiery heap. We literally ran for our lives on the heads of our fellow prisoners as on a pavement.[21]

German trawlers were sent to rescue *Cap Arcona*'s crew and guards. They managed to save sixteen sailors, four hundred SS, and twenty SS women helpers. Most of the prisoners who tried to board the trawlers were beaten off the boats. Those who reached shore were machine-gunned as they struggled in the surf to the beach. The *Cap Arcona* exploded that afternoon. Bodies would continue to float out of the wreck for six weeks. Three hundred and fifty prisoners somehow survived.[22]

At about 4 P.M., the eight Typhoons of Rumbold's 263 Squadron banked and dived on the *Deutschland*, the ship that Flight Lt. Stevens had attacked earlier that morning. He and his pilots pressed their "burst" switches, apparently unaware that the crew of the anchored hospital ship was frantically signaling surrender with white sheets. Cannon shells and thirty-two rockets burst under the bridge on the port side, igniting the vessel. The German crew abandoned ship in lifeboats—the ship ablaze from end to end. Moments later, eight Typhoons of 197 Squadron attacked the *Deutschland*, dropping 500-pound medium-capacity bombs. The ship heeled to starboard before righting herself. No one can say today if the pilots saw the red cross markings on the funnel.[23]

What happened to the barges crammed with prisoners from Stutthof concentration camp? The British found them washed up on the beach; dead bodies lying everywhere. Children had been clubbed

to death, adults shot; men, women, and children were burned to death
in the holds of those barges or drowned in the icy waters of the Baltic
Sea. Thousands died on the beach before the sun went down on
May 3, 1945.

Sergeant Cooper, who headed a British unit at the waterfront of
Neustadt, reported:

> When we arrived on the shore, I saw many bodies in the water,
> and looking closer, observed that these were terribly mutilated.
> Many of these bodies had arms, legs, or heads severed or missing
> altogether as if struck by an axe or some similar instrument. . . .
>
> Nauseated by this sight I walked down to the water's edge . . .
> and was confronted by the sight of a mass of bodies all roped to-
> gether and half-floating in the water. . . . We found this party to
> contain nine women and girls and one man. All were terribly muti-
> lated by gun wounds . . . and leaving these for burial, I boarded a
> large barge and saw the most terrible sight possible. There were bod-
> ies all over the place, either shot or axed—and in a dreadful state.
> Among these I found one girl still alive, she was about nineteen
> years of age, but in too dazed a condition to pass any information.
> She was sent to the nearest hospital in Neustadt.[24]

There were thirty to forty fishing boats in the harbor at Neustadt
that day, but not one of the German fishermen went out to help the
people in the water or on the sinking ships. The ships were five kilometers away from the town, yet Neustadt residents said they could
hear the screams of burning victims. Some of the town's residents did
open their doors to the pleading, freezing, and starving concentration
camp victims that wandered the town. They took survivors into their
homes and offered food and clothing. Even in Neustadt, a little bit of
human kindness existed here and there.[25]

In the early morning of May 4, Eva Neurath walked through
Neustadt. Eight years earlier, the Nazis had arrested her husband,
Willi, a book publisher in Cologne. The last word Eva had heard from
him was in October 1944, when she got a postcard from Buchenwald
KZ: "I'm doing well." Eva was in Neustadt because she had been
evacuated from Memel when the Red Army closed on the city. She
had been watching the ships in the harbor for days and was told by a

police officer that the ships held convicts and that they were slated to be blown up. Eva had watched as the *Cap Arcona* burned and the *Thielbek* sank. When she reached the edge of town she saw a man coming toward her. His pants were stained and burned, and he was badly injured. He walked up to Eva slowly and stopped. "Muppel, is that you?" he asked. It was Willi.[26]

On May 4, Germany surrendered its forces in the northwest. Four days later on May 8, 1945, at one minute past midnight, World War II ended in Europe.

All told, there were 4,500 prisoners on the *Cap Arcona*, 2,600 prisoners on *Thielbek*, and 1,998 on the *Athen*. There are no records concerning the number of lives lost on the *Deutschland*. Fortunately, 350 from the *Cap Arcona*, 50 from the *Thielbek*, and most of the prisoners on board the *Athen* survived. Some sources report that in all, seventy-five hundred prisoners from Neuengamme perished in Lübeck Bay or on the beaches of Neustadt that day. This figure does not include the men, women, and children from Stutthof KZ near Danzig, Poland, who were murdered when their boats were washed up on the beaches of Neustadt and aboard the barges that drifted onto the nearby shores. Thus, no one will ever know the accurate number of victims who were lost in the massacre at Lübeck Bay.[27]

Sumner Waldron Jackson disappeared into the sea. Phillip survived, as did the remarkably courageous Andre Migdal and Jean Langlet—young men who, together with family members, resisted heroically. Their survival among so many lost souls is close to miraculous.

10

SACRIFICE

Two nights after Dr. Jackson drowned in the waters of Lübeck Bay, Clemence Bock had a dream:

> Dr. Jackson was standing behind his desk in his office at the American Hospital, just as he had so many times before. He looked at me and I was struck by how pale he was. "Listen," he said. "I need to tell you something." He bit his lip and tears ran down his face. "Pete was able to swim." Then he smiled. "He made it. . . . Better him than me!"[1]

Sumner died doing what he had always done: looking after his fellow man. In 1944 they were his sick and dying comrades at Neuengamme and aboard the *Thielbek*. That is his monument. There are other monuments at Neustadt dedicated to the thousands who perished on the SS prison ships and in the cold waters of the Baltic that terrible day. Sumner Jackson would have been sixty years old in October 1945.

Toquette was fifty-six when she was evacuated from Ravensbrück. Maisie Renault tells how she later visited with her friend:

> I was to meet Toquette Jackson again after the war. She had invited us for tea at her beautiful house in d'Enghien-les-Bains. I went along with Lucienne Dixon and Beatrix de Toulouse-Lautrec (a lot younger than us: she was 20 at Ravensbrück).
>
> Everything was still. Through the large windows we could see the green lawn flowing down to the lake where sailing boats were drifting peacefully.

Toquette had remained the same affable person, very quiet about her misfortunes, but nonetheless highly emotional when talking about her husband and the Lübeck tragedy. This reminded us how much he was loved and what a good father and excellent doctor he had been, dedicated to his patients 'til the very end.

She never complained but we could feel how deep were her wounds. She told us she had decided to work again as a nurse. Little was said about the camps, but she showed us a picture taken for a magazine at the time of her liberation. She had been devoured by lice to such an extent that she still had the indelible marks of those terrible bites. It was as if her skin, from neck to chest, had been embroidered with little dots.

Her son, Pete, came to greet us. I knew that he had been rescued from the Lübeck tragedy, and I felt eager to ask him questions. My brother, Philippe, perished on one of those boats. But seeing how young Pete was, I remained silent.[2]

Toquette wrote to Sumner's sister a few weeks after returning to Paris:

July 18, 1945   11, avenue Foch, Paris XVIe
My Dear Freda,
Enclosed you will find the translations and copies of Pete's two first letters to friends in Paris, telling of what happened. He is with the English unit still.

Sumner didn't have a bad heart, but he was very short of breath since he had pneumonia a few years before the war. It was the third finger of his right hand that had to be disarticulated. He had been working in the infirmary of the camp, taking care of his fellow prisoners. Of course, hygiene was very bad and he got an infection.

They were always together, father and son, at the camp of Neuengamme, which they never left. It seems his morale was always good, he was so courageous, never knew what fear was.

We were all three arrested on May 25, 1944, not because we were Americans but because we were working for the underground liberation movement that we call the "Resistance." We were therefore political prisoners and much worse off than the regular prisoners of war.

As soon as my health permits, I am going to look for a job. Life is very expensive in France and we have not the means to live on our income.

I want you to know that I never ceased to be in love with Sumner, for whom I had moreover a great admiration and respect. He had such big qualities. . . . My sister, Alice, thanks you for your letter of June and sends greetings.

Best remembrances, Freda, I hope you are a happy wife and mother.

Affectionately, Toquette[3]

———————————————

French Resistance groups such as Goélette did heroic work. But one asks: was the loss of life and the suffering of the men, women, and youngsters—like the Jackson family—worth it?

Gen. Dwight D. Eisenhower thought so. "Invaluable," he called the French Resistance, declaring in his official report, "They had by their ceaseless harassing activities, surrounded the Germans with a terrible atmosphere of danger and hatred which ate into the confidence of the leaders and the courage of the soldiers."[4] Eisenhower's headquarters, SHAPE (Supreme Headquarters, Allied Expeditionary Force), said Resistance groups ambushed retreating German units, attacked isolated groups, and protected bridges from destruction. The actions of the Resistance resulted in an average delay of two days on all German units attempting to move to the battle in Normandy. Groups including Goélette provided SHAPE forces with priceless information on Wehrmacht troop movements and the strengths and weaknesses of their units, equipment, and leaders.[5]

The Office of Strategic Services, the forerunner of today's CIA, observed that: "The most significant discovery was the enormous importance of the French Resistance as a source of accurate tactical intelligence."[6]

The price paid in human sacrifice was heavy: twenty-four thousand members of the French Resistance were executed by the Nazis. Of the one hundred fifteen thousand who were deported, only forty thousand returned in various stages of emaciation and with innumerable disabilities—there is no accurate record of how many like Toquette and Phillip survived illness after returning to France. And 30,000 men, women, and adolescents of the *maquis,* who fought pitched battles against the German armed forces, were killed in combat. These appalling losses were suffered in darkness and only revealed after World War II.

After Phillip's miraculous escape with death, he spent a number of months as an interpreter with a British Army unit stationed at Neustadt harbor. Then he set about trying to pick up the pieces of a shattered world and to look after his mother. But life could never be the same for Phillip. People who knew him in 1945 remarked how the eighteen-year-old teenager had become a mature adult—unable to study for the BAC exam, unable to relate to and enjoy others of his age in the lighthearted, playful atmosphere of a country recently liberated from occupation and war. Yes, Phillip was a decorated hero—but there were many decorated heroes in Paris that summer and fall of 1945. Now the war was over and won, and everyone wanted to get on with life. "Survivors" like Toquette and Phillip had no easy time. And there were no post-traumatic shock facilities after the war: there was almost near famine, chaos, and total destruction of cities, towns and villages, factories and transport. The European Recovery Program was two years away and France was on her knees.

Toquette was too sick to return to nursing and talked about having a small business to afford life in Paris. And Toquette needed peace and time to heal. Phillip found work, and went to trade school after work to study engineering. He eventually married, had children, and was successful.

I am afraid this author can find no wise philosophic lessons in the Jackson story. Perhaps there is one regarding Man's inclination to do evil and his capacity for suffering. The lesson may be: Keep trying, keep fighting. Don't give up. In a world where one hears, "All my heroes are dead from an overdose,"[7] we ought to keep in mind that some sixty years ago, American, British, French, and other European peoples—men, women, children, whole families, and nations united in a common cause to defeat the German Third Reich. How are we to forget the thousands of people like the Jacksons who suffered grievously in mind and body and gave of their lives to liberate Europe?

Elie Wiesel wrote, "The victims elect to become witnesses." Maisie Renault, Toquette's friend and fellow prisoner at Ravensbrück, put it succinctly in a note she penned to the author in her book, *La grande misère:* "To the memory of all those who lost their lives in Nazi concentration camps, and particularly to Doctor Jackson: *Mort pour la France.*"

EPILOGUE

Heroes and Villains

Here is what became of the heroes of this story . . . and the villains.

Gilbert, or "Gil" (family name Asselin), who took Joe to Toulouse, was arrested by the Gestapo in 1944 for helping William Dallin, a British flyer, to escape. Gil was deported to Dachaü prison camp in July 1944. He returned to France in May 1945. After the war, agents in Gil's group claimed he had betrayed them.

Toquette's sister Alice Barrelet de Ricou, "Tat," lived out her life after the war a spinster at the lake house at Enghien where she taught English from time to time. It is not clear whether she was active in some secret Resistance work. She died in 1960.

Clemence Bock went on teaching the classics and never married. Her children were those students of Latin and French who, year after year, passed through her classroom. In her memorial to Sumner Waldron Jackson, the deeply religious Bock wonders, "What were the last thoughts of this man who never knew the comfort of faith in a higher being?"

Eleftherios Gregos ("Joe") stayed in the U.S. Air Force after the war and graduated from flight engineer school. He later flew Typhoon penetrations with the U.S. 54th Air Weather Squadron out of Guam. When he retired, he had 7,500 hours as a panel flight engineer. He is currently an instrument-rated private pilot living in Sacramento, California, with two sons and four grandchildren and 1,660 miles logged on his 1966 Cessna. He expressly asked the author not to mention him by his real name, and is reluctant to be considered a hero. "There are a lot of real heroes out there and I am the least worthy."

He is too modest to say which decorations he received other than the Purple Heart.

Squadron Leader Frank Griffiths was picked up by the British Consular Officer in Spain and returned to duty in England. He retired from the RAF in 1977 after forty-one years of service. He had a distinguished career in the Royal Air Force and wrote a book about his escape entitled *Winged Hours*, published by William Kimber, London, 1981.

Louise Heile (Agent P2, FFC) stayed on at Avenue Foch and looked out for the Jacksons' dog, Kiki, until Paris became unlivable in the last days of the German Occupation. She went to live in the country but came back to Avenue Foch when Toquette returned from Ravensbrück. Louise eventually married a man from her village. She was decorated with the Croix de Guerre for her work in Goélette.

Michael Hollard spent time recuperating in Sweden. He finally boarded an RAF DC-4 expressly ordered by RAF High Command to take him to Paris. As the plane crossed into France, it passed over Bonnetot-le-Faubourg and the ramps the Germans used to launch V-1 rockets against London. Hollard and brave men and women like Erich Posch-Pastor, *R*, and the Jackson family had helped destroy these weapons. Later, King George VI of Great Britain would decorate Hollard with the Distinguished Service Order. The French awarded him the Croix de Guerre. A book about his exploits, *The Man Who Saved London*, was published by Doubleday in 1961.

Hollard wrote after the war that Sumner never talked about his work in the Resistance and never explained why the family was arrested and deported. He did say that Sumner took life in the camp with dignity. Hollard added, "Dr. Jackson was some sixty years old with white hair, a solid build, and held himself always straight as an 'I.'" Hollard was able to send news of the Jacksons to Sumner's sister in America through Hollard's sister in Switzerland.

SS Gestapo chief Heinrich Illers fled to Germany just before Paris was liberated. He had been the subject of a French military investigation after the liberation of France, but due to a mistaken identity, the French sought to indict a Dr. *Peter* Illers instead of Heinrich. The investigation went nowhere.

Serge and Beat Klarsfeld, renowned Nazi hunters and members

of a French group that brought Klaus Barbie back to France from hiding in Bolivia, discovered Illers in Germany in 1972. At the time, Illers was employed as president of the Court of Social Affairs of Land Lower Saxony (Land de Basse Saxe) as a specialist in the problems of war victims. The Klarsfelds exposed him in a press conference at Bonn on October 3, 1972. Thanks to their efforts, Illers was indicted and tried in court. Sadly, he was never imprisoned for his war crimes. He died in his sleep, a free man.

Phillip "Pete" Jackson joined the Fourteenth British Light Ambulance, Royal Army Medical Corps, as an interpreter a few days after his escape from the sinking of the Nazi prison ship *Thielbek* in the Bay of Neustadt. (He was seventeen years old.) Thinking his mother had perished, he wrote a friend shortly after his escape:

> I am working with H.M.S. forces, living with them and sharing their life. I am not in great haste to come back for my *bachot*. [As mentioned earlier, had he not been arrested with his parents by the Milice, Pete was to have taken the French baccalaureate examination a few days later.] Either I have it or I have to pass it in September. My father is dead. I do not know if I shall see my mother.
>
> It is likely I shall still spend a few weeks here. This life is fine.
> Signed: Ph. Jackson
> O.H.M.S.! [On His Majesty's Service]

He went on to testify at a War Crimes Trial at Curio House, Hamburg, in May 1946.

Phillip Jackson was cited for L'ordre du Régiment and decorated with the Croix de Guerre 1939–45 with Etoile de Bronze. He was decorated with the Chevalier de la Légion d'Honneur and holds the Medal for the Deported for Acts of Resistance. Phillip was recently promoted to Officier de la Légion d'Honneur. He lives with his wife at the Jackson family house on the lake at Enghien outside of Paris.

Sumner Waldron Jackson, M.D., was a member of the Harvard Unit in France beginning in 1915, and then a first lieutenant and later a captain in the U.S. Army Medical Corps from 1917 to 1919. He was twice decorated with the Croix de Guerre 1939–45, awarded the U.S. Medal of Freedom, and was cited by Field Marshal Montgomery and

Air Chief Marshal Tedder for his heroic acts in the Resistance during World War II. He may have been decorated in World War I but his military records for that war have been lost or destroyed in the United States.

Dr. Morris B. Sanders, a colleague of Dr. Jackson's at the American Hospital, wrote after the war:

> If any of Sumner's friends ever thought that he had become "Frenchified" by his life in France, they can rest assured—he lived and died as a man from Maine. I could believe it if I heard that he had uttered some dry and humorous remark while he was floundering around in the water before sinking.

Sylvie Barrelet Jackson née de Ricou, "Toquette," died at the American Hospital of Paris on February 17, 1968. Though continually ill after her return from Ravensbrück, she managed her life with courage and dignity. In lonely moments at the lake house at Enghien—so full of Sumner's memories—her diary entries for some days read: "Nobody came. . . ."

This courageous American served France and the United States in the two World Wars. She was decorated with the Médaille de la Croix Rouge 1914–18 for service as a nurse in World War I, the Croix de Guerre 1939–45, Médaille des Déportés, Médaille des Combattants volontaires, and Chevalier de la Légion d'Honneur in 1946 and Officier in 1964.

Jean Langlet, sous-lieutenant, Agent P-1 F.F.C., Déporté-Résistante, was awarded the King's Medal for Courage in the Cause of Freedom for his services in France. His brother-in-law died at Neuengamme. He and his father-in-law made it home to Lyon in 1945. He now lives with his wife in Boulogne, a suburb of Paris.

Gladys Marchal was arrested in June 1944. She was released after questioning for lack of proof of having committed a crime. Some of her Resistance comrades claimed she betrayed them.

Andre Migdal, Déporté-Résistante, Caporal R.I.F., is an Officier de la Légion d'Honneur, Commandeur de l'Ordre National du Mérite, and Commandeur des Arts et Lettres. "Mickey," to his comrades and grandchildren, is a writer and poet living in Paris. His latest book, released in Paris, tells of Neuengamme and describes the massacre at Lübeck Bay. It is entitled *Les Plages de Sable Rouges* (The Beaches of Red Sand). His wife, Jeannine, lost her father, Edouard Rodde, and grandfather, Jean, when Dr. Heinrich Illers selected them as hostages. They were murdered by a Nazi firing squad at Mont Valerien on August 11, 1942. Ninety-three persons were shot that day. At the Pantin cemetery outside Paris in an area devoted to martyrs, there are two crosses bearing their names.

General Carl-Albrecht Oberg was supreme head of the SS and police in Occupied France from 1942 to 1945. At the end of the war, Oberg went into hiding at a Tyrolean village but was arrested by American Military Police in June 1945. Courts in Germany and France sentenced him to death, but his sentence was commuted to life imprisonment in France. President Charles de Gaulle finally pardoned Oberg in 1965.

Baron Erich Posch-Pastor von Camperfeld, alias Etienne Paul Pruvost, "Rickey" to his friends, was born in Innsbruck in 1915. As a lieutenant in the Austrian Army during the Anschluss, he and his regiment were among the few who resisted the Nazi takeover of Austria. He was arrested, sent to Dachaü, and then to the Russian front, where he was wounded. He arrived in France in 1943 and joined Goélette while working at Niort, where parts of V-1 rocket bombs were assembled. After the war, he was decorated with the Médaille de la Résistance and seen in Paris in the uniform of a U.S. Army officer. His life in the French Resistance is still mostly a mystery.

SS Maj. Max Pauly and the more vicious of his subordinates were hanged at Hamelin prison.

R for Renaudot, sous-lieutenant in the French Army (later captain, commandant, and head of the FFC group Goélette), was one of the founders of Goélette in Paris. Very little is known about him except that he was born in Paris in 1904. His real name was Paul Robert Ostoya Kinderfreund, and he was probably a journalist before the war. *R* was highly decorated. He was certainly close to the Jackson family and the mysterious Baron Erich Posch-Pastor von Camperfeld. Kinderfreund received the coveted Médaille de la Résistance in April 1946. After the war he had a career in journalism and was the keeper of the Goélette Archives, many of which have now disappeared.

Lawrence K. Whipp was freed from the internment camp and appointed by the Germans to play the organ at his beloved gray gothic cathedral in Paris, which became a Wehrmachtskirche—a German Chapel—during the Occupation. When Paris was liberated, he disappeared and was never seen alive again.

APPENDIX

Letter from SS General Oberg to His Chief, SS Reichsführer Himmler, Paris, August 8, 1944

[This may be the first time this now-declassified document from the National Archives has been published. The English translation is given here in full.]

Higher SS and Police Leader   Paris, 10.8.44
Under the authority of the Military Commander
in France
Diary. no. 1823 / 44
Ob/Wr.

To the
SS Reichsführer
Field Command Post

Re.: Wehrmacht arrest operation carried out on 20.7.44
Reference: Dort. FS 136 of 6.8.44

Dear Reichsführer,
    It is my duty to respectfully inform you of the events surrounding the arrest operation carried out by the Wehrmacht on the evening of 20.7. The details are as follows:
    I received a telephone call from the Commander of the Security Police and SS Security Service at about 19:00 hours, informing me of the news, broadcast over the radio at 18:30 hours, concerning the assassination attempt against the Führer. I did not hear the news di-

rectly, as Paris was without electrical power until about 22:00 hours. At about 19:30 hours, I received a telephone call from the Chief of Staff of Ob. West, General Blumentritt, who asked me whether I had heard the radio news broadcast of 18:30 hours, and whether I knew anything further about what had occurred. I had to give a negative answer, as no department of the SS or Police anywhere in the Reich, with particular reference to the Reich Department of Security, had passed any information on either to myself or to the Security Police and Security Service commander, occupied territories (BdS). (The first FS. of the SS Reichsführer, concerning Home Command staff officers, issued on 20.7 at 23:00 hours, was received here on 21.7 at 04:05 hours.)—General Blumentritt asked me to inform him immediately if I should hear any further news, as he wished to report to Field Marshall von Kluge, who was then on his way back from the front.

At between 22:15 and 22:30 hours, while I was working in my office, my adjutant, SS Hauptsturmführer and Captain d.Sch. Jungst, informed me that the commandant of the Paris Security Division Major General Brehmer (holder of the Blutorden medal) was in the reception room in a highly excited state and wished to speak to me. As I was at that moment speaking on the telephone to Ambassador Abetz, I gestured to my adjutant, indicating that he should wait a moment. A few seconds later, both the communicating door to my reception room and the door to the corridor burst open, and—although dazzled by the light from my desk lamp—(the rest of the room lay in darkness) I could make out that several persons had entered the room. As I was still speaking on the telephone, General Brehmer stepped up to my desk and immediately placed his hand on the cradle of the telephone, terminating my conversation with Ambassador Abetz. I placed the receiver down on its cradle and—still seated—said to him, "What's all this about, Mr Brehmer?"—He replied, "Acting on orders of the Military Commander, I am here to place you under arrest."

I stood up and said, "I think, Mr Brehmer, that you have come to the wrong place."—I could now make out, beyond the glare of the desk lamp, that there were eight soldiers standing behind General Brehmer and my adjutant, pointing their machine guns at me. At that moment, one of the soldiers took my pistol out of my uniform holster, which lay about three metres away from me on a card table.

I asked General Brehmer for further explanations of his actions, whereupon he replied that the SS Security Service had instigated a coup against the Führer within the Reich. The Führer had ordered the immediate arrest of the higher SS and police leaders and of the SS Security Service. I was not to enquire any further. He asked if there were any other men of officer rank in the building, to which I responded in the affirmative, telling him that my political adviser, SS-Major Hagen, was in the neighbouring room. I then explained to General Brehmer, in very strong terms, that the Führer had posted me to France, and I demanded that he immediately bring me before the military commander, General von Stulpnagel. He agreed to this request.

As I left the room and stepped into the corridor, I could see that the entire staircase of the building and the administration rooms (offices and telephone switchboard) had already been occupied by troops armed with machine pistols, some of them carrying heavy machine guns. I learned later that the switchboard was now manned by an officer who responded to all incoming calls with the words "No further connections can be made from here," and naturally also prevented the telephonist from connecting any outgoing calls. There were a total of some 25 to 30 soldiers in the building. I then called to SS-Major Hagen, who was just on the way from the administrative office to his own room. We were taken in two cars to a hotel used by the Commandant of Greater Paris, where we were confined to separate hotel rooms, each guarded by an officer with the rank of captain. Each room was guarded by a soldier armed with a machine pistol.

At about 02:15 hours, the Commandant of Greater Paris, General von Boineburg, arrived in my hotel room and took me to see General von Stulpnagel, who then asserted that the entire incident resulted from him having been on the receiving end of a false telephone call from one of General Fromm's aides-de-camp.

The manner in which General Brehmer entered the building is best explained by the written declarations (enclosed) of the two men who were on guard duty in front of the building at the time of the incident. I would personally like to draw attention to the declarations made by the two guard officers in these reports. Since the start of the invasion they have watched along the street where my official building stands over an unbroken stream of troop and vehicle movements—both day and night. For this reason, the two guards saw nothing out of the ordinary in the Wehrmacht column that passed by on 20.7. I have furthermore advised the guards, effective from 6.6 onwards, that they should furnish the occupants of vehicles going towards or coming back from the front with information, and permit them to telephone from my building. The guards were thus acting in complete good faith when they allowed the General to pass. Had it been a little lighter, they would no doubt have recognized General Brehmer as an officer who frequently entered and left my official building. The guard stationed in the entrance to the building, to which all visitors must report, accompanied General Brehmer inside on the evening in question and informed my adjutant accordingly. The soldiers accompanying General Brehmer were likewise nothing out of the ordinary for the guards, as an order has been in effect since the invasion requiring all military personnel to carry a pistol, rifle, or machine gun when out on the street. Situations have often arisen since the invasion, in which men of the Waffen SS and Wehrmacht congregate in the entrance hall of my official building, waiting to make a telephone call, taking a chance to eat, or simply having a rest.

Heil Hitler!
Your obedient servant
SS Lieutenant General and General of the Police
The Reichsführer   Field Command post, 27.8.1944
Personal staff
Diary no. 371/44 Ads
H.

Original copy
Main Personnel Office of the SS
Berlin
With the request that a copy be attached to the personal file of SS Lieutenant General Oberg.
SS Colonel

NOTES

Acknowledgments

1. Somehow, an error was made. This last date should be 1944.

Prologue

1. Martelli, *The Man Who Saved London* (New York: Doubleday, 1961), 236, 249.
2. Walter Lippmann, *Public Opinion,* "The World Outside and Pictures in Our Heads." 1922.

Chapter 1: At the Western Front on the Somme: June 1916

1. Arlen J. Hansen, *Gentlemen Volunteers* (New York: Arcade, 1996), 124–25.
2. Harvard Univ. Archives, Pusey Library, Cambridge, Mass.; Francis A. Countway Library of Medicine, Boston, Mass.; Massachusetts General Hospital Archives and Special Collections, Boston, Mass.; New York Public Library, New York; Helen Jordan Lamb, *World War I, An American Nurse with British Troops in France, November 1916–Feb. 1919* (Provo, Utah: Stevenson's Genealogical Center, 1981), 3–9, 19–23; and Mark A. De Wolfe Howe, ed., *Harvard Volunteers in Europe* (Cambridge, MA: Harvard University Press, 1916), 52–53.
3. John Lucy, *There's a Devil in the Drum* (London: Faber & Faber, 1938), 99.
4. John Keegan, *The First World War* (New York: Knopf, 1999), 314.
5. Malcolm Brown, *The Imperial War Museum Book of the Somme* (Philadelphia: Trans-Atlantic, 1996), 67.
6. Keegan, 317.
7. Lamb, 19.
8. Hansen, 105.
9. Chavasse's award is on display at the Imperial War Museum, London.
10. Hansen, 18.

11. *Harvard Alumni Bulletin* 18, no. 27 (April 5, 1916).

12. Because MGH and Harvard medical staff was rotated, there are no reliable numbers of physicians and nurses serving at Dannes. The figures given here were extrapolated from Red Cross sources, and while they are approximate, they are reliable. In the end the Dannes hospital would serve 2,380 cases with British and American medical staffs.

13. Harvey Cushing, *From a Surgeon's Journal, 1915–1918* (Boston: Little, Brown, 1936), 1–2.

14. T. Bentley Mott and Myron Herrick, *Friend of France* (New York: Doubleday Doran, 1929), 3.

15. Jay Winter and Blaine Baggett, *1914–1918: The Great War and the Shaping of the 20th Century* (London: BBC Books, 1996), 205–6.

16. Winter and Baggett, 178–95.

17. Ibid.

18. Lamb, 9, 19.

19. Ibid., 27.

20. Winter and Baggett, 220.

21. Ibid., 19.

22. U.S. General Services Administration (GSA), Statement of Service, Mass. General Hospital Archives, April 19, 1965.

23. Lamb, 27.

24. Phillip Jackson to the author in an interview at the Hôtel des Invalides, Paris, July 1, 1999.

25. Phillip Jackson to the author during interviews throughout 2000–2002 at Hôtel des Invalides, Paris.

26. Clemence Bock, *Souvenirs sur le Docteur Jackson*, a 17-page, single-spaced unpublished memoir that Phillip confirms was written with the help of Toquette sometime immediately after Toquette's escape from Ravensbrück concentration camp. *Souvenirs* relates what Toquette must have told Clemence about Sumner's childhood. "Born near the sea, Sumner drove sleds over winter snow and ice; he climbed great boulders and walked in perfumed forests of pine and maple turned red in the autumn sun." And, notes Clemence, Maine was a little like Switzerland, invigorating and bracing but on the edge of the sea. There the neighbors believed in peoples' democracy, gathering at the general store to talk about the day's events. Sumner's father worked in a quarry while his wife, a mother of three, kept house. After attending the local primary school, Sumner, already at fourteen big for his age, joined his father breaking stone. But he never gave up studying and became the stable hand to the local physician whose work fascinated him. Eventually, after working as a gardener, janitor, and aide to old people, Sumner saved enough to enter Bowdoin College, where he studied under former Civil War Brig. Gen. Joshua Lawrence Chamberlain, winner of the Congressional Medal of Honor. It was then on to Massachusetts General Hospital and to the Battle of the Somme as a volunteer medical officer.

27. Phillip Jackson believes his parents met earlier, in 1916, at a hospital near Paris, but there is no record of such a meeting.

28. From letters from Jane Graham Manson, dated Germantown, January 1918, and correspondence and conversations with M. Jean-Marc Barrelet, director, Archives de Neuchâtel, Switzerland. (M. Barrelet, a distant relative of Toquette's, has kept an archive of those Barrelet and de Ricou family members who hail from Neuchâtel.)

29. Barrelet Archives, Neuchâtel, Switzerland.

30. *War Medicine*, a monthly journal of the American Red Cross Society in France (Paris: January 1919).

31. Nicole Fouché, *Le Mouvement Perpétuel* (Paris: ETHISS, 1991).

32. Arthur W. Little, *From Harlem to the Rhine* (New York: Covici Friede, 1936), 126–41, 214–15.

33. Robert Kimball and William Bolcolm, *Reminiscing with Sissle and Blake* (New York: Viking Press, 1973), 64.

34. Winter and Baggett, 238–53.

35. Hansen, 59–78.

Chapter 2: Coming Home—Going Home

1. GSA Statement of Service, Mass. General Hospital Archives, April 19, 1965.

2. Bock, 7–8.

3. Bock, 4.

4. Phillip Jackson to the author on June 15, 2001; Dr. Maurice B. Sanders, "The Mission of Dr. Sumner Jackson"—a memorial to Sumner Jackson published in *The News of MGH* (June–July 1965); and Hansen, 70–71.

5. Sanders; and from interviews with Phillip Jackson in July 1999.

6. Bock, 8.

7. Charles Bove, *A Paris Surgeon's Story* (New York: Little, Brown, 1956), 33–39.

8. Bove, 40; and Sanders.

9. In *A Paris Surgeon's Story*, author Bove describes the trials he endured a year before Sumner as he studied for his medical exams.

10. Bove, 36–39.

11. Bock, 5.

12. In 1909, the building opened with 24 beds. In 1925, it recorded 1,626 patients hospitalized and 5,300 consultations. American Hospital of Paris Archives.

13. This mission was, and still is, written into the by-laws that govern the hospital's status as a philanthropic institution—and that allow it to raise tax-deductible contributions from the public and charitable institutions under U.S. and French law. Ibid.

14. Fouche, 54.

15. Letter dated May 25, 1961, from Morris B. Sanders, M.D., to Robert M. Cross, editor of the *Bowdoin Alumnus*, Bowdoin College, Brunswick, Maine.

16. Cummings was particularly notorious in Paris. In 1917, the French interned him for three months on a wild charge of "liking Germans." Sumner saw him in Paris again in 1928. Hansen, 82, 155–57.

17. American Hospital of Paris Medical Archives, 1928–35. It should be noted that the hospital refuses access to its medical archives. But the author did see admission cards for the period 1925–35 giving brief information. Saunders correspondence.

18. Report on Zelda Sayre Fitzgerald, Valmont Clinic, Glion, Vaud, Switzerland. Kendall Taylor, *Sometimes Madness Is Wisdom—Zelda and Scott Fitzgerald: A Marriage* (New York: Ballantine Books, 2003), 150, 159, 177, 204.

19. Taylor, 168.

20. Michael Palin and Basil Pao, *Michael Palin's Hemingway Adventure* (London: Orion Books, 2000), 51–69.

21. American Hospital of Paris Emergency Room Ledger, March 1928.

22. Ernest Hemingway, *Selected Letters 1917–1961* (New York: Scribner's, 1981), 272.

23. Palin and Pao, 51–69.

24. Taylor, 227–28, 256.

25. Bernard Grun and Daniel J. Boorstin, *The Timetables of History* (New York: Simon & Schuster, 1975), 501.

26. The Wright murder and Coty's involvement were extensively covered in the international and Parisian press from August to October 1933. Miss Wright's admission card was still on file at the American Hospital of Paris as of 1999.

27. *Le Huron*, August 10, 1933, 8–9.

28. The removal of the bullet from the anonymous man's tongue is covered in Bove's book. Phillip Jackson told the author in November 1999 that he had a keen recollection of Sumner's involvement in the procedure. It was considered an amusing "physician's anecdote" for the Jackson family at the time.

29. Fouché, 60–65.

30. Ernest R. May, *Strange Victory* (London: I. B. Tauris, 2000), 154.

31. From author's conversation with Jacques Andeiux, a Jackson family friend, at Cercle de L'Union Interalliée, Paris, on April 4, 1999. Andeiux gives credit to the stories and believes that the American Hospital was "scouted" by German agents before the war to determine if it were a secure medical facility for their top officials. According to NARA, Porfirio Rubirosa, the Dominican playboy, was a Gestapo agent in Paris before going to New York. NARA, Secret Gestapo Lists, France.

32. Bock, 5.

33. Ibid; and from Medical Board minutes from 1938 and 1939 discovered at the American Hospital of Paris Archives.

34. Alice Barrelet de Ricou (Tat), diary entries 1938–39.

35. May, 78.

Chapter 3: The Debacle: Paris 1940

1. Charles L. Robertson, *An American Poet in Paris: Pauline Avery Crawford and the Herald Tribune* (Columbia: University of Missouri Press, 2001), 212.

2. Phillip Jackson to the author, December 2002.

3. Ian Ousby, *Occupation: The Ordeal of France 1940–1944* (London: Pimlico, 1999), 24–29.

4. May, 18, 216.

5. Robert D. Murphy, *Diplomat among Warriors* (New York: Doubleday, 1964), 51–52, and Albert Kammerer, *La Vérité sur l'Armistice* (Paris: Editions Médicis, 1944), 69.

6. In the midst of a national tragedy, the Reynaud scandal threw a shadow over Charles de Gaulle, who was an obscure colonel until Reynaud appointed him a general and a subminister in his cabinet. No mention is made of the des Portes-Reynaud incidents in the de Gaulle memoirs. As the news media of the time blew up the death of Mme. des Portes and Reynaud's relation to her, the whole business had a profound effect upon the French public. Men like Marshal Pétain had contended for years that the Third Republic's politicians were weak and morally rotten. When he was French ambassador to Madrid in 1939, Pétain was invited to return to Paris and assume political power. He was said to have remarked, "What would I do in Paris? I have no mistress!" Murphy, 51.

7. Sanders, "The Mission of Dr. Sumner Jackson."

8. Bove, 188.

9. *Chasseurs alpins* were French mountain troops.

10. Henri Amouroux, *La Vie des Français sous l'Occupation: Les Routes de l'Exode* (Paris: Fayard, 1961), 10–11.

11. Paul Ritchey, *Fighter Pilot* (n.p., circa 1941–42).

12. Zouaves were French Algerian infantry troops who wore brilliant uniforms and marched at quick step.

13. Dr. Thierry de Martel was a pioneering brain surgeon in France and the medical director of the American Hospital of Paris, and was renowned in Paris society. (He was also a member of a number of anti-Semitic organizations before World War II broke out.) Fouche, 64–67; and Adam Nossiter, *Algeria Hotel* (New York: Houghton Mifflin, 2001), Introduction.

14. Sanders.

15. Bove, 80; and Sanders.

16. Amouroux, 32.

17. Dr. de Martel was one of 15 Parisians who committed suicide on June 14 when the Germans entered Paris. Six German writers exiled in France also took their lives when the country capitulated, including Albert Einstein's nephew Carl, author of a book on African sculpture, who drowned himself in the icy waters of a Pyrenees river. Ousby, 170–71.

18. Nossiter, Introduction.

19. Sanders; and from Kathleen Keating, "The American Hospital of Paris during the German Occupation" (unpublished paper, May 1981, 3); Bock; and the diaries of Alice "Tat" Barrelet from the period May 1940–41.

20. Phillip Jackson to the author on July 1, 1999, at the Hôtel des Invalides in Paris.

21. Ousby, 59.

22. Vice-Admiral Fernet, *Aux côtes du Marechal Pétain* (Paris: Plon, 1961), 33.

23. Amouroux, 23.

24. In a letter to the *New York Herald Tribune*, October 22, 1940, Beekman wrote:

> No one could conceive of an imminent capitulation with millions of unused reserves in Weygand's [commander-in-chief of French Army] "defense in depth." For days private motor cars with valises, bicycles, dogs, cats, birdcages, reserve gasoline, and the inevitable mattress on top to protect against machine gunning from the air had passed along the streets of Paris going south. But so had they before the first and second battles of the Marne in 1914 and 1918, when many of us remained in Paris. But the circumstances this time were different. On June 11 I was informed . . . that the Germans might enter Paris within twenty-four hours.
>
> On June twelfth, my small car filled with luggage and reserve gasoline, I drove across Suresnes Bridge and caught up with the fleeing refugees en route to Versailles. The congestion was so great that the progress was slow. Ahead were long lines of farm wagons drawn by Normandy horses, their owners, stalwart men of middle age walking beside them. Inside on straw or wooden chairs sat old men, women, and children. One old man in a truck jostled along with a patient look, a birdcage hanging above his head, his arms around the neck of his dog. A faster car passed with a beautiful girl, her blonde hair tossed by the wind, sitting on the forward fender. I passed a twelve-year [*sic*] boy on a bicycle with his serious-faced nine-year-old sister balanced on his handlebar. Then another bicycle with a small luggage trailer attached. Cars out of gasoline stopped alongside the roadside. Others received a tow from other cars and went on for miles. At Chartres we were obliged to detour—the city had been bombed earlier in the day—and we finally reached the main road to Tours.

It was getting dark and night brought on a cold rain. Arriving at Bonneville I found a parking place behind a church and after receiving a bowl of hot extract of beef I tried without much success to sleep in my car. As the rain fell ceaselessly I thought of the revelation I had seen of the French character and soul. Not once did I hear a sharp or petulant word—not once a note of terror or despair. Remembering the words of Clemenceau in 1918, "We will fight before Paris, we will fight in Paris, we will fight behind Paris," and the order of Weygand only a day old to "fall back on the Loire and prepare for battle there," these Frenchmen were doggedly resolved to do their duty to the country and their families by placing themselves behind the battle lines in which they still had full confidence.

At Le Mans I went to the Hotel de Paris where I had stayed before and found my old friend Col. Fabry, formerly Assistant Minister for War, and during the last war Commander of the Chasseur Alpin ["Blue Devils"]. The dining room was filled with British and French officers and after dinner, thirty of us stretched ourselves on the chairs, lounges, and floor and half-dozed, half-slept through the night. The next day I reached Angers, I noticed engineers mining the long bridge over the Loire, an ominous sign. Then toward evening I passed into another world. Instead of the France of war of devastation, of moving troops, of fleeing thousands, I found myself almost alone on the mountain routs [*sic*] nearing the sea, now with a view of green forests or cultivated fields, browsing cattle or children at play.

Saturday morning I attempted to telegraph Paris, but I was informed "It is useless, Paris has fallen." Reaching St. Jean de Luze near the Spanish frontier, at last I was met with the stunning news of the armistice and the forming of the new government under Premier Henri Pétain.

French military and political leadership during the period of Hitler's régime has been worse than mediocre. Giving Hitler full credit for brilliance, still he has had no real opposition in any of the countries he has conquered. He has yet to be tested.

Prepared for reverses but for nothing worse, these French people who crowded about the radio several times a day stood there in breathless silence, refusing to believe the worst, straining to hear a single word of encouragement, and leaving as silently as they came, their faces marked with grief and suffering. The silence was of the death chamber but without comprehension of the causes of death. Such a people, deprived by class and political divisions and treachery of its national unity, through which alone successful resistance to a powerful enemy could be achieved, with unconquerable soul will rise again to reclaim that which was lost to them in 1940.

(This letter is also cited in Dean Beekman's papers from the American Cathedral's Archives, Paris, France.)

25. "De Gaulle," *Le Figaro* magazine, June 17, 2000, 57–66.

26. Robert O. Paxton, *Vichy France: Old Guard and New Order, 1940–1944* (New York: Columbia University Press, 1982), 171.

27. Charles Williams, *The Last Great Frenchman* (London: Little, Brown, 1993), 112–13.

28. Diary entry of Alice "Tat" Barrelet, August 12, 1940.

29. Ousby, 223.

30. Ibid., 69.

31. Conversations with Phillip Jackson, Hôtel des Invalides, 1999–2003.

32. Clara Longworth de Chambrun, *Shadows Like Myself* (New York: Scribner's, 1945), 99–101.

33. Ibid., 99.

34. Confirmed to the author by Phillip Jackson in a telephone conversation, May 2002.

35. British intelligence accused René de Chambrun and his wife Jose Laval de Chambrun of being "strongly pro-Nazi" after the war and supplied proof that Jose carried secret documents from Washington to Vichy to aid the Vichy pro-German cause. William Stephenson, *A Man Called Intrepid* (New York: Harcourt Brace Jovanovich, 1976), 308–10.

36. Fouche, 66; and Longworth de Chambrun, 66.

37. The groups, Libération and Froment, are named in the files in the cases of "Joe," the American B-17 tail gunner, and the British pilot William Dallin. Dr. Sumner Jackson is mentioned, along with the American Hospital and the Foch apartment as hiding places. Goélette is not mentioned. Records of the U.S. Army Commands, 1942 (Record Group 338), National Archives and Records Administration, College Park, Maryland (NACP).

38. As Dr. Jackson kept no records, there is scant information about his early Resistance work. Brief mentions are found in the remaining archives of the American Hospital of Paris and in the Goélette files at the Château de Vincennes. There is frequent mention of "Dr. Jackson at the American Hospital" in USAAF Escape and Evasion reports located at the National Archives. Toquette and Phillip knew that Sumner used the hospital to hide people from the Gestapo, but he never talked about specific activities that went on there. Otto Gresser and Elisabeth Comte, Sumner's team at the American Hospital, waited until after the war to tell about their efforts in saving Allied soldiers and aviators.

39. Like many French officers, de Chambrun violently objected to English ambitions in French North Africa and Chad. René de Chambrun, *Général compte de Chambrun sorti du rang* (Paris: Atelier Marcel Jullian, 1980).

40. Keating, 4.

41. Ibid.

42. Amouroux, 131.

43. Don and Petie Kladstrup, *Wine and War* (New York: Broadway Books, 2002), 116.

44. Ibid., 112.

45. Pamphlets like Jean Bruller's (Vercour's) "Les Edition de Midi." Ousby, 208.

46. Ousby, back cover.

47. Henri Nogueres and M. Degliame-Fouche, *Histoire de la Résistance en France, vols. I–V* (Paris: Robert Laffont, 1981), 255.

48. René de Chambrun, 69.

49. Ousby, 70.

50. Phillip said this was one of Sumner's favorite expressions—though he insists that Sumner did not use "foul" language. Phillip Jackson to the author, November 1999.

51. Author's translation from the French.

52. Diary entry of Alice "Tat" Barrelet, October 13, 1940.

53. In a ceremony in October 9, 2001, the Croix de Guerre citation was presented to David McGovern, president of the American Hospital of Paris' Board of Governors, by George Yates, president of the American Club of Paris. The evening was attended by over 400 physicians, hospital, and club members, including Phillip Jackson. But the next day a number of Jewish staff members objected to the citation being displayed because it was dated after the dissolution of the Republic and signed by General Huntziger—then a Vichy minister. The author went to great lengths to research the history of the citation and to show Dr. Serge Kernbaum, a major figure at the hospital, that the citation was prepared before the armistice in the last days of the Republic, but was lost in the hectic days following the rapid German advance and capitulation of the French armies. The citation was found later in Paris or Vichy and signed after the Republic was dissolved, but correctly issued and entitled: République Française.

Controversy involving the Jewish community in France and the media and government is a daily event. Most French media have a very short memory or no memory at all. (A case in point is that of Maurice Papon.) But this is evolving with the publication of a number of works by Serge Klarsfeld and Internet sites with searchable databases. It is no wonder the French Jewish community is sensitive to these issues when one counts the hundreds of thousands of French and non-French refugees deported from France to German gas chambers with the aid of French authorities. More than 67,000 Jews from 37 countries were deported (largely to Auschwitz) from the main French camp at Drancy. Paxton, *Vichy France*, 181–85, 281, 296, 311; and Nogueres, (Tome 2), 10, 442, 429, 456.

54. He may have been murdered by the Nazis on November 12, 1941, in a rigged airplane accident. Nogueres, 194.

55. Ousby, 128–30; Kladstrup, 124–29.

Chapter 4: Internment

1. William D. Leahy, *I Was There* (New York: McGraw-Hill Books, 1950), 14, 62.

2. Hitler had no treaty in place obliging the Reich to follow Japan into war with the United States.

3. From the pseudo-Latin: *Illegitimis non carborundum*. The phrase seems to have originated with British Army intelligence early in World War II. It was popularized when U.S. Gen. Joseph W. "Vinegar Joe" Stilwell (1883–1946) adopted it as his motto. http://www.perseus.tufts.edu/Help/faq.html

4. Keating, 5.

5. Tat's diary entry for September 30, 1942.

6. This incident and what follows remain anchored in Phillip Jackson's mind. Phillip Jackson to the author at the Hôtel des Invalides, Paris, March 2001.

7. Dr. Jackson gave a detailed account of his internment to Clemence Bock following his release after only ten days. Bock, 9.

8. From notes of Phyllis Michaux, who has a collection of Resistance memorabilia that she shared with the author.

9. Bock, 9.

10. Newspaper reporting error. Women were taken to Besançon camp and then to Vitell camp.

11. Bock; and from L. Whipp's files at the American Cathedral of Paris Archives.

12. A State Department cable dated October 24, 1942, states that Dr. Jackson had rendered very important services to the Red Cross before and during the Occupation. It's possible that General de Chambrun was successful in obtaining Sumner's release from internment this time. But it remains a mystery as to why the general couldn't intervene when the Jacksons were ultimately arrested and deported.

13. Mme. Felix Gatier, who was a friend of Lawrence Whipp during the Occupation of Paris, wrote to the dean of the Holy Trinity Cathedral on July 5, 1944, on the inauguration of the World War II memorial. Her letter describes life at the Compiègne prison camp where Whipp was interned with Sumner. A copy of the Gatier letter was obtained from the Cathedral Archives.

14. From the diary of an unnamed French-American prisoner found in March 1999 at the American Cathedral of Paris Archives.

15. Conversation with Lindsay Siviter at the American Cathedral of Paris, March 14, 1999. Ms. Siviter, a volunteer at the Cathedral, researched its archives for the author with the permission of the Dean.

16. Letter on consulate paper dated Paris, le 25 fevrier 1944, and signed by "Le Gerant du Consulat."

17. *Time* magazine, March 12, 1945, 66.

18. Dr. Carrel was one of the founders and the director of the French Foundation for the Study of Human Problems. He received the Nobel Prize

for Medicine in 1912 for his pioneering work in organ transplants. He developed an artificial heart in 1936, discovered white corpuscles in 1922, and performed the first successful heart surgery on a dog in 1914.

19. In his book, *Man the Unknown* (New York: Harper, 1935), Carrel wrote: "Human beings are equal. But individuals are not. The equality of human rights (or their rights) is an illusion." (Author's translation from the French.) Phillipe Burrin, in *La France à l'heure allemande* (Paris: Editions du Seuil, 1995), wrote: "The Vichy Government was receptive to [Carrel's] views, created his foundation whose objective was to 'safeguard, ameliorate and develop the French population in all its activities.'" To avoid future difficulties Carrel downplayed the racist aspects of his work and remained discreet in his contacts with the German Embassy. Nevertheless, he approved the antidemocratic and eugenicist aspects of the Nazi State, though he disapproved of its mass politics. In 1943 he would write, "Only the Germans are capable of bringing order to Europe and to France in particular."

20. After the war, Sanders was appointed to the U.S. Foreign Service and was the first U.S. public health attaché for France in Paris, and later for the Middle East States of Lebanon and Syria. He retired in 1951 to Rockport, Mass., where he continued his studies on the science of man.

21. Amouroux, 140. Author's translation.

22. Michael M. Marrus and Robert O. Paxton, *Vichy France and the Jews* (Stanford, CA: Stanford University Press, 1995), 260–61.

23. There remain copies of letters sent by Jewish prisoners from the French-run camp at Drancy, written as families awaited deportation. "Dear Nana, go up to my place and take my belongings, they're a gift. I'll send you a package. Inside a pillow is all my money and jewels. Keep them. . . . I beg you to have pity for my children. This is my last letter. . . . Whatever you were going to send, keep it. I no longer need anything." *Le Monde*, July 18, 2002: 7.

24. Marrus and Paxton, 372–73.

25. Fouché, 65–66.

26. Robert S. Wistrich, *Who's Who in Nazi Germany* (London: Routledge, 1995), 108–9.

27. Ernst Kaltenbrunner oversaw the intelligence division, the Gestapo, the criminal police, and the SS security service. At the end of 1942, Oberg informed Kaltenbrunner that his agents were convinced that all French Resistance organizations were being directed by General de Gaulle in London. Kaltenbrunner then presented a 28-page report on de Gaulle's Secret Army to Adolf Hitler early in 1943. Gerard Chauvy, *Histoire secrète de l'Occupation* (Paris: Payot, 1991), 309–23; Marrus and Paxton, 372.

28. Documents in the archives of Me. Serge Klarsfeld, president, Les Fils et Filles des Déportés Juifs de France, Paris.

29. German security in France was shifted from the Army to the SS in the

spring of 1942. Vichy minister Laval entered into an arrangement with General Oberg by which French police would use German security measures including tracking down, arresting, imprisoning, and deporting Jews and Resistance agents. Oberg became head of security in France on June 1, 1942. Paxton, *Vichy France: Old Guard and New Order*, 183.

30. From caption attached to Oberg War Pool Photo, Office of War Information, 1945.

Chapter 5: Resistance

1. Goélette was an offshoot of a main network named "Phratrie" (origin unknown), which was established by Jacques Robert, an early *résistant* leader. After a spectacular escape from a French prison in Nice in May 1943, Robert was secretly flown to London where he worked for de Gaulle until the liberation of Paris.

2. Goélette numbered some 950 agents at full strength but the count varied as networks (*reseaux*) were merged or broken up by German or Vichy security services. The groups were part of the Bureau Central de Renseignement et d'Action [Militaire] B.C.R.A.[M.]. They were responsible to the Free French under Gen. Charles de Gaulle, headquartered in London and later in Algiers.

3. By 1941–42, having a radio transmitter in Paris was suicidal. The Germans had perfected a system of citywide radio detection finders.

4. Kinderfreund, or *R*, remained the surviving head of Goélette. He had been a member of the French state police (gendarmes), before the war and was highly decorated for his Resistance work after the war. *R* stayed alive and kept his cells functioning because he was clever. He kept contact between his agents to a minimum to avoid betrayal.

5. In 1944, Vichy (French) courts executed no fewer than two hundred people for crimes related to so-called terrorist activities—resistance to Vichy. The condemned were never given attorneys to represent their cases. *Le Monde*, May 30, 2003. By the end of 1944, a number of *R*'s cells, including the Vichy operations, were betrayed, their agents arrested, shot, or deported—among them the Jackson family. Goélette lost eleven agents to Nazi firing squads, twenty agents who died because of deportation (mostly in concentration camps), and two agents who were deported and never found.

6. Phillip confirms that he became fully involved in his family's underground work for Goélette in late 1943, when he was not quite sixteen years old. Interview with Phillip Jackson at Hôtel des Invalides, Paris, February 7, 2002.

7. Throughout their undercover work, the Jacksons maintained a strict "need to know" policy among themselves—even more so after their arrests

by the Gestapo, who had their own agents placed in French prisons and German concentration camps. "Need to know" was standard operating procedure among Resistance networks. Apart from the records kept in London at B.C.R.A., most of what has been written about de Gaulle's French Resistance of the Interior is based on cable traffic and the memory of clandestine agents going back to 1940. The files and history of Goélette's activities and agents were prepared by Kinderfreund after 1944.

8. There is a substantial file detailing Goélette's activities in the archives at the Château de Vincennes outside Paris. The archives are run by the French Defense Ministry, which granted the author permission to review its materials. However, some access was forbidden, presumably because the materials contained embarrassing information about an individual or the French government. The files are still classified secret. Most of the materials, typescript on what is now aged, browned paper, were prepared by Kinderfreund immediately after the war when he held the rank of commandant. He was paid as a civil servant, as most Resistance leaders were, to write up Goélette's work and to "liquidate" its operations and assets. The files that were kept in London by General de Gaulle's officers are not available. They have been lost or destroyed or are still covered by French security regulations.

9. Texts of messages are from Records of the Office of Strategic Services, Field Station Files, Paris, Record Group 226, NACP.

10. Paxton, *Vichy France: Old Guard and New Order,* 296–97.

11. Bock, 9.

12. André Migdal, *Biographie* (n.p., n.d).

13. This was Klaus Barbie's headquarters in Lyon. It's where he first questioned (tortured) General de Gaulle's representative in France, Jean Moulin, after Moulin's arrest at Caluire.

14. Langlet to the author in various interviews in Paris, 2001.

15. French *maquisards* attacked a German garrison at Tulle on June 7 and 8, 1944, killing more than fifty and executing ten of the prisoners they took in the fight. Ousby, 287.

16. Ibid., 215.

17. Phillip Jackson's reflections in an interview, December 2002, Hôtel des Invalides.

18. Goélette Archives, Château de Vincennes.

19. This incident, along with Phillip Jackson's complete escapade at Saint-Nazaire, was related to the author in a series of interviews at the Hôtel des Invalides, Paris, 2001–2002. Phillip's trip is also detailed by Paul Ostoya Kinderfreund in a dossier still classified secret at the archives of the Ministère de la Défense, Bureau Résistance, Château de Vincennes.

Chapter 6: Flying Fortresses—Secret Agents

1. Virginia Kays Veenswijk, *Coudert Brothers* (New York: Truman Talley Books/Dutton, 1994), 252.

2. Ibid.

3. The Nazi Security Service—Gestapo, SS, SD, etc.—were installed all along Avenue Foch. The Jacksons, at 11, avenue Foch, were within a stone's throw of the SD building at number 19. Pierre Pean, *Vies et morts de Jean Moulin* (Paris: Fayard, 1998), 563–65.

4. The events described were related to the author by Sgt. Buck Moro at Keesler Field, Mississippi, in the winter of 1946. Moro had been a Fortress crewman stationed in England, flying missions over Germany and France in 1944, though Moro did not know Joe. The author was also an airman at Keesler.

5. Allen Mikaelian and Mike Wallace, *Medal of Honor* (New York: Hyperion/Bill Adler Books, 2002) 141–42, 190.

6. This name is a pseudonym used at Joe's request.

7. Joe's letter to the author explains:

> While in training one of the waist gunners told me he would be flying the tail position. He was a S/Sgt. (staff); I was plain buck Sgt. But he had been to armorer's school at Denver, Col. before he went to gunnery school. I approached Lt. Kordus and told him what was going on—saying if he was an armorer gunner, what good would it do the crew for him to be in the tail since he was more checked out on the bomb racks and turrets than I was . . . it would be more logical for him to be close to these systems. Kordus told the gunner, 'Joe will be in the tail.' As luck would have it he was one of the waist gunners that was killed on 7/14/43.

Joe did not give the gunner's name; both waist gunners were killed that day.

8. Mikaelian and Wallace, 146.

9. Sergeant Moro to author.

10. Joe says the copilot's name was spelled "Beiger" but the USAAF Escape and Evasion reports all spell his name as John W. Bieger.

11. This is standard operating procedure (S.O.P.) for pilot to crew after reaching the channel.

12. The descriptions and notations for this action are contained in USAAF Escape and Evasion reports filled in by Joe after his escape from France, and in Joe's letters to the author.

13. From Joe's USAAF Escape and Evasion report, NARA.

14. Ibid.

15. Flying Fortress action sequences over England and France are drawn from Records of Headquarters MIS-X (Military Intelligence Service, Escape and Evasion Section Detachment, Record Group 332.2.2 [NACP]); and from correspondence and telephone conversations with Joe. Also essential were documents and reports contained in *Nostalgic Notes*, the newsletter of the 94 Bomb Group Memorial Association, along with Col. Ralph Saltsman's unpublished autobiography, *My Story*. In Paris, the author met with former Flying Fortress pilots who told of what it was like up in the big blue. The

author drew on Harry Slater's *Lingering Contrails of the Big Square A*, a publication of the 94 Bomb Group, for part of the action sequences.

16. Other than Harrison, the pilot of Five-by-Five, and his copilot Dave Turner, no records are available of the names of other crew members and which ones escaped from France to England.

17. Joe's outfit, the 331 Squadron of the 94 Group, Eighth U.S. Air Force, flew their B-17 Flying Fortresses in bombing missions over France and Germany between May 1943 and April 1945. Their exploits—particularly the attempt to destroy German naval works and submarine pens at Saint-Nazaire, France—are detailed by Michael Lugez in his book, *Missions de Bombardements Américains sur Saint-Nazaire* (France: Edilarge S.A.-Editions Ouest, 1998), 196–201. In a note to the author, Lugez wrote: "Their [the airmen's] missions were a tragic and barely known episode in the history of World War II."

18. Conversations with Phillip Jackson, Hôtel des Invalides, 2000.

19. Joe's letter to author dated May 3, 2000.

20. Slater, *Lingering Contrails*.

21. From Potvin's USAAF Escape and Evasion report, NARA.

22. Potvin later died in an airplane crash in 1944 while serving with an Air Force unit in the United States.

23. From Joe's USAAF Escape and Evasion report.

24. Thomas Childers, *In the Shadows of War* (New York: Henry Holt, 2002), Prologue, 352.

25. Keating, 6.

26. Reports to Headquarters, 6801 MIS-K Detachment, U.S. Forces, European Theatre, U.S. Army, February 1946.

27. Bock.

28. Flight commander Frank Griffiths escaped with Joe to Spain. Frank Griffiths, *Winged Hours* (London: William Kimber, 1981), 92–163.

29. From Joe's letter to the author dated May 3, 2000.

30. Ibid.

31. Excerpted from Missing Air Crew Report no. 113 and Escape and Evasion Reports filled out by Joe upon his return to England in 1943. Records of the Office of the Quartermaster General, Record Group 92, NACP.

32. Ibid.

33. Ibid.

34. Ibid.

35. Rutabaga turnips were served in school meals in England where food supplies were also desperate, though less so than in France. People said they were "disgusting . . . great knotty roots which rent the bowels and filled the hospitals with appendicitis cases and ulcerated stomachs." Ousby, 137.

36. From a report dated October 30, 1945, Headquarters, 6801 MIS-X Detachment, U.S. Forces, European Theater, U.S. Army, NARA.

37. Griffiths, 129.

38. Ibid.

39. Bernard Eyheralde, whom the author met while doing research about the French Resistance, was a member of the French *maquis* (General de Gaulle's secret army of the interior) in the Haute Savoie in 1943. He sent me a publication: *Meythet, de l'an II a l'an 2000*. In it the story of squadron leader Frank Griffiths and the crash of his Halifax bomber is described by residents who lived through the experience.

40. *Meythet*.

41. Ibid.

42. Ibid.

43. Griffiths, 49–51.

44. Griffiths's wife, Ruth Fuller, was serving with the British WAAF (Women's Army Air Corps) in England.

45. From Joe's letter to the author, April 2002.

46. The Lysander was a high-winged monoplane with a high rate of climb and descent: perfect for landing in small fields even when surrounded by trees. It was used extensively by the British SOE to infiltrate and exfiltrate agents from secret airfields prepared by Resistance groups on the European continent. The Halifax, a four-engine aircraft, was used by SOE to parachute "Joes," arms and supplies to the Resistance.

47. Griffiths, 182–87.

48. Ibid., 106–7.

49. In *Winged Hours*, Griffiths explains that after the liberation of France he was able to track down many of the Resistance and *maquis* people who had helped him. Françoise Dissart turned out to be a schoolteacher from Toulouse. There is a full-size statue of her erected in the courtyard of the girls' school where she taught before the war.

50. Griffiths, 184.

51. October 13, 1943.

52. George Martelli, *The Man Who Saved London* (New York: Doubleday, 1961), 143–45.

53. Eric Posch-Pastor von Camperfeld was the grandson of Dr. von Camperfeld, the last ambassador of the Austrian-Hungarian Empire to the Vatican. In 1938 Eric was a twenty-three-year-old lieutenant in the Austrian Army when his regiment fought against the German troops that had entered Vienna to annex Austria to Germany. Posch-Pastor was imprisoned at Dachau concentration camp, one of the first Nazi camps to be run by the notorious SS Death's Head Formations (Totenkopfverbande). He managed to escape by joining a German Army unit as a second-class soldier. He was wounded on the Russian front in 1940 and sent to France as a security officer to supervise the production of German armaments. His secret file at the French Ministère de la Défense mentions that before being posted to a fac-

tory at Niort, France, he was arrested and sent to Fresne prison for 15 days when he tried to help a French Jew named Madame Marie-Antoinette Verne escape deportation to a Nazi death camp. Ministère de la Défense files, Bureau "Résistance," Château de Vincennes, Paris; and from the footnotes contained in Larry Collins and Dominique Lapierre, *Is Paris Burning?* (New York: Simon & Schuster, 1965).

54. Posch-Pastor's work resulted in French railroad workers sabotaging German arms shipments, as well as Allied bombers destroying arms factories, troop movements, Atlantic coast defenses, and submarine bases in the west of France. He is credited with stopping a major Gestapo operation against a Resistance unit in Dijon.

55. In May 1945, Kinderfreund hosted a meeting of his surviving agents in Paris to establish an after-war association: Amicale du Reseau Goélette (Friends of Goélette). Toquette, Phillip, and Posch-Pastor were in attendance. From Renaudot's letter to agents, Paris, April 15, 1945.

56. Phillip Jackson tells how he was often sent to the lake house at Enghien to stay with his Aunt Tat, either because there was a meeting of Goélette agents at the Avenue Foch apartment and no one wanted Phillip to witness it, or because Toquette was away on a mission.

57. Brooks Richards, *Secret Flotillas: Clandestine Sea Lines to France and French North Africa 1940–1944* (London: HMSO, 1996), 216.

58. *Encyclopédie Petit Larousse* (Paris: Larousse, 1995).

59. Winston Churchill, *The Second World War*, vol. 6 (Boston: Houghton Mifflin Company, 1948), 43.

60. Martelli, 167.

61. By the liberation of Paris in August 1944, twenty thousand French *résistant* agents had been shot by German firing squads. Of the sixty thousand agents who had been deported to SS concentration camps, only one-half would return. The men, women, and adolescents deported came home often in a pitiful physical and mental state. Michel, 124.

62. From Reports Headquarters, Paris, 6801 MIS-X Detachment, U.S. Forces European Theatre, 1946, on Gilbert Asselin, Gladys Marchal, Louise Russ et al., NARA.

63. Department of State telegram from Bern to Washington, August 7, 1944, NACP.

64. Goélette files, Château de Vincennes.

65. Ibid.

66. Martelli, 171.

67. Interviews with Phillip Jackson and Andre Migdal at the Hôtel des Invalides, Paris, December 2002.

Chapter 7: Betrayal, Arrest, Deportation

1. AP report in *Boston Herald* dated September 1944 (after the Jackson family had been arrested by the Gestapo) stating that Elizabeth Ravina was

trying to trace Dr. Jackson. Miss Ravina discusses receiving a letter from Dr. Jackson describing his family's deprivations.

2. Bock, 9–10; and from Jackson family documents of 1945.

3. Ibid.

4. Ibid.

5. Ibid.

6. Ibid., 10–11

7. The hospital part of the monument is named L'Institution nationale des Invalides.

8. Interview with Phillip Jackson in May 2000 at the Hôtel des Invalides, Paris; and from Bock, 10.

9. It should be noted that when the officers arrived at the Jacksons' apartment that day, they had been given a simple order to pick up the family for questioning. Their instructions from Vichy headquarters contained no specific details. It wasn't until the next day, Thursday, May 25, that the Milice talked by telephone with their superiors at Vichy and learned that the Jacksons were wanted for espionage. The order to pick up the Jacksons had been sent from Vichy to the Paris office of the Milice by wireless, because a tornado had knocked down telephone lines between Vichy and Paris. Ibid.

10. Stolz saw Sumner briefly at a German holding prison at Moulins before Sumner and Phillip were deported. Stolz was saved from deportation by the intervention of his wealthy wife.

11. Conversation between the author and a representative of the Vichy Office de Tourism, May 2000.

12. Letter dated June 12, 1944, from the brother of a family friend named Jeanine. The letter reports that the Jacksons were handed over to the Gestapo at Vichy on June 3, 1944, and that if the family were involved in matters concerning German security, they would be sent to the prison at Moulins—and after that . . . "unknown." Jackson Family Archives.

13. Bock; interview with Phillip Jackson, Hôtel des Invalides, December 2002; and from testimony of Phillip Jackson on May 23, 1945, to Noel Till, official of Second War Crimes Investigating Team.

14. Phillip Jackson to Noel Till, May 23, 1945; and from Phillip's letter addressed to "Dear Friends" and dated May 10, 1945. Sumner never knew how Toquette was treated nor what she said to the Gestapo. Phillip thought "very little." Conversation with Phillip Jackson, 2002.

15. The letter was enclosed in an envelope postmarked Vichy, 9:30 P.M., June 1, 1944. The author believes that much of the text contains secret meanings alluding to Toquette's treatment, and telling her sister to do certain things connected with Toquette's Resistance work. Parts of the letter make no sense coming from a Resistance fighter who had been arrested with her husband and son, questioned by the French Gestapo police—the Milice— and imprisoned. Letter courtesy of the Jackson Family Archives.

16. Scottish kilts were very popular at the time.

17. A person unknown to Phillip.

18. The aunt of Toquette and Tat.

19. The family maid at the lake house.

20. Unidentifiable acronym.

21. Miss Comte was not the director of the hospital but the head of nursing. This may have been Toquette's way of asking Tat to get in touch with General de Chambrun.

22. An impossibility at this point in the war.

23. This sentence makes no sense. Was it meant to tell Tat to look in a particular sack?

24. This penultimate phrase is totally unlike Toquette, a woman dedicated to the French Resistance movement and staunchly anti-Vichy.

25. Neutral Switzerland represented the United States vis-à-vis the German government during World War II. State Department telegrams courtesy of NACP.

26. From despatch [*sic*] from American Embassy Paris, France, dated February 27, 1945, and revealing events in 1944 related to the Jackson family.

27. Phillip Jackson to the author in May 2000 at the Hôtel des Invalides, Paris. In a report after the war, Phillip mistakenly wrote "Portuguese Embassy" for "Hôtel du Portugal."

28. The correct name of the city is Clermont-Ferrand.

29. Leahy, 71–73.

30. Vichy witnesses to the Occupation as quoted in Nossiter, 138–39 and 141.

31. Ibid.

32. Ibid., 124–39.

33. A German transit camp.

34. All extracts are from Jackson family documents, courtesy of Phillip Jackson.

35. When Phillip wrote this in June 1945, he believed Toquette had died in a German concentration camp.

36. From Phillip Jackson's testimony to Noel Till; and from Phillip's letter addressed to "Dear Friends" and dated May 10, 1945.

37. From Reports Headquarters, Paris, 6801 MIS-X Detachment, U.S. Forces, European Theatre, 1946, on Gilbert Asselin, Gladys Marchal, Louise Russ et al., NARA.

38. Phillip can shed no light on who might have authored the letter to Clemence.

39. Department of State incoming telegram from Bern, August 7, 1944, NACP.

40. Citation letter dated May 29, 1951, and signed and sealed by Kinderfreund, chief of Goélette.

41. David Stafford, *Secret Agent* (London: BBC Worldwide, 2000), 20.

42. In a letter to the author in the spring of 2000, Maisie Renault wrote, "Toquette was very secretive about the reasons she was arrested."

43. It was Dr. Heinrich Illers who signed the deportation orders of the Jackson family. Illers was deputy to Kurt Lischka, commander of the Sipo-SD of Paris, and as such was the real chief of the Paris Gestapo. During his reign, Illers signed documents that specified the type of camp and severity of punishment for a prisoner (1 *leicht*: light; 2 *mitteler fall*: medium treatment; 3 *schwer*: heavy). His orders were then confirmed in Berlin and carried out in France and later at the concentration camp where the prisoner was assigned. All prisoners (including the Jacksons) had a dossier that chronicled their movements throughout the camp system, along with the signed orders for each transfer.

Illers was personally responsible for the deportation of prisoners from the camps at Compiègne (Sumner and Phillip's cases) and Romainville (Toquette's case). He blatantly ignored an agreement between Swedish Consul Nordling and General Choltitz that called for turning over *résistant* (political) prisoners to the Red Cross; instead, he ordered the deportation of sixteen hundred *résistants* to Nazi death camps on August 17, 1944. Witness testimony, Cologne trial of Dr. Illers 26/11 dossier Lischka.

44. Serge Klarsfeld to the author in a letter dated March 3, 2003.

45. Regardless of Dr. Jackson's status, it still remains a mystery as to why General de Chambrun did nothing to save the family from deportation. It was probably in his power to do so even as late as June 1944—despite the confusion in Vichy. Was he angry at Sumner for having cooperated with de Gaulle's FFI and the British Special Operations Executive (SOE)?

46. Department of State telegrams dated August 24 and 28, 1944, NACP.

47. Air Pouch [*sic*] from American Legation at Bern, July 24, 1944, from Interagency Working Group (IWG): Record Group 226: Entries 215–20, NACP.

48. State Department telegram to American Legation, Bern, classified Secret, August 31, 1944, NACP.

49. Letter from Albert E. Clattenburg, assistant chief, Special War Problems Division, U.S. Department of State, to Julia Barrelet de Ricou on December 14, 1944, NACP.

50. Clipping from *Waldoboro Press Herald* of Sept. 6, 1944, from Jackson Family Archives.

51. In a letter dated May 25, 2000, the author asked Mr. René de Chambrun if he had any memory of Dr. Jackson's arrest. He replied, "I know nothing nor remember any event concerning Dr. Jackson."

52. There is an extraordinary document in the National Archives: a letter from SS General Oberg to his chief, SS Reichsführer Himmler, dated (Paris) August 8, 1944. It tells how Oberg was arrested by Wehrmacht General

Brehmer following the attempted assassination of Hitler at the Führer's headquarters in Rastenberg on July 20, 1944. See the Appendix of this book for the English translation of the full text.

53. All of the archives of the Gestapo service IV (Dr. Illers' domain) were shipped to Berlin, where they were destroyed by the Allied bombardments. Illers must have found a way to have his personnel file in the SS Archives in Berlin destroyed. At the National Archives, College Park, Maryland, there are two mostly blank pages on Illers. They list only his name, SS number: 90172, birth date: 12.5.08, and the mention of Paris as his post. The file on SS General Oberg contains sixty-seven pages, NACP.

54. The vast majority of those deported were Jews. Documents show that after deportation, more than 100,000 Jews from France went to their deaths in concentration camp gas chambers. Archives of Me. Serge Klarsfeld, president, Les Fils et Filles des Déportés Juifs de France, Paris.

55. On his way back to Berlin, Stulpnagel stopped at Verdun, where he had served as a soldier in World War I. He tried to kill himself but failed. He was hanged on August 30, 1944. Ousby, 288

56. Ibid.

57. Collins and Lapierre, 112–20.

58. Fouche, 69.

59. James Grier Miller, *Behavioral Science* (Santa Barbara) 41, no. 4: 245–61.

Chapter 8: Ravensbrück—Neuengamme

1. Letter from Julia Barrelet de Ricou, Toquette's sister-in-law, to Mrs. Franklin Delano Roosevelt, dated Nov. 1, 1944. From the Jackson Family Archives.

2. Bock, 12.

3. Maisie (May) Renault, *La grand misère* (Pontivy, France: n.p., 1948), 20–21.

4. Posch-Pastor's file at Château de Vincennes.

5. Catherine Rothman-Le Dret, *L'Amérique déportée: Virginia d'Albert-Lake de la Résistance à Ravensbrück* (Nancy, France: Presses Universitaires de Nancy, 1994), 95.

6. Renault, 20–23; and from a letter to the author from Mme. Renault circa June 1999.

7. No further mention is made of Professor Gebhardt in Madame de Gaulle Anthonioz's book, *La Traversée de la nuit* (Paris: Editions du Seuil, 1998). The author presumes he was an SS physician who carried out medical experiments on prisoners. This was frequent in Nazi concentration camps.

8. De Gaulle Anthonioz, 9.

9. Himmler thus hoped to ingratiate himself with the Allies and enter into a contract with General Eisenhower to negotiate the release of prisoners with important connections. Rothman-Le Dret, 115.

10. ICRC covering letter and note in Toquette's handwriting from Jackson Family Archives.

11. Ibid., 114–17.

12. Renault, 20–23; and from a letter to the author from Mme. Renault circa June 1999.

13. Enclosure to despatch [*sic*] no. 5542 addressed to Herschel V. Johnson, Minister, Legation of the United States of America, Stockholm, Sweden, April 30, 1945, and signed by Glen Whisler, special representative, American Red Cross. Document 760050 NARS 9 [*sic*]—NACP.

14. Directives issued December 7, 1941, by the Führer and supreme commander of the Armed Forces for prosecuting offenses committed within German-occupied territories. The sentences spelled out death to offenders or deportation to Germany. Avalon Project at Yale Law School, "Nazi Conspiracy and Aggression", vol. 7, 1–2.

15. *Pitchi Poi* is Yiddish for a very small shtetl—a village, but a tiny one. At Drancy, one of the principal French-German–run camps for Jews where they were held before deportation, the term *Pitchi Poi* was taken to mean "nowhere." Courtesy of Andre Migdal, Paris teleconference with author, March 12, 2003.

16. Bruno Manz, *A Mind in Prison* (Washington, D.C.: Brassey's, 2000), 45–46.

17. Marcel Ruby, *Le Livre de la Déportation* (Paris: Robert Laffont, 1957), 193.

18. Wistrich, 51.

19. Ibid.

20. Report to U.S. State Department from H. Gasser, Swiss Legation, Berlin, May 26, 1945, 10, NACP.

21. Combined (Allied) Intelligence Objectives Sub-Committee, Evaluation Report no. 341, August 28, 1945. Public Records Office, United Kingdom.

22. Martelli, 216.

23. The SS recruited a brass band among talented prisoners to accompany hangings and other punishments with well-known military marches. Martelli, 225.

24. Gunther Schwarberg, *The Murders at Bullenhuser Damm: The SS Doctor and the Children* (Bloomington: Indiana University Press, 1984), 3–9, 23–29, 40–41.

25. The physicians were Dr. Quenouille of Villeneuve St. George and Drs. Florence and Thouert, both of the Faculty of Science at Lyons, France. Ibid.

26. United Nations War Crimes Commission, classified Secret, June 1,

1945, no.16081/4; Report of Combined Intelligence Objectives Sub-Committee, August 28,1945; Prisoner of War Intelligence Bulletin no. 2/59: Neuengamme, April 27, 1945 (SHAEF Handbook, German Concentration Camps; Swiss Legation in Germany, dealing with German Penal Matters, May 26, 1945). All documents from Public Records Office, United Kingdom, courtesy of Lawrence Bond, Producer, "The Last Typhoons," History Channel.

27. Martelli, 225–27.

28. Bock, 12.

29. Ibid.

30. Ibid; and Martelli, 217–42.

31. There was a relentless process of human destruction at Neuengamme, as nobody was intended to return alive. Martelli, 217–42.

32. The description of Neuengamme concentration camp and the experiences of Sumner, Phillip, and fellow prisoners are taken from Phillip's testimony to Noel Till, May 23, 1945; U.S. and British War Crimes documents found at Public Records Office, Kew, Richmond, Surrey; and Martelli.

33. Gunther Schwarberg, "There Shall Be No Survivors, Part II," *Der Stern* magazine series, 1983.

34. Schwarberg, *Murders at Bullenhuser Damm*. Neuengamme inmate Emil Johannes Henrik Morgan gave testimony in a report to American Consul, Malmo, May 30, 1945; Records of the Office of the Judge Advocate General (Army) (Record Group 153), NACP.

35. Migdal, *Biographie*, 3.

36. Phillip Jackson's testimony at the trial of Max Pauly, Hamburg, March 20, 1946, 63–72; Public Records Office, Kew, Richmond, Surrey, United Kingdom.

37. Martelli.

38. Jackson Family Archives.

39. Correspondence of Toquette dated May 11 and 15 and June 10, 1945. Jackson Family Archives.

Chapter 9: SS Death Ships

1. The author has drawn on multiple sources to describe the events related in chapter 9, "SS Death Ships." Every fact and incident has been verified against eyewitness reports, sworn testimony contained in official British documents now declassified, and against German and French sources. The *Der Stern* citations relate to material paraphrased from an English-language translation of the German text done for the author by Alfred Barthel of Munich in April 2000. Gunther Schwarberg, a prisoner at Neuengamme and author of *The Murders at Bullenhuser Damm* (Bloomington: Indiana

University Press, 1983), wrote the *Der Stern* series, six in number, published in the spring of 1983. Because the material is taken from a translation, the author only cites the number of the series from which the material was paraphrased.

2. There was one other ship in the port of Lübeck that the SS used as a prison ship: the *Elmenhorst*. But she never left port. Schwarberg, *Der Stern*, II. The article cites testimony at the War Crimes Trial of Max Pauly, Hamburg, April 5, 1946.

3. On-camera interview during the filming of "The Typhoons' Last Storm," History Channel.

4. Schwarberg, *Der Stern*, IV.

5. "The Typhoons' Last Storm."

6. Schwarberg, *Der Stern*, III.

7. Ibid.

8. From Phillip Jackson's letter dated Neustadt, May 8. He wrote a series of letters after being freed—some in English and some in French. The letters tell the same story but vary slightly in detail. And from Max Arthur, "RAF Pilots Tricked," *The Independent*, London, October 16, 2000.

9. Ibid.

10. A report to Command 8 Corps, dated May 14, 1945, signed by J. Christopher, colonel.

11. Ibid; and from the deposition under oath by Kurt Rickert, May 17, 1946, at No. 1 C.I.C. Neumunster. From Public Records Office, Kew, Richmond, Surrey, United Kingdom.

12. The International Committee Red Cross (ICRC) delegate at Neustadt, Mr. de Blonay, stated to Maj. Noel O. Till that on May 2, 1945, de Blonay informed Major General Roberts commanding the British Eleventh Armored Division that seven thousand to eight thousand prisoners were on board the ships in Neustadt Bay. He also stated to Major Till that he heard that his message, concerning the prisoners, was passed on to a "higher authority."

Major Till himself submitted an official report in 1945 titled "Disaster at Lübeck Bay," in which Till writes that British senior officers knew in advance that KZ prisoners were put aboard the ships anchored in Lübeck Bay. On page 15, he stated: "From the facts and from the statement volunteered by the RAF Intelligence Officer (Intelligence Officer 83 Group RAF), it appears that primary responsibility for the great loss of life must fall on the British RAF personnel who failed to pass to the pilots. . . . It is strongly urged that an official enquiry be held by the responsible authorities into the failure to pass vital information, as it is understood that no such enquiry has taken place."

Later in the Till report concerning the *SS Deutschland*, he wrote, "In view of the fact that the Resident Naval Officer at Neustadt and also the witness de Blonay had both heard rumors that approximately two thousand women were aboard [the *Deutschland*], a request has been made to the Royal Navy for a diver to investigate the wreck, and the Flag Officer Schleswig-Holstein has personally ordered this to be done forthwith. This report will be forwarded as soon as it is received."

Till collected 387 exhibits related to the massacre at Lübeck Bay, including a statement from Mr. de Blonay. However, the author was only able to locate Part B of Till's report (cited above) in the Public Records Office at Kew, Richmond, Surrey, United Kingdom. The exhibits are missing. Mr. de Blonay's report is missing in the ICRC Archives at Geneva. There is no record of the report by the diver who was ordered to survey the *Deutschland*.

The British government has never made official reference to the disaster at Lübeck Bay. To this day, the RAF and the other services responsible for the catastrophe refuse to acknowledge the human error despite multiple inquiries to British authorities, documented recommendations from British officers on the scene at Neustadt, and war crimes investigators. Since 1945, the government simply maintains that the event is still under investigation. See: Letter from Ministry of Defense, Clive Richards, MOD Air Historical Branch, September 22, 1999; Schwarberg, *Der Stern* magazine series, VI; Part B from "Disaster at Neustadt Bay," report by Major Noel O. Till, British Army War Crimes Investigation Team No. 2 (undated, 11–17), Public Records Office, UK; author's inquiry September 25, 2000, to Air Commander David Adams, Defense Section, British Embassy, Paris, France; author's research at ICRC, Geneva, Switzerland; and conversations with History Channel producer Lawrence Bond on December 19, 1999.

13. These passages are drawn from George Duncan's "Maritime Disasters of the Second World War," found at http://members.iinet.net.au/~gduncan/maritime.html; Schwarberg, *Der Stern*, VI; and from *"Cap Arcona*: Atrocity or Accident?" by Roy Nesbit, *Aeroplane Monthly*, June 1984. Nesbit's narrative is based on "A Survey of Damaged Shipping in North Germany and Denmark, June 1945," British Bombing Survey Unit. There were other RAF squadrons in the air over Lübeck Bay on May 3, 1945, including 122 Squadron flying Tempests out of Fassberg air base. They also attacked the *Cap Arcona*. But the Typhoons of the Second Tactical Air Force made the principal attacks on the SS prison ships that day.

14. SHAEF Memo to 21 Army Group, June 2, 1945, signed H.G. Sheen, Colonel GSC, G-2 CI. Public Records Office, United Kingdom.

15. Jean Langlet, *Aboard the Cap Arcona* (n.p., n.d).

16. Baldwin was labeled an "Ace" because in July he had shot up General Rommel's staff car, wounding him. Baldwin stayed in the RAF and was lost over Korea in 1952.

17. Letters dated May 8 and May 10, 1945, from the Jackson Family Archives.

18. André Migdal, *Les Plages de Sable Rouges*, NM7, Paris, 2001, 235–43 [author's translation].

19. From a letter from Phillip dated May 8, 1945 to a friend in Paris.

20. Jean Langlet, *Aboard the Cap Arcona* (n.p., n.d).

21. Schwarberg, *Der Stern*, VI; Nesbit, *Aeroplane Monthly*, 288–92. The author was unable to find Mehringer's KZ number from Neuengamme.

22. Schwarberg, *Der Stern*, IV.

23. Eyewitnesses claim the red cross was clearly visible.

24. Appendix to War Diary L.A.D. att. 5 Recce. Regt. R.A.C. Report on Mass Murder Area at Neustadt. Signed, May 1945, B.L.A. From Public Records Office, United Kingdom.

25. Schwarberg, *The Murders at Bullenhuser Damm*, 90.

26. Schwarberg, *Der Stern*, VI.

27. Ibid; Langlet; and from the University of Hamburg Archives.

Chapter 10: Sacrifice

1. Bock, 17.

2. Letter from Mme. Renault to the author, circa 2000.

3. Jackson Family Archives.

4. Stephen E. Ambrose, Richard H. Immerman, and Douglas Brinkley, *Ike's Spies: Eisenhower and the Espionage Establishment* (Jackson: University Press of Mississippi, 1999), 107–8.

5. Ibid., 106.

6. Ibid., 107.

7. The author heard this phrase spoken in an exchange between two American students in the Paris Metro.

BIBLIOGRAPHY

The bibliography for this work is considerable and cited in the book's footnotes. For those readers who wish to delve further into this dark period of France's history, I recommend the following reading.

Anthonioz, Geneviève de Gaulle. *La Traversée de la nuit.* Paris: Editions du Seuil, 1998.

Aubrac, Lucie. *Outwitting the Gestapo.* Lincoln: University of Nebraska Press, 1993.

Collins, Larry, and Dominique Lapierre. *Is Paris Burning?* New York: Simon & Schuster, 1965.

Fouché, Nicole. *Le Mouvement Perpétuel.* Paris: ETHISS, 1991.

Marrus, Michael M., and Robert O. Paxton. *Vichy France and the Jews.* Stanford, CA: Stanford University Press, 1995.

Migdal, Andre, *Les Plages de Sable Rouges.* Paris: NM Editions, 2001.

Nossiter, Adam. *Algeria Hotel.* New York: Houghton Mifflin, 2001.

Ousby, Ian. *Occupation: The Ordeal of France 1940–1944.* London: Pimlico, 1999.

Paxton, Robert O. *Vichy France: Old Guard and New Order, 1940–1944.* New York: Columbia University Press, 1982.

Robertson, Charles L. *An American Poet in Paris: Pauline Avery Crawford and the Herald Tribune.* Columbia: University of Missouri Press, 2001.

———. *The International Herald Tribune: The First Hundred Years.* New York: Columbia University Press, 1987.

Stafford, David. *Secret Agent.* London: BBC Worldwide, 2000.

Wistrich, Robert S. *Who's Who in Nazi Germany.* London: Routledge, 1995.

INDEX

ABOUT THE AUTHOR

HAL W. VAUGHAN, American journalist, documentary film producer, and former U.S. Foreign Service officer, spent the past twenty-four months researching the story of the French Resistance and the Jackson family saga. As a diplomat and newsman, he has lived and worked in Europe, the Middle East, and Asia. He and his physician wife live just a few steps from the Madeleine Cathedral in Paris.